TRAUMA-AWARE EDUCATION

Essential information and guidance for educators, education sites and education systems.

DR JUDITH A. HOWARD

First published 2022 by:
Australian Academic Press Group Pty. Ltd.
Samford Valley QLD, Australia
www.australianacademicpress.com.au

Copyright © 2022 Judith Howard.

Copying for educational purposes
The *Australian Copyright Act 1968* (Cwlth) allows a maximum of one chapter or 10% of this book, whichever is the greater, to be reproduced and/or communicated by any educational institution for its educational purposes provided that the educational institution (or the body that administers it) has given a remuneration notice to Copyright Agency Limited (CAL) under the Act.
For details of the CAL licence for educational institutions contact:
Copyright Agency Limited, 19/157 Liverpool Street, Sydney, NSW 2000.
E-mail info@copyright.com.au

Production and communication for other purposes
Except as permitted under the Act, for example a fair dealing for the purposes of study, research, criticism or review, no part of this book may be reproduced, stored in a retrieval system, or transmitted in any form or by any means electronic, mechanical, photocopying, recording or otherwise without prior written permission of the copyright holder.

 A catalogue record for this book is available from the National Library of Australia

Trauma-Aware Education: Essential information and guidance for educators, education sites and education systems.

ISBN 9781925644593   (paperback)

Disclaimer
Every effort has been made in preparing this work to provide information based on accepted standards and practice at the time of publication. The publisher and author, however, make no representations or warranties with respect to the accuracy or completeness of the contents of this book and specifically disclaim any implied warranties of merchantability or fitness for a particular purpose. It is sold on the understanding that the publisher is not engaged in rendering professional services and neither the publisher nor the author shall be liable for damages arising herefrom. If professional advice or other expert assistance is required, the services of a competent professional should be sought.

Publisher & Editor: Stephen May
Cover design: Luke Harris, Working Type Studio
Cover photo: the author
Page design & typesetting: Australian Academic Press
Printing: Lightning Source

This book is dedicated to Professor Susan Cole (1948–2021).

Susan dedicated her life's work to developing the influential *Trauma and Learning Policy Initiative* and the *Trauma Sensitive Schools Framework* through leading a collaboration between her university, Harvard Law School and the Massachusetts Advocates for Children, a children's rights organisation.

During a career that spanned more than 30 years, Susan built a movement that has brought critical awareness to the need for trauma-sensitive schools. Her expertise took her all over the world where she inspired many educators to become trauma-sensitive, and she trained hundreds of trauma-sensitive lawyers to represent trauma-impacted students and to promote relevant legislation — lawyers who will continue her important work for years to come.

I had the pleasure of spending time with Susan and her lovely husband, David — at my home in 2019, where we engaged in many robust conversations and truly enjoyed each other's company.

So it is with sincere gratitude, that I dedicate this book to the life and work of the wonderful Susan Cole.

Praise for *Trauma-Aware Education*

In *Trauma-Aware Education*, Judith Howard effectively opens the door for all educational professionals and policy makers to enter into what has become an international movement for trauma-aware schooling. At once comprehensive and accessible, Prof. Howard's book carefully delineates the neurobiological and psychological underpinnings for a trauma-aware approach to teaching and learning, showing that it is indispensable in our current age. Most importantly, the book shows compassion for educators by suggesting practical and commonsense measures for taking action on the insights provided by research. Prof. Howard's book is a gift to education sites and systems — and the children they serve — in Australia and around the world.

Professor Michael Gregory, *Clinical Professor of Law, Faculty Director, Trauma and Learning Policy Initiative at Harvard Law School, Massachusetts, USA.*

Dr Judith Howard's new book is an essential guide for teachers, school leaders, allied professionals, and educational systems leaders. While certainly practical for education professionals, this book has the rigorous breadth and depth required to be mandated reading for pre-service teachers and university teacher training courses. As one of Australia's pioneers in the emerging and much needed paradigm of trauma-aware education, Dr Howard calls us into action by providing the developmental story of the field itself, the growing evidence base, and the need to frame trauma-aware education as a multi-disciplinary and interconnected practice approach.

Dr Tom Brunzell, *Director, Berry Street Education Model & Honorary Fellow, University of Melbourne Graduate School of Education.*

Dr. Judith Howard is cultivating leading-edge work in the areas of trauma awareness and trauma-informed education. In this book, she not only defines what trauma is in its varying degrees and complexities but explains the need for higher education to prepare pre-service teachers to deeply understand how adversity and trauma impact the developing nervous systems of learners. This book is critical for practitioners in education but also a lighthouse for faculty in teacher preparation programs, along with all those who sit beside our children and youth in our communities.

Dr Lori Desautels, *Assistant Professor in educational neuroscience and trauma at Butler University, Indianapolis, USA.*

Dr. Judith Howard, a leader in trauma-aware education, utilises her knowledge, experience, and research in this book to ensure the reader can make a change in whatever role they fulfill. This is a must-read book for anyone who works with children and young people!

Mathew Portell, *Director of Communities (PACES Connection), Founder of the Trauma-Informed Educators Network, and Nashville Public Schools 2022 Elementary Principal of the Year, USA.*

Terminology used in this book

'Trauma-Aware'
It is acknowledged that scholars and practitioners use different terms when they refer to policy and practice that is informed by an understanding and response to trauma. Common terms include 'trauma-informed', 'trauma-sensitive', and 'trauma-responsive'. Much of the work led by the author and the author's university has been branded by the term 'trauma-aware education'. So, this will be the term used throughout this book, and the reader should consider the term synonymous with other commonly used terms. So, in this book, 'Trauma-aware education' refers to education policy and practice that is informed by research examining and responding to the impact of trauma on children and young people and their education experiences.

'Learners'
As this book will be referring to children and young people, from birth to approximately 18 years, who are attending early childhood services and schools, the collective term 'learners' will mostly (but not always) be used.

'Caregivers'
This book will refer to learners living in various caring contexts. The contexts include those who live with one or more biological caregivers or relatives, those who are adopted, those who are in a range of out-of-home care contexts due to child protection concerns, and perhaps others. The collective term 'caregiver' will be used to represent parents or legal guardians of children and young people.

'Education sites'
This book refers to education during early childhood and the schooling years. It will refer to the places where this education occurs as 'education sites', which include schools and the places and services where early childhood education and care and alternative education occur.

'Education systems'
This book will examine a systemic response to trauma-aware education and acknowledges that education systems vary in size, structure, and function in various parts of the country and the world and for differing organisations. For example, in Australia, three main bodies oversee schooling — state or government education, catholic education, and independent schooling. Early childhood education and care is overseen by an independent national authority that assists federal and state governments in administering a nationally approved approach to service delivery. Each of these 'systems' has networks of further systems that branch out to provide hierarchies of governance. It is proposed by the author of this book that all levels of systemic governance need to be 'trauma-aware' for education sites to have the sustained support to deliver trauma-aware education services and for all trauma-impacted learners to have equitable access to these services.

Personal Pronouns
To avoid the potential exclusion of people from any gender, the author has chosen to use the general pronoun 'they', when referring to children, young people, learners, or adults in general.

Author Note

It has been my privilege to work in the area of trauma-aware education for much of my career. I commenced working in the education field as a teacher who was intrigued by and who often worked with trauma-impacted learners. After gaining postgraduate qualifications as a school counsellor, I supported many schools struggling to manage the needs of learners who exhibited chronic and challenging behaviour. More often than not, these young learners had lived through complex trauma. My intrigue grew as I discovered important learnings from various bodies of research and literature that helped explain the concerns these learners experienced and recommended a 'trauma-aware' response. I became increasingly aware that these understandings were very much lacking in schools and that schools were resorting to behaviour management techniques that they found worked for the bulk of learners but that often failed quite badly when used with trauma-impacted learners.

So, schools felt like they lacked options and were often resorting to punishment, suspension, and exclusion to deal with the behaviours of these learners.

I completed my PhD examining educators' beliefs regarding the use of suspension and exclusion from school. I continued to read and listen to experts in the field of complex trauma and trauma-aware responses more and more. I also listened closely to the stories of these learners who expressed repeated themes of feeling unsafe, fearful, anxious, depressed, and sometimes terrified, not trusting, lacking hope, and feeling alone. They expressed anger for what they perceived as undeserved relational rejection by their caregivers, support workers, educators, and peers. They were disheartened that the bulk (or perhaps all) of people who worked with or cared for them were paid to do so. They were also disheartened that the people who took on these roles were often changing and that their relationships with caregivers and support personnel were often short-lived. Yet, these children and young people mostly remained relationally thirsty, consistently seeking connection with others but often failing in their attempts. These learners rarely spoke of the details of any trauma that they had experienced in the past but rather were very focused on and very emotionally responsive to what was happening to them and around them in the present.

I also listened to educators who were working with these learners at school. They spoke of how much they felt they had invested into working with these learners and how much it hurt when these learners seemed to purposefully sabotage their work and their relationships with them. Some spoke of impacts on their mental wellbeing, physical wellbeing, sleep, and relationships at home. They mentioned taking 'sick days' and 'mental health days' more regularly than usual. They mentioned the 'guilt' associated with feeling powerless to help or to improve things for trauma-impacted learners. Teachers spoke of frustration with the behaviours of these students and how much these behaviours interfered with their teaching and the learning of other students. They spoke of what they perceived as a lack of effective solutions coming from school leadership and how they often felt responsible for and blamed for, allowing the behaviours of these learners to continue. School leaders spoke of their concerns regarding the effect that behaviours of trauma-impacted learners were having on their staff and other learners, the reputations of their schools, and their professional reputations as leaders. They also spoke of the impact on their personal and family lives and their own mental health and wellbeing. Teachers, school leaders, and other school personnel questioned their capacities to do their jobs and whether or not they should continue with their current choice of career.

During this time, health and mental health organisations and specialists supporting trauma impacted learners were starting to draw from Attachment Theory and a gradually increasing understanding of the neuroscience explaining the impact of complex trauma. More and more, these understandings were informing their work and more and more they were becoming frustrated with schools, where staff had not yet had access to this information. Increasingly, I was witness to disagreements during case meetings where specialists wanted to address trauma-impacted learners' concerns through a trauma-aware lens, whereas schools wanted to resort to behaviourist informed methodologies, often including suspension and expulsion, believing whole-heartedly that these approaches were more likely to lead to 'better choices' and student behavioural improvement.

I noticed that professionals working for support services would often recommend to schools that processes should be adopted during school hours, which were deemed by these services as supporting the mental health, wellbeing, and engagement of their young clients. These recommendations were often grounded in Attachment Theory and an understanding of the impact of complex trauma on brain development and functioning. They also focused on developing and maintaining in-school relationships for the students and enhancing their capacities for emotional self-regulation. Aligning with this, it was often strongly recommended by child and adolescent support specialists that schools avoid suspension and exclusion and work consistently towards the full-time attendance and participation of these young learners.

I noticed that schools almost always struggled to accept the recommendations from these sources. School leaders and teachers expressed a sincere concern that the support organisations and specialists did not 'get it' from a school or classroom perspective. Teachers expressed their need to support 'all the other students in their classrooms' and their worries regarding the disproportionate effort required to implement recommendations.

They expressed concern that implementing the recommendations of specialists could impair their capacities to teach according to system and school expectations and their own professional standards, preventing them from doing what they felt they were qualified and paid to do. Teachers worried about the extra time and effort required, and school leaders expressed concerns associated with the resourcing (both human and material) that was needed to implement recommendations. School leaders were also justifiably concerned about the safety implications associated with the recommendations, the impact on the professional and personal wellbeing of their teachers, and asking their teachers to take on the work of what they perceived as the work of 'therapists'.

What was very clear is that both groups were just as concerned for young trauma-impacted learners and both were really wanting to find solutions to address the complexities faced by these learners, their educators, their caregivers, and their support personnel. However, it also became clear that there were gaps in understanding from both groups. People working in and leading schools had often not had access to the theory and science explaining the impact of complex trauma and ways to address this impact and, therefore, found it difficult to understand and respond adequately to the recommendations of organisations and specialists. Organisations and specialists had little-to-no clarity or experience regarding the complexity of running a classroom or a school. Both groups had sincere concerns for the same learners, but neither was able to work with the other in a way that aligned in process and led to successful outcomes for the young people who were the focus of their efforts.

I wondered at this stage, 'How could I help?'. So, I developed an initial version of a training program for educators that explained the impact of complex trauma and recommended a trauma-aware response. I was amazed at the thirst in schools for this information, but I quite quickly recognised that a systemic response was needed to have a clear impact on many schools, educators, and learners. I moved into a number of systemic leadership roles and made training in 'trauma-aware education' an important inclusion in my work for my systems. The word 'got out', and increasingly, I received requests to run seminars across Australia and New Zealand. I was amazed at how often participants in seminars would comment to me, 'Why wasn't I taught this at university?' and 'I wish I had known this years ago!' and 'I wish I had known this when I taught him/her! I would have done things so differently!'.

Again, I wondered, 'How can I help more effectively?'. 'How can this information reach more educators?' So, I wrote a short book, *Distressed or deliberately defiant? Managing challenging student behaviour due to trauma and disorganised attachment* (Howard, 2013). This is a short and inexpensive text that is written in easily accessible terms for busy educators, that is not heavily referenced and was definitely not written in academic language. However, I am so happy that I had the opportunity to publish this little book, as it has reached and helped many thousands of educators. Many school leaders bought a copy for every staff member as they realised the importance of developing an initial understanding of trauma-aware education.

I moved into academia (a long-term career goal) with my current university in 2015. Since then, my work has strongly focused on systemic responses to trauma-aware education, and my attention has expanded from school focus to including early childhood education and care. My colleagues and I have developed courses for pre-service and postgraduate educators in trauma-aware education and short courses that reach thousands across the world each year. We continue to have important discussions with systemic leadership across the country. We have developed 'National Guidelines for Trauma-Aware Education' in collaboration with the Australian Childhood Foundation (Queensland University of Technology & Australian Childhood Foundation, 2021) [1,2], and we run the large and influential biennial *Trauma-Aware Schooling Conference*. The thirst for this work in schools and early childhood education is ever-increasing, along with our passion for helping and contributing. Our main focus now is to continually 'grow' more leaders in trauma-aware education.

This book is my latest attempt to continue to contribute to this important work.

---

1. Howard, J., L'Estrange, L., & Brown, M. (2022). National Guidelines for Trauma-Aware Education in Australia. *Frontiers in Education*. 7. 1–11.

2. QUT & Australian Childhood Foundation (2021). *National Guidelines for Trauma-Aware Education* https://eprints.qut.edu.au/207800/

Contents

Terminology used in this book vii
Author Note ix

Introduction 1

CHAPTER 1
Becoming Aware of the Impact of Trauma and Trauma-Aware Education 5
Understanding Trauma 5
Who are these trauma-impacted learners? 8
    First Nations children and young people 10
    Very young children 11
    Adolescent students 12
The Costs of Unresolved Ttrauma 16
Understanding Trauma-Aware Education 18
Summary 21

CHAPTER 2
The Research Informing Trauma-Aware Education 23
Is Trauma-Aware Education Evidence-Based? 23
The Adverse Childhood Experiences Study 25
Romanian Orphanages Studies 26
Studies Examining Attachment 28
Prevalence Studies 33
Longitudinal Studies 36
Systematic Reviews 37
Summary 39

CHAPTER 3
The Neuroscience of Learning and Complex Trauma 41
Research Powerhouses: Sources for the Science 43
The Nervous System 45
The Human Brain 48
    The Brain Stem 48

The Diencephalon 49
　　　Cerebellum 49
　　　The Limbic System 50
　　　The Insula 51
　　　The Cerebral Cortex 52
　　　The Pre-frontal cortex 52
　　　The Hemispheres of the brain 53
　Human Altriciality and Human Potential 54
　Neurons 54
　　　Neurotransmitters 56
　　　Neural development and neural pruning 57
　The Mirror Neuron System 58
　Genetics, Epigenetics, and Intergenerational transmission 60
　Hyperarousal and Hypoarousal 63
　　　The Window of Tolerance 63
　　　The Poly Vagal Theory 65
　The Endocrine System and the HPA Axis 67
　The Immune System 68
　Dissociation 69
　Memory 72
　　　Explicit Memory 72
　　　Implicit Memory 73
　Executive Function 74
　Oral Language 76
　Sensory Issues 78
　Resilience 84
　Summary 86

CHAPTER 4

Behaviour Management (Behaviourism verses Neuroscience) 89

　Considerations for Classroom Behaviour Management 89
　Considerations for Whole-School Behaviour Management 92
　Considerations for Intensive Behaviour Support 94
　Considerations for Crisis Management 96
　The Process of Co-Regulation 99
　Suspension and Time Away from School 101
　Re-Entry Meetings 102
　Exclusion from School 103
　Behaviour Management Policy 104

Case Management and Individual Support Planning 108
Summary 110

CHAPTER 5
Trauma-Aware Strategies (Safety, Relationships, Emotional Regulation) 113

The Mentor, Check In and Check Out 114
Safe Spaces 116
Emotional Regulation Strategies 116
Check Curriculum and Assessment Triggers 117
Pick Your Battles 120
Non-verbal Messages 121
Exploring Exceptions 122
Relational Rewards 123
A Better Way to Use Detention 124
Use Inclusive Education Strategies 124
Cognitive Scripts 125
Look for the Gold! 126
Model and Coach 127
Whole Class Lessons 128
Brain Breaks 128
Mindfulness 130
The Assistance of Animals 131
Summary 133

CHAPTER 6
The Complex Intersection Between Trauma and Disability 135

Legislation and Models of Disability 136
Problems with Diagnosis of Complex Trauma 'Disorders' 138
Prevalence of the Intersection 140
What about Universal Screening for Trauma? 146
   Arguments to support the use of universal screening 147
   Arguments against the use of universal screening 148
   Prevalence, time, and cost of universal screening 152
   A 'middle-of-the-road' approach? 152
Summary 153

Chapter 7
Trauma-Aware Early Childhood Education and Care 155
- Play and Brain Development 156
- Secure Base and Safe Haven 158
- Serve and Return 159
- Investing in Early Brain Development..159
- Summary 160

CHAPTER 8
Trauma-Aware Staff Support: Looking after our Educators 161
- A Team Approach..161
- Vicarious Trauma...163
- Vicarious Trauma and Supervisors 167
- Responding to Vicarious Trauma 168
- Research of Vicarious Trauma 168
- Prevention is Better than Cure: Initial Teacher Education 170
- Summary 171

CHAPTER 9
Leading Trauma-Aware Education 173
- Leaders in Education Systems 175
- Complexities and Opportunities..175
- Advocacy 177
- Building a Staff Leadership Framework..178
- Collaboration 179
- Leaders of Education Sites...179
    - *Design of Service Delivery* 180
    - *Policy Review* 181
    - *Collaborations*...181
- The School Counsellor 181
- Spheres of Influence...183
- Leading People in a Trauma-Aware Manner 185
    - *It starts with you and your nervous system!* 185
    - *Then, You Can Lead Others* 187
    - *Summary*..189

CHAPTER 10
A final word from the author **191**

REFERENCES **195**
Chapter 1… 195
Chapter 2 201
Chapter 3 207
Chapter 4 219
Chapter 5 221
Chapter 6 225
Chapter 7 235
Chapter 8 239
Chapter 9 243

Introduction

This book focuses on trauma-aware education in Australia, the author's home country. However, the content discussed is relevant for many parts of the world, as sadly, no part of the world is immune to trauma impacting children and young people. This book is written at a critical time for all early childhood education and care services and all schools. At the time of writing, the COVID-19 pandemic has exacerbated and complicated concerns for the mental health and wellbeing of learners, their caregivers, and their educators. There have also been traumatic global events (war, famine, political upheaval) and local traumatic events (for example, Australia has experienced widespread and destructive drought, fire, and floods). So, trauma-aware education that is thoughtfully delivered by all education sites and comprehensively supported by all education systems, has never been more important!

It needs to be acknowledged that over many years, many education sites and systems across Australia have struggled with managing the challenging needs and behaviours of some of our most disadvantaged and vulnerable learners, including those who come from trauma backgrounds, in a manner that does not involve suspension, exclusion, and other exclusionary practices. This is despite education sites being staffed by incredibly talented and learner-focused practitioners and the field of education increasingly adopting admirable, often whole-site practices that emphasise positive behavioural and restorative responses. Some of the challenges faced by education sites are now being explained through a growing understanding of how complex trauma can impact the educational experience of learners. These explanations are increasingly informing how sites and systems need to respond.

Complex trauma is also referred to as 'Developmental Trauma', 'Type II Trauma', 'Big T Trauma', and 'Betrayal Trauma'. We now understand that this type of trauma stems from repeated interpersonal harm done to children, including physical, emotional, or sexual abuse, significant neglect, and the experience of family or other relational violence. This type of trauma can be understood as distinct from other types of trauma, as it disrupts important attachments. It is often directed at infants and children by the very people on whom they depend for love, nurture, and protection. Research has clarified that complex childhood trauma can impact the development of children (their bodies and their brains) throughout the early childhood and schooling years, and, if not resolved, this impact can extend into adulthood and can even influence the future caregiving styles and behaviours of victims.

Drawing from a combination of the science of infant, child, and adolescent development, the prevalence and impact of adverse childhood experiences, the long-term biomedical and intergenerational consequences of complex trauma, and the science of developmental resilience, research is revolutionising practice in the areas such as health and mental health, social services, youth services, and youth justice, and now early childhood education and schooling. Indeed, this continually growing body of research and literature is now driving an international reassessment of classroom, education site, and education system approaches for supporting and managing the needs and behaviours of trauma-impacted learners, and there is a tangible and increasing 'thirst' for trauma-aware knowledge and practice among educators in Australia and beyond.

This increasing focus on trauma-aware practice is certainly due to concerns for the wellbeing of children and young people who have been harmed, but it is also due to the significant impact that engaging with young trauma victims can have on the personal and professional wellbeing of the people working with them. There are also increasing concerns that these impacts can influence whether people choose to leave their career in education, either for a time or permanently. So, an additional and significant consideration within trauma-aware education is to address compassion fatigue and enhance the compassion resilience of educators.

To support the many educators and schools, and early childhood education services that are now working within, or aspiring to develop trauma-aware education frameworks, this book will examine and discuss the impacts of complex and other trauma on learners and how trauma-aware education provides an informed approach to remedy these concerns. Trauma-aware education is grounded on the premise that — whilst the very plastic or malleable nature of the child or adolescent brain leaves young people quite vulnerable to the neural, health, and mental health impacts of trauma — there is also great hope, as neural repair can be achieved through informed and consistent practice to address harm. The first chapter of this book provides some introductory information regarding the impacts of complex trauma and trauma-aware education. Chapter two will explore the research that provides the evidence base for trauma-aware education, and chapter three will expand on this by examining, in more depth, the science that informs this response and practice. Chapter four unpacks how learnings from research inform a paradigm shift in how learner behaviours are 'managed', and chapter five will outline examples of strategies that can be employed as part of a trauma-aware education response. Chapter six examines the complex intersection between complex trauma and disability and key learnings for educators working with learners who live with disability. Chapter seven focuses on a trauma-aware approach to early childhood education and care. Chapter eight discusses important issues regarding the wellbeing of educators, and chapter nine examines aspects regarding the leadership of trauma-aware education in sites and systems.

I find as I finalise the manuscript for this book, I already recognise that several other chapters could be written as this topic of trauma-aware education reaches into so many education (and other) contexts that are worthy of consideration. However, I hope that the book in its current shape will prove helpful for education practitioners and leaders and others who are keen to enhance how we support and educate the vulnerable and victimised group of young learners who have lived through complex trauma.

Chapter 1

Becoming Aware of the Impact of Trauma and Trauma-Aware Education

Understanding Trauma

There is now abundant evidence, particularly from the field of neuroscience, that complex trauma can damage the development and functioning of the nervous systems of young victims. If left unaddressed, this impact can lead to concerning emotional, relational, and behavioural outcomes that can continue throughout the schooling years and beyond. Children and young people living with the outcomes of complex trauma can suffer many challenges during their experiences of education. Some of these challenges relate to their perceptions of safety, some to their capacities for relating to others, and some to their capacities for emotional self-regulation. The impacts on these capacities can overlap and interact with each other and the capacities of learners to learn. As a result of these challenges, these young learners can exhibit the types of challenging behaviours that can lead to their experiencing quite serious disciplinary responses, including suspension and exclusion from school. If not addressed, the effects of complex trauma can extend into adulthood, where there can be an unfortunate impact on the capacity for safe and effective caregiving, which can lead to the intergenerational transmission of this type of trauma.

Research also highlights important information regarding other categories of trauma, including simple, acute, or single-incident trauma, cultural trauma, community trauma, intergenerational trauma, domestic and family violence, grief and loss, and trauma associated with natural and other disasters. In addition, the complex interaction between these different categories of trauma is increasingly being discussed, particularly in the light of the COVID-19 global pandemic and international political upheaval that includes persistent violence and discrimination and invasion and war.

Trauma that is categorised as 'simple', 'Type I', 'small t' or 'acute' can involve single-incident, sudden, time-limited, and unexpected events that are perceived as traumatic, or even life-threatening, by those who experience them (Amin et al., 2020). Experiencing a natural or other disaster or a severe accident can fall into this category of trauma. Although this type of trauma can have a significant impact on the mental health and wellbeing of children and adolescents for a time, this is often shorter-term, and there is a lower risk of victims developing posttraumatic stress symptoms or disorder (Astitene et al., 2020).

'Complex', 'Type II', or 'big T' trauma is also sometimes referred to as 'betrayal trauma' or 'developmental trauma'. It involves the repeated relational harm experienced by children at the hands of those who should be loving and protecting them (Choi & Kangas, 2020). This trauma can include physical, sexual, and emotional abuse, physical and emotional neglect, and the experience of family or other relational violence. Neuroscience has explained clearly that this type of harm can have a detrimental impact on developing nervous systems leading to an array of longer-term relational, emotional, and behavioural symptoms that can impair education and life outcomes for victims if not resolved (Kimble et al., 2018). This trauma can also involve a higher risk of victims developing posttraumatic stress symptoms or disorder (Astitene et al., 2020).

Sometimes there can be a 'blurring of the lines' between what is conceptualised as simple trauma and complex trauma. To illustrate this, let's examine some worrying events that happened across Australia in 2020. After many years of significant drought in many parts of Australia, 2020 commenced with devastating bushfires. The deaths and other serious impacts resulting from these natural disasters led to grief, personal and economic loss, and serious and widespread family mental health and wellbeing concerns. Children and young people lost their homes, schools, and sometimes their whole community infrastructure in the fires. Families in farming communities lost their livelihoods, slaughtering starving livestock and watching crops wither or be destroyed, and some experienced increased mental illness and suicides (Office of the Advocate for Children & Young People, 2020).

The global COVID-19 pandemic then exacerbated these concerns in many ways, including the impacts associated with social restrictions. The pandemic revealed inequalities in income, employment, resources, and supports available to families (Davidson, et al., 2020) and heightened the risk of adverse experiences and outcomes for children and young people living in unsafe home environments (Teo & Griffiths, 2020). The pandemic coincided with the onset or increase in frequency and severity of intimate partner and family violence in many homes (Boxall, et al., 2020). Mechanisms put in place to prevent the COVID-19 virus from spreading left victims locked down with their abusers and isolated from vital social supports and services such as courts, therapy, and crisis aid. Economic challenges and alcohol usage increased in families, and mental health concerns were exacerbated by the impacts of COVID-19 (Newby, et al., 2020; Tran et al., 2020). Adults were suffering anxiety, and kids were becoming anxious about their caregivers' anxiety — whilst dealing with their own growing anxiety.

Concerns were also exacerbated by the closure of schools and early childhood services, which had previously acted as safe havens for children and young people who had lived through complex or other trauma or were currently living in unsafe or unsupportive homes. These sites provide education services and social networking for young learners, emotional and relational support, and, importantly, careful monitoring of any evidence of harm. In Australia, educators are mandated to report child protection concerns, but, unfortunately, during school closures and the move to home-schooling from 2020, this monitoring mechanism was removed, and many children were denied this safely net.

Due to the devastating impact of all this on the capacity for safe and effective caregiving of children and young people, it became too simplistic to classify the trauma associated with the natural disasters and disease that was overwhelming children and young people, as simple trauma, with predictably shorter-term impacts. The lines between the trauma 'types' were truly blurring due to children and young people experiencing multiple traumatic events and circumstances, the length of time that the trauma was experienced, and the harmful impact of the traumatic experience on parenting and caring.

However, despite this 'blurring of the lines', it remains imperative that the emphasis on preventing and addressing complex childhood trauma stays strong. It is important that organisations (including education sites and systems) continue to address the concerns of the vulnerable and victimised group of children and young people who have experienced complex trauma. It is vital that educators and other professionals are equipped and supported to work in trauma-aware ways to help traumatised learners as they engage or re-engage with their education.

Who are these Trauma-Impacted Learners?

It is also important to consider how being a member of a particular social cohort or living in particular social contexts can lead to a 'blurring of the lines' between types of trauma. Clearly, children who have suffered child protection concerns are trauma-impacted. In Australia, many (but not all) of these children are identified through child protection processes, such as mandated reporting, substantiation of concerns through investigation, and interventions, including out-of-home care placements. However, in many parts of the world, these processes may not be available or may not be working effectively, and children can remain unidentified, unprotected, and unsupported. Sadly, of those who are placed in out-of-home care, there is a proportion who suffer ongoing trauma at the hands of their new caregivers, or in residential placements, or due to a series of unsuccessful placements and the need for regular changes in care context.

There are others to consider. Some children are living in traumatic circumstances in war-torn parts of the world, where terror, grief, and loss can be regular experiences. Some live with the outcomes of intergenerational trauma due to the traumatic, historical events and circumstances suffered by their relatives and those of their culture, race, and ancestry. Some have suffered chronic neglect during placements in under-resourced orphanages. Some of these children have lived through severe deprivation with long-term impacts, and some may or may not end up being adopted within their home country or by a family overseas. Some who experience the trauma associated with being forcibly displaced are refugees or asylum seekers who have needed to flee their home countries. Some of these children need to persevere through complex and often lengthy assessment of their cases, and some are placed in detention centres during this time. Then there are children whose families need to assimilate into foreign and sometimes unwelcoming new parts of the world with unfamiliar languages and cultures, who can face racism, discrimination, and disadvantage. Some poor children have suffered the cruelty of torture, or their family members have suffered this indignity and harm. Some have survived the horror of being trafficked. Some have been victims of online or other predators, and it is important to acknowledge that there are children who are currently experiencing this who are yet to be identified as victims. Some children are incarcerated at a young age or may have parents who are incarcerated. Some are living with the trauma associated with being severely mentally ill or physically ill or who live with a family member suffering serious mental illness. Some endure significant and traumatic medical interventions. Some suffer the trauma associated with severe bullying that can be associated with all sorts of things, including religion, race, and culture. Some young people suffer trauma when treated poorly due to their being diverse according to sexual orientation or gender identity, or if they are gender questioning. Some are children who are responsible at a very young age for family members who live with illness or disability, which can compromise their own wellbeing and life outcomes. Some live in poverty or are homeless, and some live in violent and terrifying homes in which their loved ones or even their pets are at risk of harm. Some survivors of trauma end up pregnant and parenting at very young ages. Some suffer trauma due to their living with a disability or become disabled due to suffering trauma. Some exhibit problematic or even harmful sexualised behaviours as a result of their experience of trauma, or exposure to sexually explicit material or pornography, which can lead to their being branded and treated as 'perpetrators' and 'offenders' at very young ages. Tragically, many are still living in traumatic circumstances, but this is hidden and silent. They remain unidentified. Of course, all of these types of trauma also cause serious psychological harm to children.

Children and young people from all these categories are sitting in classrooms across Australia and the world, and each of them is more than deserving of safe and supported access to education and support. A trauma-aware response from schools and early childhood education and care services becomes undeniably vital and necessary in the light of information about the various types of trauma suffered by some young learners.

First Nations Children and Young People

The ongoing impact of trauma on First Nations peoples in Australia, Canada, areas throughout Africa, Alaska, and throughout Oceania, and other parts of the world can be explained through a transgenerational trauma lens. Not only have these peoples experienced the impacts and associated grief from violent and socially disruptive invasion and colonisation of their homelands, but also from compounding institutional and interpersonal discrimination, marginalisation, racism, and oppression (Kirmayer, et al., 2014; Koea, 2008; Nicolai & Saus, 2013; Yellow Horse Brave Heart, et al., 2011). Milroy (2005) explains that trauma is transmitted across generations in First Nations communities due to the impact on attachment relationships and parenting and family functioning, the impact on parental physical and mental wellbeing, and the disconnection and alienation of individuals from extended family, culture, land, and society. These effects can be worsened by exposure to continuing high levels of stress, including multiple bereavements and personal losses and the process of vicarious traumatisation whereby children witness the ongoing impacts of trauma that family members have experienced (Milroy, 2013).

Despite this transgenerational impact, the strength and resilience of the First Nations peoples of Australia (and other parts of the world) must be acknowledged. Strong kinship systems and connections to spiritual traditions, ancestry, lands, and community, are protective factors that have helped many First Nations Peoples to overcome personal, communal, and historical pain (Atkinson, 2013; Caruana, 2010; Kelly, et al., 2009). Atkinson expresses the admirable and logical view that any solutions to help these peoples heal from trauma must draw from research into risk and protective factors affecting Indigenous populations and be driven and supported by these peoples, their elders, and their leaders (Atkinson, 2013).

However, the ongoing health disparities between First Nations peoples compared to non-Indigenous populations are well understood and yet continue to be under-addressed. In Australia, the intergenerational impacts of European colonisation, the subsequent forced removal of children from families and communities, and the ongoing effects of interpersonal and institutional racism continue to impact the health and lives of First Nations communities and families and continue to add complexity to the wellbeing and schooling of their children (White, 2015). The way that First Nations children are treated can have a significant influence on their health and life outcomes, and therefore, they are deserving of a culturally safe, trauma-informed model of care in many areas of service delivery, including their education (Milroy, 2013). It is worth implementing trauma-aware education to strengthen relationships between communities and schools, to help First Nations young people engage well with their education, and to improve the rates of First Nations young people who complete their schooling.

Very Young Children

Much of the rapid neural development from birth and throughout early childhood occurs as a response to interactions with caregivers and educators (Hughes & Baylin, 2012). As adults and young children respond to each other's cues, sets of neurons in the brain that manage human emotion — and the body's physiological responses to emotion are busily firing. This interactive process forms the foundation of human attachment, which develops and matures throughout life to assist with all relationships. As young children grow and then start to crawl, walk, and run, they increasingly engage in exploring their environments and playing and connecting with other children. To do this successfully, they initially need the support of the caregiver to initially encourage them to be brave and confident enough to physically separate from them so that they can explore their environment and play. They also need the caregiver to be available to co-regulate their unregulated emotions when they become upset, unwell, or frightened (Powell, Cooper, Hoffman, & Marvin, 2014). This type of activity happens multiple times throughout each day during early childhood. As a result, neurons are rapidly firing and connecting, and important neural development occurs.

However, if an infant's or young child's environment is frightening and abusive, where a person who should be loving, nurturing, and protecting them is actually the source of harm and terror, there can be a tragic impact on the development and future functioning of the early nervous system, including the brain. There can also be a worrying impact if access to warm and supportive adult attention is unpredictable or absent. How educators engage with very young children is important. How educators engage with very young children who have experienced complex trauma is vital! Not only does this very rapid period of neural development leave these children vulnerable to the impacts of complex trauma, there is also a wonderful window of opportunity for the trauma-aware work of educators to remediate this impact. Please see chapter seven of this book for more information on what a trauma-aware approach to early childhood education and care might entail.

Adolescent Students
During puberty and adolescence, the regulatory systems of the brain stem (fight, flight, freeze) and limbic system (emotional regulation, relationships) are gradually bought more and more under the control of the maturing pre-frontal cortex (executive functioning). However, this takes time. Caregivers and schools generally acknowledge that young people will need guidance to help them steer through this period to be safe and

well and achieve at school. So, this period of development can require the sustained support of caregivers and educators to connect with and work with adolescents in a manner that strengthens neural pathways that are responsible for impulse control and rational decision-making.

During adolescence, young people can experience physical, emotional, and relational changes that are directly associated with changes in the structure and activity of the brain. These changes are necessary for successful adaption into adulthood, allowing them to move in a more autonomous way towards becoming an adult and preparing them to eventually 'leave the nest'. However, these changes are also associated with increased emotionality, impulsivity, and a drive for reward, which can present adolescents and those around them with challenges.

It is helpful if the adults in the adolescent world take the time to understand at least some of the neurobiology of adolescence, to help them understand and respond adequately to these challenges. For example, it is helpful to know that the pre-frontal cortex goes through a period of integrating and linking differently to other parts of the brain during adolescence. Cells, circuits, pathways, and networks that are no longer needed are pruned away, and as a result, the brain becomes more differentiated and eventually, more coordinated and integrated, leading to a well-structured and well-functioning adult brain. However, it does take a number of years to get there, and during this period of neural change, there can be physical, psychological, relational, and behavioural impacts.

It is also helpful to know that there are changes during adolescence in the neural circuitry that manages the availability of a neurotransmitter called dopamine, which is a chemical that can enhance experiences associated with reward and feelings of pleasure. The baseline of dopamine can reduce, and this can lead to increased restlessness and feelings of boredom. It can also take a lot more stimulus to release more dopamine and for the young person to feel really good. However, when dopamine is released, it is released in more intense amounts, which feels great! Therefore, these interactions with the changing dopamine circuit can increase the adolescent's drive for novelty, danger, and high-risk behaviours.

There are benefits and challenges associated with the intense neural changes that occur during adolescence. Important sensations that are more intense during adolescence can create passion and vitality in young people, allowing them to become more creative and engage in thoughtful processes as they search for deeper meanings in their lives. However, these more intense sensations can also lead to emotional ups and downs, relationship issues, and difficulties focusing on schoolwork. There can be an exciting drive towards novelty, and new experiences and information during adolescence, which can lead to important development in knowledge and understanding. However, the risk with this drive is that young people can be drawn towards unevaluated or risky information or activities that may do harm. Also, adolescents may become frustrated with the mostly 'status quo' thinking and activity of the adults in their lives, which can help them to develop their conceptual thinking, courage, and creativity. However, it can also lead to disagreements and relationship difficulties and may be viewed as pushing boundaries or rebellion. There can be an increased desire for social engagement outside of the home, which is an opportunity for young people to develop important social skills and connections and to prepare for the quantity and types of relationships that will come more readily with adulthood. However, this can also come with risk, as this is a time when young people are vulnerable to relational pressures and complexities such as peer pressure, bullying, and managing the intense and confusing feelings associated with romance, intimacy and sexual attraction, as well as challenges with relationships with family members. So, adolescence is a time when caregivers and educators are continually balancing the need to allow for this development in young people with the need to keep them and those around them safe and emotionally, relationally, and educationally sound (Siegel, 2014).

So, adolescence is a time of change, possibilities, and challenge, but we need to consider what this period of development might be like, for young people living with unresolved complex trauma. In addition to the usual challenges faced during adolescence, these young people may also be negotiating feelings of injustice about their lives and circumstances, perhaps shame, guilt, or worry as they ponder their life experiences, or maybe self-consciousness when they compare themselves to their non-traumatised peers. In serious cases, some of these unresolved adolescents may become preoccupied with negative thoughts and behaviours (Jensen & Nutt, 2015). There may be a deep-seated distrust of adults, causing them to become hypersensitive to perceptions of threat. This can all impact the capacity to engage well with their education and to learn, as their attention is focused on survival and self-protection, and their emotions can too readily become dysregulated (Craig, 2017). Adolescents living with the outcomes of complex trauma are not the only young people who might suffer mental health concerns, but they are greatly at risk of mental health concerns if they are not supported adequately. By being informed and working in a trauma-aware way with at-risk adolescents, schools can recognise and respond to concerns and seek extra help for those young people who require this help.

Sometimes secondary school educators can be less tolerant towards behaviours exhibited by adolescents who are impulsive and deemed as behaving in a developmentally inappropriate manner due to the belief that they should have developed reasonable self-control during the primary school years. This presents challenges for those living with the outcomes of complex trauma, and they may not have had the opportunities to develop these capacities and skills by developmentally typical standards. If complex-trauma surviving secondary school students don't get the support and help that they need and deserve, the emotional and relational dynamics associated with puberty and adolescence can result in even more intensive behavioural (and mental health) concerns.

Also, during the secondary schooling years, students often need to manage the complexity of high school organisation, relationships with multiple teachers, negotiating multiple classroom changes, and the substantial expectations regarding performance and assessment, all of which can provide significant challenges for trauma-impacted students (Bomber, 2009). As a result, these students who struggle with their emotions and behaviours can be the recipients of quite serious punitive responses such as suspension or exclusion from school, in the hope that this will alleviate their concerns and the impacts of their behaviours on their peers, their educators, and the learning environment. Unfortunately, these approaches are rarely successful and can actually lead to students becoming even more ingrained in maladaptive thinking and behaviour, even to the extent that they can disengage from school.

It takes time, practice, and effort for adolescent, trauma-impacted students to learn to trust and feel safe with others and to manage the multiple daily transitions within each day at high school without becoming overwhelmed (Hertel & Johnson, 2013). To minimise concerns, schools can investigate possibilities to minimise the number of adults and room changes these students need to encounter each day, particularly when they are new to a school. Teachers should be made aware that students could face these challenges and aim to build constructive relationships, make classrooms feel safe, and provide time and spaces for students to emotionally self-regulate when needed. Behaviours that arise due to students feeling unsafe or overwhelmed should not be viewed as purposeful behavioural choices. They should not automatically be responded to with punitive or excluding sanctions. Rather, these students need repeated opportunities to experience help with their emotional regulation and unconditional positive regard from their educators.

The great news is that adolescence provides a window of opportunity to have a powerful influence on the brain development of all young people, particularly those impacted by trauma. There is already intensive 'rewiring' happening in the adolescent brain, so it is a great time to work towards helping young people to feel safe, to relate adaptively, and to become better and better at emotional self-regulation. All of this can contribute to the development of vital neural networks that can benefit trauma-impacted students throughout their schooling years and beyond. In other words, secondary schools have a marvellous opportunity to help move these adolescent learners closer and closer to becoming 'resolved' from the impacts of complex trauma.

The Costs of Unresolved Trauma

If childhood trauma is not addressed and left unresolved, studies have shown significant longer-term and sometimes lifetime costs associated with managing the impacts (Kezelman, 2015). If not addressed effectively, the impact of complex trauma can lead to already vulnerable students disengaging from their education (sometimes voluntarily and sometimes not) which can lead to worrying educational and life outcomes as well as significant societal expenses, including those associated with service areas such as health, welfare, child protection and care, crime, and accommodation. In addition, there are longer-term productivity losses as unresolved trauma victims are often unemployed due to the life complexities that they face (Jaffee et al. 2018).

International researchers agree that the economic impacts of unresolved complex trauma are substantial and very concerning. A study in Japan reported the annual costs of dealing with the outcomes of complex trauma to total at least $US16 billion (Wada & Igarashi, 2014). A later study found that the national lifetime cost was equivalent to 1.3 million GDP per capita and the burden of disease was equal to that of colon and rectum cancers or stomach cancer (Mo et al., 2020). A review in China estimated that 26.3% of overall disability-adjusted life-years (DALYs) were lost due to emotional abuse and 12.2% due to physical abuse (Fang et al., 2015). A study in the USA estimated the average lifetime cost, per child, of non-fatal maltreatment to be $US210,012 and fatal maltreatment to be $US1,272,900 and the total lifetime economic burden to be between $US124 billion and $US585 billion (Fang et al., 2011). A later systematic review and meta-analysis examined the impact of adverse childhood experiences in Europe and North America in terms of life course health consequences and associated annual costs (Bellis, et al., 2019). The study found that total annual costs were approximately US$581 billion in Europe and US$748 billion in North America. The researchers of this review suggest that a 10% reduction in adverse childhood experience prevalence could equate to annual savings of US$105 billion and that prioritising expenditure towards ensuring safe and nurturing childhoods would dramatically reduce pressures on health-care systems and be economically beneficial to both continents. A study from the United Kingdom estimated the average lifetime cost per child of non-fatal maltreatment as £UK89,390, with the bulk of this being due to welfare costs, short-term health costs, and long-term labour market outcomes (Conti, et al., 2021). Researchers in the Netherlands found that child maltreatment leads to profound mental health consequences and 'staggering long-term economic costs rendering lack of action very costly' (Thielen et al., 2016: p.1297). An Australian study estimated annual costs totalling $AU9.3 billion or $AU176,437 per child and estimated costs associated with reduced quality of life and premature death as $AU17.4 billion, or $AU328,757 per child (McCarthy et al., 2016). Moore, et al. (2015) explained that child maltreatment in Australia contributes to a substantial proportion of health costs related to depressive and anxiety disorders and intentional self-harm. A current study in Australia will identify associations between child maltreatment and adverse mental and physical health concerns and will estimate the costs and burden of disease attributable to child maltreatment (Mathews et al., 2021).

There is also evidence that the outcomes of unaddressed complex trauma can be transmitted across generations, so this social expense is compounded. Of course, in addition to these economic impacts, the human costs are incalculable. It is now evident that these costs to the individuals, families, communities and societies are considerable and concerning and warrant an expansion of investment into proactive support services for children, youth, and families, and hopefully, whole-of-government and systemic responses including those from the education systems. The early childhood and schooling years provide a window of opportunity to remedy harm associated with complex childhood trauma, given the substantial amount of time students spend in early childhood services and at school and the very malleable nature of the child or adolescent brain (Baylin & Hughes, 2012). It is in society's interest to invest in addressing the impacts of complex trauma in all learners during the education years, to minimise these worrying costs and maximise outcomes in areas such as education, health, and the workforce.

Understanding Trauma-Aware Education

Enthusiasm for trauma-awareness and trauma-aware practice within education settings is increasing rapidly, suggesting that education settings are starting to acknowledge that they play an important role in addressing the impacts of complex childhood trauma (Berger, 2019; Chafouleas, et al., 2018). It is increasingly being acknowledged that schools and early childhood services are critically positioned to support the resolution of complex, psychological trauma suffered by children and young people through the relational and learning environments they can offer and the amount of time that young learners spend in these environments (Berger, 2019; Dorado et al., 2016; Fondren et al., 2020). These sites are staffed with professionals who are dedicated to improving education and life outcomes for children and young people and they are increasingly informed by inclusive education policies and practices aimed to respond to the needs of learners with a broad array of backgrounds and needs (Morgan et al., 2015).

Trauma-aware education draws from various bodies of research, including neuroscience describing and analysing the impact of complex trauma on developing young bodies and brains, to inform a more effective means to educate and support children and young people who have lived through complex trauma. It is a shift away from a more traditional means of managing student behaviour that draws from behaviourist (reward/consequence) methodologies that can lead to behavioural and learning complexities that place learners at increased risk of disengagement from education (Barr 2018). It is a shift towards processes informed by neuroscience that develop learner capacities for feeling safe in education settings, for effective relationships whilst in these settings, and for emotional self-regulation; three areas that are negatively impacted by the experience of complex childhood trauma (Desautels, 2020; Thompson et al., 2014).

Trauma-aware education focuses on three main areas of learner support.

- First, strategies and processes are put in place to enhance the capacities of trauma-impacted learners to feel safe: to perceive their environment and the relationships within that environment as safe and non-threatening. The perception of safety is vital for children and young people to want to be in an educational environment and for the brain and the entire nervous system to function in a manner that allows for the learning process to occur and be effective.

- Second, trauma-aware education is dependent on relationships. It acknowledges that relationships that are perceived as safe, supportive, and unconditional can be a source of healing for trauma-impacted learners and their bodies and their brains.
- Third, trauma-aware education emphasises strategies and processes to help children and young people to develop their capacities for emotional regulation. As emotional dysregulation can lead to behaviours that can result in disciplinary responses and disengagement from learning and relationships, it is vital that work is done to develop capacities for emotional regulation. Often this starts with time spent co-regulating, where adults work with young learners to calm and soothe their emotions. Then with practice and support, these children and young people can gradually develop their capacities for self-regulation, where they become more and more able to calm and sooth their emotions themselves.

Of these three foci of trauma-aware education, relationships are the key. It is through relationships that we can help young learners to feel safe, and it is through relationships that we can help young learners to emotionally regulate. It is suggested that any of the activities involved in a trauma-aware education approach can be narrowed down to these three main areas of learner support and development.

Another important aspect of trauma-aware education is to improve education and life outcomes not only for trauma-impacted learners but also for their classmates. A trauma-aware approach is deemed appropriate and helpful for all learners as all children and young people can benefit from feeling safe, from engaging effectively in relationships, and from successful emotional self-regulation. Also, all learners benefit when the needs and behaviours of trauma-impacted learners are addressed. Disruptions to teaching and learning can be minimised, and peer-to-peer empathy and understanding (and friendships) can be enhanced.

An additional and vital aspect of trauma-aware education is to support and enhance the personal and professional wellbeing of the adults working hard to deliver inclusive education programs to trauma-impacted children and young people. This approach acknowledges that engaging with these young learners, day after day, can be very taxing and challenging. Therefore purposeful activity must be embedded into organisational processes to prevent harm and enhance outcomes for educators and any other practitioners who are working in schools and early childhood services.

Ideally, the journey of a school, early childhood service, or education system towards becoming trauma-aware should commence with, and receive continual support from, staff training and/or professional learning. This is to ensure all personnel are aware of the neurobiological impacts of complex trauma on developing nervous systems and the effect that this can have on the education experience for young learners. This will help educators develop ways of thinking, understanding, believing, and acting so that the harm that trauma exerts on the functioning of children and young people is minimised or alleviated.

Summary

This chapter has provided a brief introduction explaining a little of what complex trauma is, who it impacts, how it impacts, and what a trauma-aware response might entail. The following two chapters provide an overview of research and neuroscience that explains the impact of child maltreatment. It is certainly not necessary for all educators to know or remember all that is covered in these chapters. However, these chapters are written to provide a resource that explains the incredible evidence that informs trauma-aware education. The chapters draw from the work of devoted researchers and scientists who have dedicated their careers over decades to helping the world understand the impact of complex trauma and to develop effective ways to address this impact

Chapter 2

The Research Informing Trauma-Aware Education

Is Trauma-Aware Education Evidence-Based?

One of the common questions that people from education sites and education systems ask about trauma-aware education is, 'Is this evidence-based'? Most often, when people enquire into this, they are referring to whether trauma-aware interventions in places like schools have been evaluated using scientific research methodologies and, as a result, have been deemed successful. These types of evaluations are increasing each year. However, this type of research is certainly in an early stage of emergence compared to some other areas of research and is but one small component of an impressive body of research that truly informs trauma-aware education practice and policy reform. So, it is important that when we ask the question, 'Is trauma-aware education evidence based?' we do not limit our understanding of 'evidence' to only these studies.

Hoover (2018) discusses the frustration experienced when academic research exploring the mental health and wellbeing of school students falls short of having the desired impact for these learners. She mentions obstacles, including mutual distrust between researchers, practitioners in schools, and policymakers. She speaks of potentially misaligned incentives for the research and poor articulation of research findings by researchers to end-users. Hoover (2018) emphasises the importance of researchers translating their findings into brief synopses for end-users (such as educators, education sites and systems, and policymakers) and increasing networks to share their findings among researchers, practitioners, and policymakers through events like conferences and research-practice meetings. She proposes that, 'The science we produce in school mental health research is only as good as the meaning and impact it produces in the real world of schools' (Hoover, 2018, p. 195). It is vital that research examining trauma-aware education is negotiated, designed, and disseminated in ways that avoid the obstacles disclosed by Hoover (2018). In this way, it can contribute effectively and ethically in a time-efficient manner to policy and practice reform that aims to address the harm of complex trauma and to enhance education and life outcomes for trauma-impacted children and young people. The work is just too important!

Also, it may be important to question whether it is appropriate to restrict the design of studies evaluating implementation of trauma-aware education to only those that use experimental or quasi-experimental research methodologies. It is acknowledged that this is a very controversial topic among researchers and publishers of research literature. However, there may be ethical implications when applying strict research requirements to studies, particularly when experimental, random controlled trials allocate participants to control or treatment groups, leading to some trauma-impacted learners being denied access to interventions (Chafouleas et al., 2018; Zakszeski, et al., 2017). There may be concerns with using data from short-term studies, as it is known that recovery from the impacts of complex trauma can be a long journey for many young people. There may be concerns when deciding what aspects to examine or track in evaluation studies; should this be learning outcomes, behaviour outcomes, or the capacity for relatedness, empathy, or emotional regulation? There are certainly concerns with minimising data collection to only the items that are of more interest to schools, for example, academic outcomes, attendance, or the frequency of disciplinary responses such as suspension or detentions, as there are so many other important aspects to the education experience of a trauma-impacted learner. There may be concerns with waiting for findings from longitudinal studies when so many children and young people need help now. Research that is designed to influence practice, policy, and the experiences of 'end-users' is certainly recommended and required to contribute to the growing evidence base for trauma-aware education. However, this may mean becoming more comfortable with moving away from some of the more traditional and expected research methodologies.

The Adverse Childhood Experiences Study

One of the more significant bodies of research that informs trauma-aware education and trauma-aware practice more generally is the 'Centre for Disease Control and Prevention' (CDC) 'Kaiser Permanente' 'Adverse Childhood Experiences' (ACE) Study. The original version of this much-replicated study was conducted through Kaiser Permanente, an American health care insurance organisation. Researchers collected data from over 17,000 insured members of Kaiser Permanente in California, who were receiving medical examinations from 1995 to 1997. Participants, who were mostly middle-income, white, and tertiary educated, completed confidential surveys asking for retrospective information about their childhood experiences and current health status and behaviours.

This initial, large-scale medical study examined the long-term impacts of ten influential adverse childhood experiences (ACEs). It was the first study to identify childhood trauma as a costly and global public health issue rather than only a social issue. Of the many important discoveries that came from these initial and subsequent studies, three stand out. First, it was revealed that the more ACE's experienced during early life, the more likely individuals are to experience concerning, sometimes debilitating, sometimes deadly, health, mental health, and life impacts. Second, it was discovered that ACEs are far more common than previously believed, with approximately two-thirds of the population having experienced one or more ACEs and approximately 12% reporting four or more ACEs. Third, the initial ACE study and subsequent versions of this study that examine more diverse populations have found that ACEs do not discriminate, with individuals experiencing ACEs regardless of level of education, socioeconomic status, gender, religion, race, or culture. Prior to these studies, the effects and prevalence of ACEs were underestimated or misunderstood. These studies confirmed that, sadly, child maltreatment is far more prevalent than previously understood and if unresolved, can have devastating impacts on health (Felitti, et al., 1998; Hughes, et al., 2017).

Ongoing research examining the impacts of ACEs explores many areas of life experience, including employment, income potential, and poverty (for example, Metzler, et al., 2017). ACE researchers have also explored the impact on the behaviours of children and young people and their experience of education and on education outcomes for survivors of child maltreatment (for example, Hunt, 2017; Jimenez, 2016). It is now understood that addressing the potential impact of early adversity across the life course is critical if societies and systems are to address many of their health and welfare expenses and concerns.

Romanian Orphanages Studies

Another very significant and informative body of research comes from studies examining the very tragic impact of institutionalising babies and children in impoverished orphanages in Romania. Many of these institutionalised children in Romania suffered severe impacts on their development, which led to a wave of studies seeking to understand these impacts. However, it is important that this sad time in history is contextualised and explained before we look into the research.

Nicolae Ceausescu, Romania's last Communist dictator, ruled for 24 years. During his regime, he declared new policies designed to increase Romania's population so the economy would grow and flourish. These policies dictated that abortion and contraception were banned, that tax penalties would be imposed on people who were childless, and that women were required to have at least five children. In Romania during this time, women who gave birth to 10 or more children were declared as 'heroine mothers' and were celebrated! As a result of these policies and the resultant political pressure on women and families, levels of poverty increased dramatically. As a result, large numbers of infants and children were abandoned and institutionalised, including many who were born with disabilities. 'Child gulags,' were established, which were hidden from the outside world, and in which an estimated 170,000 abandoned infants and children were placed. These institutions were under-staffed and under-resourced, and abuse and neglect were rampant. After the fall of Ceausescu in 1989, the outside world discovered the existence of the 'child gulags' and the plight of the children and teenagers who were being raised in them. Many were adopted by Romanian or international families, but some remained institutionalised. Many continued to experience long-term and complex concerns.

These institutionalised children and adolescents exhibited alarming physiological and psychological symptoms that led to an abundance of research designed to understand this impact on child development. Neuroscience studies show the devastating effects of severe neglect on the brain development of institutionalised children. A severe lack of neural development and a disastrous amount of neural pruning led to brains having less mass and being malformed. Random controlled studies compared treatment and non-treatment groups. For example, some studies revealed significant differences in the brain composition of children who spent their first years in these institutions when compared to those who were randomly assigned to foster care in their early years. Longitudinal studies tracked the outcomes for these children over years. Retrospective studies describe the journeys of children who stayed in these institutions or were adopted and escaped the orphanages. Video data from studies describes the heart-breaking impact on the life experiences of babies, children, and adolescents. Studies have also examined the lives and circumstances of the biological parents of these children and the impacts of intergenerational harm.

Through this body of research, it became clear that extreme stimulus deprivation during the early years can lead to severe developmental delays, social and mental health concerns, and even early death, due to the tragic impact on brain development (Sempowicz, 2017; Sempowicz et al., 2018). This type of deprivation can lead to behaviours that are associated with, or are similar to, behaviours of those living with Autism, including self-soothing and self-stimulating behaviour such as finger sucking, hair twisting, body spinning and rocking, and head banging. Many post-institutionalised children experience persistent dissociation (Gindis, 2019). Gindis suggests that the trauma suffered by these children is:

> A complex somatic and neuropsychological phenomenon, which is chronic, relational (caused by humans), and significant enough to affect the development of a child'. (2019, p. 37)

One important outcome of this body of research is that societies now have a greater understanding of the impact of neglect. We now understand the seriousness of this impact and we no longer view neglect as less severe than overt physical or sexual abuse. We understand the devastating impact of physical, emotional, and relational neglect on brain development and functioning, and we are more responsive to intervene in child protection concerns that include neglect. We are also more aware of, and responsive to, concerns related to post-natal depression as this mental health concern can lead to the emotional and relational neglect of infants and young children.

Studies Examining Attachment

Attachment research has complemented other areas of research examining child development by exploring the impact of early childhood bonding experiences between a child and the parent or caregiver. When complex trauma occurs during infancy and early childhood, it can significantly impact a child's early attachment to their caregiver. This can then impact future behaviours, the capacity to negotiate future relationships, and even mental health and wellbeing.

Attachment research examining human bonding behaviours built upon earlier research using animals. One influential example was Harry Harlow's (1905–1981) studies in the 1950s and 1960s that examined the impact of contact comfort on primate development (Harlow, et al., 1965). His studies were conducted before the development of modern ethics research guidelines and remain controversial today for what is seen by many as the cruel treatment of animals. The studies involved removing infant rhesus monkeys from their mothers, raising them in a laboratory in cages, and isolating them from other monkeys. His studies showed that isolated, non-parented monkeys exhibited very unusual, concerning, and sometimes self-mutilating behaviours. When they were reintroduced to other monkeys, they were unable to engage effectively, and some refused to eat. Harlow continued to experiment by taking isolated infant monkeys and providing them with two 'surrogate mothers'. One was a 'mother' made of wire and wood with a bottle of milk, and the other was a 'mother' covered in soft cloth that did not have any milk. It was found that the infant monkeys spent significantly more time with the cloth mother and mostly visited the wire mother for food only, suggesting that the drive for maternal comfort was more important to these young animals than food. Harlow continued with other experiments to examine primate bonding and other behaviours, and his findings later informed experiments with humans (Harlow, et al., 1965).

British psychoanalyst John Bowlby (1907-1990) built on Harlow's findings and formulated the basic tenets of 'Attachment Theory' during his early studies in the 1940s and 1950s, which examined the interplay between parenting behaviours and child development. Initially, this work was informed by observations of the distress displayed by orphans and children separated from their parents in hospitals during and after World War II. He found that babies and young children who had been separated from their parents experienced difficulty forming or re-forming quality attachments with primary caregivers, leading to anxiety or what was initially referred to as 'insecure attachment'. He claimed that grief and mourning processes in children occur when attachment behaviours are activated but the attachment figure is unavailable. Bowlby worked with other researchers and eventually concluded that, based on his research findings, adult mental wellbeing was dependent on the quality and availability of the early relationship of the child and the mother, or mother substitute (Bowlby, 1951, 1958; Bowlby & Ainsworth, 1951; Bretherton, 1992). He referred to this type of relationship as a 'secure base' for developing children (Bowlby, 1988).

Bowlby's work was further developed during the 1960s and 1970s by Canadian psychologist Mary Ainsworth. Ainsworth was actually examining attachment at the same time as Bowlby and collaborated with Bowlby during this time. Amongst other work, she and her colleagues drew from Bowlby's seminal ideas to develop a methodology to categorise different types of attachment between child and caregiver. She developed the experimental procedure known as the 'Strange Situation', which involved placing a parent and their child in a play context in a room and observing and filming their interactions from behind a two-way mirror. After the child had settled into play, either a stranger entered the room and attempted to interact with the child, or the parent left the room, or both occurred. After a short period, these stressors were removed by the stranger leaving the room, the parent returning, or both. The responses of the parent and child to being separated, but more importantly, to being reunited, were recorded, analysed, and categorised. Ainsworth initially identified two broad categories of attachment; 'secure' and 'insecure'. 'Secure attachment' was identified when the infant or child used the parent as a source of security when playing and exploring their environment, and although they may have been distressed during separation, they sought contact and comfort with their carer when reunited. The reunion behaviours were warm and effective and allowed the child to emotionally regulate enough to resume playing and exploring their environment.

Ainsworth divided the category of 'insecure attachment' into two further subcategories. The first was 'anxious-ambivalent', which can be displayed when the child becomes extremely distressed by the separation, and although they may seek contact upon the reunion, they may not settle emotionally very quickly or effectively. The child can seem to both desire and repel parental contact and support. Within this category, parents may not have been consistently or adequately responsive to their child's needs. They may have exhibited poor timing in response to their child's distress and may exhibit a pattern of obtrusively interrupting their child's play. Ainsworth's category of 'anxious-avoidant' attachment may be identified when the child shows little or no distress when the parent leaves and may actively avoid and ignore the parent upon reunion, perhaps looking down or away, even when in the parent's arms. Historically, the parent may have also avoided the child or at least emotional engagement with the child at times. They may have been unresponsive to their child's needs and may have avoided the child's attempts to get relationally or physically close. Ainsworth suggested that these responses and categories may not only reflect the history of the parent-child relationship and the parenting style but may also predict the child's later psychosocial functioning.

Mary Main, a doctoral student of Ainsworth's, also researched in this area and worked with colleague Judith Solomon to develop a further category of 'insecure attachment' (Main & Soloman, 1986, 1990). 'Disorganised attachment' was identified during the 'Strange Situation' experiment when out-of-context, anomalous, or contradictory behaviours were observed that suggested the child was disorientated, feared the caregiver, or experienced significant levels of conflict about approaching the caregiver. Researchers observed children exhibiting undirected, misdirected, mistimed, or incomplete movements and anomalous postures such as freezing. There was no predictable or effective pattern to the behaviours exhibited by the stressed child to elicit effective caregiving from their parent (Main & Solomon, 1986, 1990). Main and Hesse (1990) suggested that when a child experiences their caregiver as frightening to them, or frightened of them, this can have a very influential and detrimental impact on the attachment system. They also explained that any psychological dissociation experienced by caregivers could result in significant distress for young children. Solomon and George (2011) suggested that caregivers of young children classified as having 'disorganised attachment' can feel helpless or out of control or can become very emotionally dependent upon the child. The 'disorganised' classification has been found to be substantially more common in at-risk samples of children and also predictive of later child mental health problems (Cyr et al., 2010).

Main also found that how adults remember their own childhood experiences might influence the attachment categorisation of their children (Main et al., 1985). As a result, she developed 'Adult Attachment Theory' and the 'Adult Attachment Theory Interview' (Main, 2000). Consequent research into adult attachment suggests that 'secure attachment' serves as a foundation for healthy expression and regulation of emotions and communication in future relationships, and the varying forms of 'insecure attachment' can lead to difficulties with adult and parenting relationships.

The work of these early attachment theorists has been instrumental in the development of many years of research examining child development. One example is the work of Ed Tronick (1978), who was one of the first researchers to show that babies are profoundly affected by their caregivers' emotional states and behaviours. In 1975, Tronick developed an experimental procedure known as the 'Still Face Experiment' (Tronicket al., 1978). The experiment involved filming (simultaneously) the face of a caregiver and the face of their infant or young child. The caregiver was asked to engage actively and relationally with the child for a period of time, then to turn away, and then to turn back expressionless and silent for a period of time (two to three minutes), not responding in any way to the child's cues or attempts to regain their attention. Children in this context usually become sombre and wary quite quickly, and when their repeated attempts to engage with their caregiver fail, they can become quite distressed, their posture can slump, and they can withdraw emotionally. This period of relational disconnect is quite short during this experiment, and when securely attached caregivers and their children begin to connect again, it doesn't take too long for the child to recover. Tronick would suggest that this experiment explains the wonderful and positive impact that engaging and responsive interactions between caregivers and their children can have on the child's experience, development, and resilience. The experiment shows that the withdrawal of carer interaction can have an immediate and significant impact on the emotions and behaviours of infants and young children, but that impact is often short-term and is certainly minimised if the caregiver readily resumes interaction. Tronick's work was, however, able to show that when there are more serious attachment challenges between caregiver and child, the relational repair might take longer or become more problematic. This type of 'relational neglect' can seriously impact how the Mirror Neuron System develops and functions (see Chapter Three), and therefore, the emotional wellbeing of children and their capacities for relationships. Tronick also researched the impact of post-partum depression on infants, showing that when the 'still face' that a young child experiences from their carer, continues repeatedly and for long periods, emotional recovery is impaired (Tronick, 1978). These learnings also apply to those infants and young children who have suffered child maltreatment and neglect at the hands of their main caregivers (Beebe, 2015).

A multitude of subsequent studies has been implemented examining the impact that different types of attachment, and child maltreatment, can have throughout the lifespan, and this has informed various therapeutic and parenting interventions. One influential intervention was developed by clinicians Powell, Cooper, Hoffman and Marvin (2014) and is known as the 'Circle of Security'. This intervention builds upon Attachment Theory and Bowlby's concepts of caregivers being a 'secure base' and a 'safe haven' for their children. The authors developed an assessment and intervention protocol and training regime that can be used by clinicians, parent educators, and others to work with groups of caregivers, couples, or individual caregivers who need help with their caring and attachment with their children. Empirical evaluation of the intervention is continuing (Kim, et al., 2018, Maxwell, et al., 2021) and the intervention has now expanded to include applications in classrooms and in early childhood care (Cooper, et al., 2017; Gray, 2015).

Prevalence Studies

Countries and systems collect prevalence data to provide a picture of the pervasiveness of child maltreatment and the importance of addressing the harm associated with child maltreatment. For example, the 'Violence Against Children and Youth Surveys' (VACS) data is collected annually by national governments and the CDC, and findings suggest that half of all the children in the world succumb to violence each year, with some areas of the world having significantly greater density of prevalence than others (https://www.cdc.gov/violenceprevention/childabuseandneglect/vacs/). However, much of the information that helps us understand the prevalence of child maltreatment in individual countries comes from child protection service data. There are generally two approaches to this data collection, with the most common being annual collection of incidence data.

Some countries (including Australia) report on annual data regarding the numbers and types of children receiving child protection services (The Australia Institute of Health and Wellbeing (AIHW), 2021). Examples of findings from the time of writing this book suggest that one in 32 Australian children aged from birth to 17 years receive child protection services due to reported or substantiated reports of child maltreatment. Annual findings also suggest that First Nations children were almost eight times as likely as non-Indigenous children to have received these services, and 42% of children placed in long-term, out-of-home care, were First Nations children. Children from geographically remote areas were three times more likely than children from major cities in Australia to have a report of harm substantiated or to be placed in out-of-home care. Infants under the age of one year were most likely (38 per 1,000 children) to have received child protection services. For all children, emotional abuse (54%) was most common, followed by neglect (22%), physical abuse (14%), and then sexual abuse (9%). About twice as many girls experienced sexual abuse than boys, and slightly more boys experienced neglect and physical abuse than girls (AIHW, 2021). At the time of writing, a large and comprehensive research project is in play that aims, amongst other goals, to generate population-based data on the prevalence of child maltreatment in Australia (Mathews, et al., 2021).

A second approach to understanding the prevalence of involvement with child protection services adopts a life course perspective or the cumulative risk of ever having received child protective services during a life stage (for example, birth to 17 years). Life course data provide an important measure of child protection service information that is additional to annual incidence data. Some would consider these data allow for a more accurate description of the prevalence of this concern. For example, research in the United States shows that although experience with child protection services can appear relatively rare in annual figures a much larger proportion of children are reported to receive child protection services over the course of their childhood years (Kim et al., 2017).

Child protection data also explains that service delivery is not spread evenly across countries and communities but rather disproportionately affects families who are marginalised by race and socioeconomic status.

However, it is important to understand that these social groups are often those for whom social resources are lacking and other stressors are exacerbating the likelihood of maltreatment. Due to these and potentially other important reasons, including social bias and racist thinking, these communities may become more visible to professionals who are mandated to report and respond to child maltreatment. These dynamics can lead to children from certain groups of society being more easily, or less likely, to be represented in child protection data. Importantly, some children who experience maltreatment are not represented in this data at all and yet are just as deserving of safety and support.

Research shows that children who have experienced maltreatment are at greater risk of eventually engaging in criminal activity and entering the youth justice system (Cashmore 2011; Currie & Tekin 2006; Malvaso et al. 2017). Another prevalence study from the AIHW explored the intersection of youth justice and child protection data in Australia (AIHW, 2020). Around 54% of young people who are in youth justice supervision in Australia have also received child protection services. About one-third were the subject of a substantiated report for abuse or neglect, and around 22% were placed in out-of-home care within the previous five years of data collection. Although girls made up only 21% of the youth justice population, they were far more likely to have had involvement with child protection services. Around 71% of girls under youth justice supervision during 2018–19 had received a child protection service in the previous five years compared to 49% of boys. Again, and unfortunately, First Nations youth were also disproportionately represented in these data. Approximately 61% of Indigenous young people who were in youth justice supervision had received child protection services in the previous five years, compared to 48% of their non-Indigenous counterparts (AIHW, 2020).

From data sets analysed through prevalence studies, we can understand more fully the pervasiveness of child maltreatment in countries, other geographic areas, and the global community (Mathews, 2021). However, it must be acknowledged that the number of children who have experienced harm according to child protection data must be considered an underestimate of the total number of children who have been maltreated as there continue to be unidentified children who have been or who still are being, harmed. These studies help us to begin to grasp the likelihood of childhood maltreatment leading to long-term consequences, including involvement in crime and the justice system. They also help us to become aware that children who are of a certain 'type' can be more likely to experience maltreatment or incarceration due to circumstances beyond their control, including how old they are, their gender, where they live, or their race or culture.

So, prevalence studies add to the evidence base that reinforces the importance of a trauma-aware response in schools and early childhood education and care, as the likelihood of trauma-impacted learners enrolling or participating in these education settings is high. These studies also remind us of the importance of proactively addressing the harm done to children through an informed and supportive approach to education during childhood and youth. In tandem with child protection services, schools and early childhood services in marginalised (and indeed, all) areas can work to prevent and address the harm of child maltreatment by being equipped to work in trauma-aware ways to support children.

Longitudinal Studies

Most research on ACEs, including the original study, collects data retrospectively, whereas longitudinal studies collect data from or about participants over a defined or extended time period. The Dunedin Study (Dunedin Multidisciplinary Health and Development Research Unit, n.d.) is a good example of this. This study started as a much smaller examination of developmental and health problems identified in a cohort of approximately one thousand one-year-old children, who were to be followed up at age three. This study has been expanded and funded to collect and analyse lifetime data on this cohort, who are now all in their 40s. The physical and mental health of each participant is regularly assessed and has resulted in hundreds of published research projects. Some of these have contributed well to our understanding of the impact of child maltreatment. For example, brain imaging studies and data on participants' childhood experiences have shown that childhood adversity is clearly associated with alterations in brain structure (Gehred, et al., 2021).

In another example of a longitudinal study, researchers in Sweden examined a cohort of over 13,000 participants born in 1953 to explore the impact of childhood adversity on education outcomes. By examining those who had received child protection services or who lived in out-of-home care as children and comparing this group to those who did not have these experiences, researchers were able to identify that child welfare involvement is a strong indicator for midlife educational disadvantage (Forsman & Jackisch, 2021).

Systematic Reviews

Systematic reviews are sophisticated and in-depth literature reviews that appraise and synthesise primary research using rigorous, clearly defined, and documented methodologies. First, researchers decide on and document their search strategies for finding research publications on their topic. Then, they decide on and document how they select from this group of publications those that they will include in their analysis. These approaches to research, while considered more robust evidence than individual studies, can also be more abstract and less connected to the reality of actual education practice.

There are a growing number of systematic reviews that examine topics associated with trauma-aware education, and these mostly have identified that there is a sincere need for ongoing research in this emerging area of study. Maynard et al. (2019) provides a good example of this. The researchers explored the effects of trauma-informed approaches in schools and came to the conclusion that despite the growing support for, and increased rate of which trauma-informed approaches are being promoted and implemented in schools, solid evidence to support this approach was still lacking. The aim of their review was to assess how trauma-informed approaches in schools impacted student trauma symptoms, mental health, academic performance, behaviour, and social-emotional functioning. The studies they included in their review needed to be published between 2007 and 2017 and needed to be experimental in design. So, the studies needed to compare learners who received a trauma-aware intervention with other learners who did not. The researchers found that no studies met their selection criteria to be included in their review. However, Maynard et al.

(2019) state that while caution is warranted when moving forward, this 'does not preclude schools from continuing to implement evidence-informed programs that target trauma symptoms in youth, or that they should wait for the research to provide unequivocal answers' (p. 3). They suggest that:

> The adoption of a trauma-informed approach is relatively new, and it is likely that there has not been sufficient time for the research to catch up to the enthusiasm for this approach in schools. Furthermore, conducting rigorous research on multi-component and multi-tiered approaches can be complex and expensive, often requiring large grants to help fund the research, which can also delay the conduct of rigorous research (Maynard et al., 2019, p.12).

Fondren et al. (2020) also engaged in a systematic review evaluating trauma-informed interventions in schools, but they had a more expansive criteria to include studies in their review compared to Maynard et al. (2019). After their search and selection process, they examined 62 peer-reviewed studies of trauma-aware interventions that included a three-tiered system of service delivery. They found that most interventions included in their review focused on tier three interventions for students requiring intensive support, and few integrated all three tiers effectively. They concluded that there is strong evidence for the feasibility of whole-school, trauma-aware, multi-tiered interventions where support increases across tiers depending on the needs of students. However, they recommended that more work needed to be done to understand how to tailor trauma-informed approaches for individual students or individual schools, and there was an ongoing need for more rigorous research.

A scoping review by Stratford et al. (2020) also examined school-based, trauma-aware interventions. They included peer-reviewed research publications and grey literature in their review. Grey literature is published informally or not published at all and is not usually peer-reviewed, but still might include helpful and reliable information. This type of literature can include documents such as government or organisational reports and conference papers. The authors of this scoping review examined 91 publications after their search and selection process. They noted that most interventions focused on counselling services, psychoeducation, and parent engagement but that there was a lack of interventions that were designed to be implemented by non-clinical personnel at schools. They suggested that more rigorous evaluations of whole-school approaches were needed and, in particular, examination of work that could be implemented by school personnel. They highlighted the need for quality professional learning for school personnel and the need to make high-quality research accessible to schools and policymakers.

There is also a systematic review by an Australian researcher that focuses on trauma-aware education. Berger (2019) implemented a review examining multi-tiered approaches to trauma-informed care in schools. She included published and unpublished sources, such as conference proceedings and doctoral theses, in her review. After her search and select process, 13 studies were examined. Her findings suggested that there was evidence that multi-tiered approaches to trauma-aware schooling were effective, but the evidence, although increasing, still remained limited. She recommended greater consistency in interventions and in research methods to add to this growing body of evidence and to inform the ongoing uptake of trauma-aware approaches in schools.

Roseby and Gascoigne (2021) conducted a systematic review exploring the impact of trauma-informed education programs on the academic and academic-related functions of trauma-impacted students in preschool, primary, and high school settings. Academic-related functions for this study referred to student attendance, disciplinary referrals, suspension, resilience, school attachment, and emotional presentation. After the search and select process, these researchers examined 15 studies that met their criteria for inclusion, including that the programs were implemented in a whole-of-school manner and that they measured the academic and academic-related outcomes of interest to the researchers. Despite results not being consistent across all the studies, this review did find that trauma-informed education programs had the potential to positively impact students' academic and academic-related outcomes.

Summary

There is a rapidly growing enthusiasm for exploring the impacts of complex trauma on children and young people and on trauma-aware education responses. Some of the research examining education responses include studies and literature (some peer-reviewed and some not, some published in journals and some not) that may or may not be considered 'academic' or 'rigorous'. Indeed, much of what we currently know is drawn from the dedicated explorations of non-government organisations that focus (full-time) on a trauma-aware response to remediate the harm of complex trauma. So, what is becoming clear, is that findings from many sources are contributing to a growing global understanding of, and a growing conversation about, trauma-aware education. These deserve to be read and considered alongside the growing impetus for more research and publications on this topic. What is vitally important is the contribution of the studies examining the **science of complex trauma** to help us understand what complex trauma and trauma-aware education are, why it is important to respond in a trauma-aware manner in education sites and systems, and how we should respond. The following chapter will examine this science in detail.

Chapter 3

The Neuroscience of Learning and Complex Trauma

The brain of a young learner is wired to survive and thrive and it is through social connectedness that they have the chance to reach their potential (Ziegler, 2011). Interpersonal neurobiology is one body of science that helps to explain neuroplasticity, which is the capacity for neurons to change in their structure and relationship to one another in reaction to experience. Interpersonal neurobiology also helps to bridge the gap between the biological sciences (bodies and parts of bodies) and the social sciences (interactions between bodies). It explores the way in which human relationships and nervous systems interact to shape the mental worlds of individuals and groups (Siegel, 2012). It also helps us to understand more fully the relational components of the educational experience for all learners, and particularly for trauma-impacted learners.

The brain began to be understood as a social organ during the 1970s as neuroscientists started exploring the interconnections between human anatomy, biochemistry, and social relationships. Since then, thousands of studies have testified to the influence that relationships have on health, neuroplasticity, and learning. We can conceptualise interpersonal neurobiology by thinking about the micro (very tiny) relationships — through to the macro (very large) relationships in our bodies and our worlds. I will step you through this in the next paragraph in very simple (but still intriguing) terms.

It all starts with relationships between my neurons (nerve cells) and my synapses (the connections between my nerve cells) within my brain. These interactions lead to the rapid and complex development of, and interactions between, neural pathways and networks within specialised parts of my brain. This then leads to relationships between parts of my brain and parts of my entire nervous system throughout my body. At this stage, we can conceptualise this as 'Me'. This then leads to relationships between my nervous system and your nervous system, and we can think of this as 'We'. This then leads to growth in my relationship with myself as it develops with my relationship with you and with others, and can be conceptualised as 'Us'. All of this leads to (and is dependent on) the development and functioning of the social, learning brain and entire nervous system (Cozolino, 2013; Seigel, 2012).

So, what does this mean for education? In education settings, teachers and others use their personalities, interpersonal skills, and teaching methods to create physical, emotional, conceptual, and social environments that stimulate neural plasticity for their students, which leads to learning and development at the 'Me', 'We', and 'Us' levels. While teachers may be focussing on what they are teaching, neuroscience suggests that the relational and emotional environments in which teaching occurs are very important for cognitive and social growth and for the mental health and wellbeing of children and young people in learning environments. Indeed, interpersonal neurobiology would assure us that relational interactions in and beyond the classroom are the fundamental regulators for neuroplasticity in the young brains of learners and therefore their learning.

In the classroom, young brains are especially attuned to detecting and evaluating new and unexpected information and experience. When a teacher introduces novel events or concepts or information that has previously not been known by learners or that provides some challenge to learners, a cascade of electrical and chemical interactions in the brain is triggered. This can then heighten the attention of learners and the functioning of their memory. This also happens when a teacher behaves unexpectedly or interestingly by using new and varying types of pedagogy (Willis, 2009). Great teachers know that the way that they teach matters, and now we can explain why this matters through the lens of neurobiology.

It is important to recognise that this exciting process is enhanced if learning occurs in what the learner perceives to be a safe, relational, and inclusive context. Unfortunately, this process is hindered if children or young people perceive that they are not safe, not connected, or not included. We know that the experience of complex trauma can interfere with how students perceive their relational and learning environments, and despite the best efforts of creative and dedicated teachers, feelings of safety, relationships, and emotional regulation can be impaired. So, for the education experience of trauma-impacted learners to be successful, it is vital that educators have some understanding from the perspective of neurobiology of the impacts of trauma and of recommended trauma-aware responses.

It is important to acknowledge when looking at neurobiology that all the various parts of the brain and nervous system are interdependent. They all communicate with each other and have an overall, integrated function. When this integration is working well, people can present as physically, emotionally, mentally, relationally, and behaviourally well. When this integration is not functioning well, individuals might feel physically, emotionally, or mentally unwell. They may struggle with their relationships and behaviours. Thus, healthy neural integration could be considered one of the goals of a trauma-aware approach to the education and support of learners.

Research Powerhouses: Sources for the Science

In 2000, the *Institute of Medicine and National Research Council Committee on Integrating the Science of Early Childhood Development* produced 'From Neurons to Neighborhoods: The Science of Early Childhood Development' (Shonkoff & Phillips, 2000), which was a landmark report in the field of early childhood development. At around the same time, a second group, the *John D. and Catherine T. MacArthur Foundation Research Network on Early Experience and Brain*

Development was examining the transformative impact of working at the intersection of neuroscience and developmental psychology. In 2003, members of these two groups joined together to form the *National Scientific Council on the Developing Child*, which became a multidisciplinary, multi-university collaboration that was committed to research examining learning, behaviour, and physical and mental health for young children. From this group, the *Harvard Center on the Developing Child* was founded in 2006. This centre has since become a nationally recognised and extremely influential research and development platform for translating complex neuroscience related to childhood adversity into language and resources that are highly credible yet understandable to non-scientists and informative and useful for public and policy decision-makers. They design, implement, and evaluate their ideas and findings in collaboration with a comprehensive network of scientists, researchers, practice, policy, community leaders, and philanthropic organisations. Research findings, publications, and resources developed by the centre are freely and widely available on their website (https://developingchild.harvard.edu). The centre describes its overall mission as driving scientific innovation to achieve innovative and successful outcomes for children who are facing adversity (Center on the Developing Child at Harvard University, 2014).

One important source of scientific research that informs the outputs of the *Harvard Center on the Developing Child* and certainly informs trauma-aware work internationally, is the *Developmental Biopsychiatry Research Program* at McLean Hospital in Massachusetts. This program was founded in 1988 to enhance the lives of people afflicted by psychiatric disorders that arise during development. Martin Teicher is the founding director of this program and is also an Associate Professor at Harvard Medical School. Teicher comes from an illustrious career as a multi-award-winning scientist and oversees the work of a research laboratory exploring the enduring impacts of child maltreatment. Research from this laboratory shows clearly that childhood maltreatment alters brain structure and function, depending on the type of abuse, the stage of development during which the harm occurs, and the severity and multiplicity of exposure to maltreatment. Studies identify stages of development, referred to as sensitive or critical periods, during which exposure to maltreatment mostly affects genetic factors, neural development, and particular parts of brain anatomy. The laboratory has also examined in depth whether alterations in brain structure can predict future risk for substance abuse and mental illness.

So, these are two contemporary and important examples of increasingly prolific, science-informed learning sources that allow us to assure educators that trauma-aware education is indeed evidence-based. The remainder of this chapter will outline some elements of the science that help us to understand how the human body is supposed to develop and function and the potential impact of complex trauma during childhood and adolescence, and if not resolved, throughout life. Again, educators are not neuroscientists and certainly should not be expected to know and memorise the science in depth. However, a general awareness of what is shared in this chapter is certainly helpful and very much recommended if we are to contribute towards the resolution of complex childhood trauma as individual practitioners, as part of a school or early childhood education and care service, and as part of broader education systems.

During the following explanation of the various parts of the nervous system, I will not always provide regular in-text references, as the information comes from so many sources. However, a substantial list of references is provided in the references for this chapter to help the reader grasp the amount and quality of scientific research that has contributed to our ever-growing understanding of the impact of complex trauma on the human nervous system.

The Nervous System

First, to understand the neurobiological impact of complex trauma on bodies and brains, we need a basic understanding of the 'usual' development, structure, and functioning of the human nervous system. We understand the nervous system as a network within the body that functions to manipulate external and internal information. It is responsible for receiving, interpreting, and sending information to and from all parts of the body and the brain. It receives sensory input from the environment, integrates this within its processes, and then manages motor output via the body's muscles, glands, and organs. The two main parts of the human nervous system that manage all these processes are the **Central Nervous System** and the **Peripheral Nervous System**.

The Central Nervous System is made up of all the neural matter within the brain and the spinal cord. It is the processing centre for the whole nervous system. The brain processes and interprets sensory information sent up from the spinal cord, which is the major conduit for information travelling between brain and body.

The Peripheral Nervous System consists of networks of nerves that connect the Central Nervous System to the rest of the body. It can be broken down into two further systems, the **Somatic Nervous System** and the **Autonomic Nervous System**.

The Somatic Nervous System processes and responds to sensory information from the environment and consists of two types of nerves. Afferent (sensory) nerves register sensory information or sensations from the peripheral or distant parts of the body (those away from the brain — like the arms and legs) and carry them to the Central Nervous System. Efferent (motor) nerves extend out of the brain and take the messages for movement and action to the skeletal muscles. For example, if you touch a hot object, the sensory nerves carry information about the heat to your brain. Then the motor nerves transmit information back down to the muscles of your hand that cause you to move away from the hot object. The whole process takes less than a second to happen. Due to the important interconnection of the Somatic Nervous System and the Autonomic Nervous System, interventions to support trauma-impacted students can often include activities to sometimes stimulate, and sometimes calm, activity in the Somatic Nervous System.

The Autonomic Nervous System controls the nerves of the inner organs of the body. We have no conscious control over this part of our nervous system. The Autonomic Nervous System can influence heartbeat, digestion, and breathing (except conscious breathing). It relays information to the smooth, involuntary muscles of internal organs and glands and causes them to function and secrete hormones (chemical messengers that trigger many functions) and enzymes (proteins that can accelerate chemical reactions). The Autonomic Nervous System can be further broken down into the **Sympathetic Nervous System** and the

Parasympathetic Nervous System, both of which have important functions necessary for survival.

The Sympathetic Nervous System mobilises the body for action in response to a perceived threat (referred to as 'mobilising defences'). This part of our nervous system is best known for its stimulation of the fight, flight, or freeze response. During fight, flight or freeze, our field of consciousness narrows to include only those elements in the environment that we perceive are pertinent to our survival (for example, a possible escape route). Our senses become hyperalert and emotional states might emerge to support our defence against any perceived threat (for example, anger can accompany a fight response and fear can accompany a flight response). Our pupils dilate, digestion can be interrupted, respiration rate can heighten, and there can be increased blood supply to our large, skeletal muscles to prepare our bodies for a physical response. If escape is not likely or available, sympathetic nervous system (fight or flight) reactions can become more frantic, or they can lead to the freeze response (referred to as 'immobilising defences'). The freeze response can lead to a slowing of heart rate and respiration, physical limpness and passivity, and psychological distancing or dissociation. One quite serious outcome of complex trauma is that victims suffer from an overactive and sensitive, Sympathetic Nervous System.

The Parasympathetic Nervous System counteracts the action of the Sympathetic Nervous System by reversing or calming the sympathetic nervous system response. The job of this system is to help the body reach what is known as 'homeostasis', a calming and balancing of the nervous system responses so that the body can get back to optimal functioning. A parasympathetic nervous system response can cause the pupils in your eyes to constrict and your heart rate to slow down. In your lungs, it can cause bronchial musculature to contract and stimulate bronchial secretions, both of which help slow and regulate breathing. It can also enhance gut motility for digestion to occur effectively. All of this can be summarised as the 'rest, digest, and repair' response. The Parasympathetic Nervous System is also responsible for internal functions while resting and relaxing. The aim when working with trauma-impacted learners is to engage the Parasympathetic Nervous System to help children and young people calm, their bodies to reach homeostasis, and for them to rest, digest and repair, and then re-engage with their social and learning environments.

The Human Brain

The human brain is perhaps the most complex structure known. This complexity is embodied in its makeup as it consists of several hundreds of billions of cells interconnected by hundreds of trillions of connections constantly interacting and changing. Each connection is a locus of signal transfer between neurons (nerve cells), so that (at all times) there are vast networks of cells intercommunicating in some manner. In the following section, I will describe and explain the 'usual' anatomy and function of parts of the human brain. As you read through this information, I am sure you will become increasingly aware of how intricate, integrated, and incredible the human brain is. This remarkable organ is so very well designed, so powerful, and yet so very malleable. Sadly, the brain is also very susceptible to the impacts of complex childhood trauma.

The Brain Stem

The brain stem is the first region of the brain to develop after conception. It starts as a microscopic neural tube and develops and specialises quickly. The brain stem is directly connected to the spinal cord and is the conduit for information to and from the brain and spinal cord. It controls functions needed for survival, even before birth, including heart rate, blood pressure, body temperature and respiration. It is the centre of autonomic nervous system responses, including the fight, flight, or freeze response associated with the Sympathetic Nervous System. In unresolved trauma victims, this part of the brain can be too regularly and too severely overactive.

The brain stem includes the **medulla oblongata**, the **pons**, and the **midbrain**. Information travels back and forth from brain and spinal cord through each of these sections. The medulla oblongata controls autonomic functions such as breathing, digestion, heart, and blood vessel function, swallowing, and sneezing. Both sensory and motor neurons travel through this area. The pons is one of the smallest parts of the brain (only 2.5cm in length) but is involved in many autonomic and sensory processes, including arousal, respiration, fine motor control, equilibrium, muscle tone, and the circadian (sleep regulation) cycle. The midbrain is associated with many functions, including the management of auditory and visual sensory information.

The Diencephalon
The diencephalon is a small section, just under and between the two hemispheres of the brain and just above the brain stem. This part of the brain helps to manage motor regulation, internal recharging and healing, the body's ability to negotiate its environment, arousal, appetite, and regulation of sleep patterns. It also helps the body to manage the energy required to respond to challenges placed upon it by the environment. The diencephalon includes the **epithalamus**, the **hypothalamus**, and the **thalamus**. The epithalamus is located bottom of the diencephalon. It helps with the sense of smell and includes the pineal gland, an endocrine gland that secretes the hormone melatonin, which helps with sleep cycles. The hypothalamus is approximately the size of an almond. It controls many autonomic functions through the release of hormones and helps to maintain homeostasis. When an unanticipated imbalance is detected in the body, this part of the brain employs a mechanism to counteract the disparity. The thalamus acts as a relay station for almost all sensory information (except for smell) and assists with regulation of motor function, sleep cycles, and consciousness.

In humans, the bulk of the development of the brain stem (medulla oblongata, pons, midbrain) and the diencephalon (thalamus, hypothalamus, epithalamus) is complete before a baby is born. There is rapid development of these parts of the brain in utero.

The Cerebellum
The cerebellum (which means 'little brain') is located just below the cerebrum and just behind the upper brain stem (the area at the base of the skull where the head meets the neck). It is the densest part of the brain, accounting for about half of the neurons in the brain but only being a tenth of the total brain size. The cerebellum receives information from other areas of the nervous system. It uses this to regulate and coordinate motor functions, including voluntary movements, balance and posture, motor learning, and the movements associated with speaking.

In human beings, the cerebellum takes approximately three years after birth to reach a level of maturity whereby children can start to manage their motor functions effectively (e.g., walking and running). This is in stark contrast to other animals that are born with cerebellums that are quite mature and developed and therefore, are able to move quite effectively immediately or soon after birth. Due to this, these animals are more likely to survive even if they don't receive consistent and adequate attention and care from caregiver animals. However, human babies are very dependent on the care and protection of adults if they are to survive infancy and very early childhood due to their underdeveloped cerebellum and minimal capacity for movement. This is why the attachment phenomenon between children and their caregivers is so important and why harm can be exacerbated when it comes from the hands of people who should be nurturing and caring for very young children.

The brain stem and diencephalon areas of the brain are referred to as the 'lower' or 'subcortical' parts of the brain. Some refer to them as 'older', 'primitive', or 'survival' parts of the brain. Add to these the cerebellum, and this is often referred to as the 'reptilian' part of the brain as reptile brains consist only of these areas.

The Limbic System

The limbic system rests in the middle of both hemispheres of the brain. This system helps to regulate emotions (through complex interactions of perception, experience, memory, and body chemistry) and aspects of sexual behaviour, relationships, attachment, and motivation. It determines the body's emotional and behavioural responses to perceived threat and environmental influences and connects to cortical (higher) and sub-cortical (lower) parts of the brain. The limbic system includes the **amygdala,** the **hippocampus,** and the **cingulate cortex**. In humans, the bulk of the limbic system development happens from conception to the (approximate) third year of life. This is a period of rapid development. If the relational harm of complex trauma happens during this time, there can be longer-term emotional, relational, and behavioural outcomes due to the impact on the developing limbic system and the parts within this system.

- The amygdala is deep within the limbic system and is responsible for responding to and recalling emotions, especially fear. It controls how we react to certain stimuli or events that cause emotion, particularly those we see as potentially threatening or dangerous. The amygdala of trauma victims can be particularly sensitive.

- Close by is the hippocampus, which assists with storing, retrieving, and using different types of memory. It is responsible for the processing of long-term memories that are associated with emotional responses. The experience of complex childhood trauma can have a worrying impact on the development and functioning of the hippocampus. Cells within the hippocampus are particularly sensitive to harmful reactions to stress hormones, especially when stress is prolonged and severe.

- The cingulate cortex (also known as cingulate gyrus) is involved with emotion formation and processing, learning, inhibitory control, and memory. It is described as a neural interface between emotion, sensation, and action as anatomical connections link the cingulate cortex with brain areas closely associated with each of these functions. Child maltreatment has been shown to impact the healthy functioning of this part of the limbic system.

The combined brain stem, diencephalon, cerebellum, and limbic system is referred to as the 'mammalian brain'. Both human and non-human mammal brains include these areas.

The Insula

A part of the brain that has a strong connection to the limbic system is the insula. The insula is not large, but it is a very complex part of the brain that manages many interrelated functions. It is situated deep within a fissure separating the temporal lobe from the parietal and frontal lobes (within each hemisphere). Due to its position in the brain, it is able to bring information up from lower parts of the brain and can send this information to the many other neural networks that it connects to and to all the lobes of the cerebral cortex (outer layer) of the brain. It is believed to be involved in consciousness, awareness and perception, functions associated with emotion, compassion, and empathy, interoceptive processing (how much or how little attention one pays to sensory information within the body), interpersonal experience, regulation of homeostasis, motor control, and taste. The relational activity associated with attachment and bonding strengthens and thickens the insula, as does engagement in deep relaxation activities such as mindfulness. A thicker and more well-developed insula is said to be related to an enhanced capacity for relatedness and empathy, which is often a concern for trauma-impacted learners.

The Cerebral Cortex
The outer layer of the brain, the cerebral cortex, is divided by a bumps and grooves known as gyri (bumps) and sulci (groves or fissures). The gyri and sulci increase the surface area of the cerebral cortex and enable more brain matter to fit inside the skull. Each half of the brain can be divided into four lobes (Parietal, Temporal, Occipital, and Frontal). Although most brain functions rely on many different regions working together across the entire brain, it is still true that each lobe carries out the bulk of particular functions. The **parietal lobe** helps the body to process sensory information, including touch, temperature, pressure, and pain. The **temporal lobe** also helps with processing sensory information, but mainly in the area of hearing, and it has an important role in recognising language and forming memories. The **occipital lobe** is the visual processing centre of the brain. It receives visual information from the eyes, which is then relayed to processing areas in the brain that help interpret depth, distance, location, and the identity of things that are seen. The **frontal lobe** manages higher executive functions, including emotional regulation, planning, reasoning, and problem-solving. Even these higher areas of the young brain can be impacted by child maltreatment. For example, Tomoda et al. (2011) explained that exposure to the verbal abuse of a caregiver can lead to an increase in neural matter in the superior temporal gyrus. Tomoda et al. (2012) showed that there is reduced neural matter in the visual cortex in young adults who had witnessed domestic violence when children.

The Pre-Frontal Cortex

The pre-frontal cortex is the section of the frontal lobe that lies at the very front of the brain. It is more developed in primates and highly developed in humans. It manages complex mental functions to regulate cognitive, emotional, and behavioural functions in response to novel and challenging demands. One of the major tasks of the pre-frontal cortex is executive function. In humans, the bulk of pre-frontal cortex development happens from conception through to approximately the mid to late 20s. There is rapid and ongoing development during this time. Adolescence is an important time for the re-modelling and ongoing development of the pre-frontal cortex. Neural activity in the pre-frontal cortex is compromised if there is too much activity in the brain stem, the part of the brain acutely involved in our survival response to a perceived threat and the fight, flight, or freeze response. This will be discussed in further depth, a little later in this chapter, as this part of the brain is so important when discussing the impact of complex childhood trauma on the capacity for learning.

The Hemispheres of the Brain

The brain is divided into two halves or hemispheres, and within each, particular regions control certain functions. Neuroscientists continue mapping the hemispheres, and insight is growing regarding the functions of each. The two hemispheres look very similar, and they do work interdependently, but they can differ in how they process information. Each side of the brain controls movement and feeling in the opposite half of the body but it is important to understand that the two halves of the brain work together and complement each other and no matter what task you are involved in, you are receiving input from both sides of your brain. A thick band of more than 200 million nerve fibres (known as the **corpus callosum)** provides a neural bridge between the right and left hemispheres. The corpus callosum is approximately ten centimetres in length and is shaped like the letter 'C.' Research has shown that the development and integrity of the corpus callosum can be impaired in response to complex childhood trauma, which can compromise inter-hemisphere neural communication.

Human Altriciality and Human Potential

Based on what is known about brain development and functioning in human beings, we are the least suited of all animals for independent survival at birth and during infancy and early childhood. Humans are distinguished by their altriciality, meaning they need a caregiver to survive and thrive early in life. Human children are born with an immature cerebellum, and so it takes much longer for them to move independently, and this inhibits their capacities to fend for themselves or nourish themselves. They are born with few built-in survival skills. No member of the animal kingdom takes as long to be able to survive without direct assistance from others. Human beings also have a much longer adolescence than other animals, which is a time of rewiring of the brain in preparation for independence from external caregiving.

However, humans are the most likely to survive and thrive in the longer-term, due to the specialised anatomy, development, and functioning of the human brain. The bulk of development of the human brain occurs very rapidly and then continually throughout life in response to ever-changing environmental stimuli. This process of adaptation, which is led by a very sophisticated pre-frontal cortex, allows us to manipulate environments and negotiate responses in ways that benefit us. So, despite a vulnerable period during very early childhood, humans are the most suited to adapt to all sorts of environmental possibilities and challenges. We just need to ensure very young children are loved, nurtured, and protected from the harm of complex trauma.

Neurons

Now that we have covered the main (larger) parts of the nervous system, the next section of this chapter will examine the cells within the nervous system to go a little deeper in our understanding. Neurons, or nerve cells, are the building blocks of the nervous system. Although neurons don't make up the largest number of cells in the nervous system, they can be considered the most important as they drive neural development through the constant transmission of electrical and chemical information. They vary in length and size, ranging from those that are microscopic through to some that are approximately a metre long. Neurons are both resilient and vulnerable. They are resilient because, unlike other cells that die and regenerate continuously, most neurons live as long as a person lives. However, they are vulnerable because they cannot survive more than a few minutes without continuous nourishment and oxygen.

To understand how the nervous system develops and works, it is helpful to learn about key components of the neuron and their important functions. The **cell body (or soma)** is the metabolic centre of the cell that provides energy to drive all the activities of the neuron. It is enclosed by a membrane that both protects it and allows it to interact with its immediate surroundings and it includes a number of important parts. The cell body includes the **nucleus** which is an organelle that contains the genetic properties of the cell. The **dendrites** are fibrous roots that branch out from the cell body. The job of the dendrites is to receive and process electrical and chemical information from other neurons. Neurons can have more than one set of dendrites, depending on their role, and these are known as dendritic trees.

Neurons also have an **axon**, a long, tail-like structure that connects to the cell body (at a junction called the **axon hillock**) and extends down to one or more **axon terminals** at the end of the axon. The job of the axon is to relay electrical impulses transmitted from the dendrites, through the cell body, and down to the axon terminals so that information can then be transmitted to other neurons. The axon is enclosed in an amount of a fatty substance called **myelin**. The greater the coverage of myelin on the axon, the more efficient the conduction of electrical impulses. The axon terminals include tiny pockets, known as **synaptic vesicles**, which contain a multitude of various types of chemicals called **neurotransmitters.** Neurotransmitters are molecules used by the nervous system to transmit messages between neurons.

The **synapse** (or synaptic cleft) is a microscopic gap between the axon terminal of one neuron and the dendrites of neighbouring neurons. When an electrical impulse arrives at the axon terminal, it causes the synaptic vesicles to release their neurotransmitters into the synapse. Some of these chemicals will be reabsorbed by the original neuron (this is called reuptake). Others will bind with receptors on the dendrites of neighbouring neurons. This can cause these cells to experience an electrical change, leading to the electrical impulse continuing through the next neuron. An excitatory neurotransmitter can generate an electrical signal called an **action potential** in the receiving neuron, while an inhibitory transmitter prevents this. The generation of an action potential is often referred to as neurons 'firing'.

Neurotransmitters

There are many different categories of neurotransmitters, and each serves vital functions. The following briefly explains the work of only a small number of neurotransmitters. These explanations are certainly not comprehensive, but rather are just to provide you with some examples of the tasks of these important chemicals.

Glutamate is the primary excitatory transmitter that enhances the transmission of electrical impulses, and **gamma-aminobutyric acid (GABA)** is a major inhibitory transmitter that prevents transmission. These two neurochemicals work in combination. When this is done effectively, the body is more likely to be in a state of homeostasis. **Norepinephrine** is the primary neurotransmitter for the Sympathetic Nervous System. It has a role in the fight, flight, or freeze response and influences the activity of various organs to control blood pressure, heart rate, liver function, and many other functions. **Acetylcholine** is the Parasympathetic Nervous System's main neurotransmitter and has a key role in the 'rest, digest, and repair' process. It also has a key role in the Central Nervous System functions that manage memory and learning. **Dopamine** is involved in many functions, including motor control, the perception of reward and pleasure, and motivation. **Serotonin** influences functions such as mood, sleep, memory, and appetite. **Histamine** has a role in metabolism, managing the body's temperature, regulating the release of hormones, and managing the sleep-wake cycle. It is also released when the immune system is defending against a potential allergen.

So, despite their tiny size, these microscopic chemicals have vital and multiple roles in how we perceive ourselves and how we interact with our environments, our physical and mental health and wellbeing, and how we function. They also direct the process referred to as neural development which involves neurogenesis (the growth and development of neural tissue), and synaptogenesis, (the formation of synapses between neurons).

Neural Development and Neural Pruning

During neural development, the electrical and chemical interactions at synapses lead to neurons firing and joining up with each other and forming neural pathways and networks. Each neuron has the capacity to develop and communicate with up to 10,000 to 15,000 other neurons, and each of these can, in turn, communicate with the same amount. Neurons are so prolific that one month after conception, the brain is generating 500,000 neurons every minute, and at birth, an infant has approximately 100 billion neurons. Once a baby is born and starts to experience and respond to an ever-expanding range of environmental stimuli, neural development becomes more rapid. During the early childhood period (particularly during the first three years), intense neural development occurs, and the brain becomes increasingly dense with neural matter.

There are also peaks in neural activity during 'sensitive periods' or 'critical periods' of development throughout life. A 'sensitive period' is a limited time window in development during which the effects of experience on the brain are unusually strong. Early childhood, pre-adolescence, and adolescence are examples of sensitive periods. A 'critical period' is a special class of sensitive period where behaviours (and neural development that supports these behaviours) do not develop normally if appropriate stimulation is not received during a restricted time window. Examples of 'critical periods' would be the periods in very early life where sight and hearing develop. Suppose an infant (child or animal) did not receive visual or auditory stimuli during this period. In that case, they can be at risk of sight or hearing impairment and, for children, possible language delays or impairments. A number of paediatric neurological disorders can be attributed to impaired neural plasticity during 'critical periods'. Knowing about these periods of opportunity for maximal neural development can help professionals time their interventions to help towards the optimal development of children (Ismail & Johnston, 2016; Teicher, 2019).

Neural pruning is an additional process that occurs alongside neural development. This involves the removal of neurons, synapses, pathways, or networks that are no longer used or useful in the brain. This process happens throughout life but is particularly active during adolescence when unused or no longer useful neural matter is pruned away, particularly in the pre-frontal cortex. Over time, the remaining neural matter goes through a period of integrating and linking differently to other parts of the brain. Eventually, the adult brain evolves as a more differentiated yet integrated organ with faster, more coordinated, and more effective neural communication. Adolescence can prove to be a 'rocky road' for young people (and those who care for and educate them) as these rapid and significant changes occur, but it is a necessary period of neural activity that leads to the maturation of the adult human brain.

The Mirror Neuron System

Research into the Mirror Neuron System has radically altered how we think about our brains, ourselves, and our connection to others. This system includes a special class of neurons that fire not only when an individual performs an action but also when the same individual observes someone else performing the same action. It appears to let us simulate not only the actions of other people but also the intentions and emotions behind these actions. For example, when you see someone smile, your mirror neurons fire and initiate a reaction in your mind of the feeling associated with smiling. You don't have to think about what the other person intends by smiling. You just experience the meaning immediately and without conscious effort, and often, you will smile in response.

Early research examining the interactions of this system within the brain occurred in the 1980s and 1990s. Using intrusive microsensors surgically placed deep in the brain, researchers recorded the firing of neurons in the brains of macaque monkeys as they observed the behaviours of other monkeys. It was noted that neurons in the premotor areas of the frontal lobe of a monkey's brain would fire (preparing the monkey's muscles for the movements it will make) when another monkey was observed in a specific behaviour, such as grasping an object. It was also noted that the same neurons fire when the original monkey engaged in the same task in response. Later, researchers using surface electrodes discovered that these same sets of neurons were active in infant monkeys as they responded to human facial gestures. They recorded monkeys up to one-week-old that repeated the actions of humans that they observed, such as when they stuck out their tongues. As these neurons fire both when observing and when performing an action and are involved in the 'mirroring' of behaviours of others, they were dubbed 'mirror neurons'.

Human studies followed and have continued to examine the Mirror Neuron System. Brain scanning technologies (including Functional Magnetic Resonance Imaging [fMRI]; Electroencephalography [EEG], and Magnetoencephalography [MEG]) were used to further explore this phenomenon in humans and discovered that mirror neurons are situated in much broader brain areas than originally thought through monkey studies. They were mostly found in networks in the frontal lobe of the left hemisphere and the parietal lobes of the right hemisphere. These studies expanded the understanding of mirror neurons from the behaviour of specific (mirror) cells to the behaviour of complex (mirror) neural networks. They also began to explain how synergies created by interactions between these networks are activated during observation, imagination, empathy, and the execution of actions.

Researchers investigating the psychological and social implications of this body of neuroscience became excited about how this could inform a deeper understanding of how humans connect with and respond to each other. This was particularly helpful in advancing our understanding of human attachment and the development of relational capacities such as compassion and empathy. 'Theory of Mind' refers to our ability to infer another person's mental state (for example, their beliefs and desires) from their experiences or behaviour. 'Theory of Mind' is available because we subconsciously empathise with the person we are observing, and we imagine what it would be like for us if we were 'in their shoes'.

Brain scanning experiments suggest that interactions of mirror neuron systems can trigger 'Theory of Mind' responses. They have shown that mirror neurons in brain regions (such as the anterior insula, anterior cingulate cortex, and inferior frontal cortex) are particularly active both when people experience an emotion (such as disgust, happiness, or pain) and when they observe another person experiencing a similar emotion. Findings suggest that the Mirror Neuron System plays a key role in our ability to empathise and socialise because we communicate our emotions mostly through facial expressions. The Mirror Neuron System helps us decode (receive and interpret) facial expressions, and the same mirror neuron areas become activated whether we are observing or making a facial expression.

Researchers examining human attachment have explored the activity of the Mirror Neuron System by examining human interactions. Mirror neuron driven behaviours can be witnessed when caregivers interact with their infants. For example, an infant might mimic aspects of the facial expressions of a caregiver, such as opening their mouth, smiling, or sticking out their tongue. A baby might cry and frown when distressed, and almost immediately, the face of the caregiver will change to match the emotional tone expressed by the baby. With healthy and active Mirror Neuron Systems, caregivers and their infants cannot help but respond to each other's social cues.

Genetics, Epigenetics, and Intergenerational Transmission

The science of epigenetics is adding more depth to what we see in the 'real world' through the behaviours and experiences of human beings. It is quite usual for people to see 'real world' evidence of intergenerational transmission of circumstances such as poverty, violence, maltreatment, neglect, and other negative impacts on families and children. It is also quite usual for this type of 'real world' evidence to be explained in behavioural terms. For example, the maltreatment of a young child by a parent can impact the attachment relationship between parent and child, whereby they may not be adequately able to read and respond to each other's social cues. This could then lead to an impact on how the child is cared for or treated, and if this impact is not resolved, the child could then grow up to have a child of their own and treat that child in a similar manner to the way that they were treated. You may have heard this explained as being 'the cycle of abuse', or as 'learnt behaviour', which are ways of understanding intergenerational transmission through behaviourist and psychological understandings that explain how 'whole bodies' behave in the 'real world'. The science of epigenetics explains this same phenomenon but at a cellular, genetic, and epigenetic level. So rather than looking at how whole bodies (people) behave, it examines how the cells and parts of cells within whole bodies behave when child maltreatment is experienced. Epigenetics is helping us to understand the impact of harm and is also helping us to grasp the potential for healing inherent in trauma-aware support.

One of the main functions of the nucleus inside human cells is to manage the hereditary traits of individuals (those you inherit from your biological parents). Inside the nucleus are **chromosomes**, which are thread-like structures made up of strands of **deoxyribonucleic acid (DNA)** and **histones** (alkaline proteins on which the DNA strands are packed). Chromosomes in the nucleus are tightly packed with approximately three billion pairs in each cell. If stretched, the DNA in a single cell would be about two metres long. An organism's complete set of (inherited) DNA is referred to as its **genome**.

A **gene** is a unit of hereditary information that occupies a position on a chromosome, and each cell in the human body contains approximately 25,000 to 35,000 genes. Genes carry the information that determines your traits (features or characteristics that are passed on to you from your biological parents). Gene expression refers to a complex series of processes through which information that is encoded in a gene is used to modify how much protein is made by a gene, effectively turning the gene 'on' or 'off.' What we experience in life can leave a chemical 'signature' on our genes, determining whether and how they will be expressed. Collectively, these signatures are referred to as the **epigenome**. So, the genetic makeup that you have inherited from your parents and were born with, is referred to as the *genome*, then as you interact with your environment and experiences throughout life and chemical markers modify the structure and behaviour of some of your genes, this is referred to as the *epigenome*.

Epigenetics is a body of research that explains how environmental influences (experiences) can affect the expression of genes. It is an area of science that is increasingly contributing to our understanding of both positive and negative intergenerational transmission of genetic information and traits. This science disproves the idea that your genetic makeup is 'set in stone' and has shown that 'nature versus nurture' is no longer a debate. Epigenetics explains that genetic makeup is clearly influenced by both.

An important message gleaned from epigenetics is that genetic changes in an individual that can result from both positive and negative experiences can then be passed on to their offspring. Early studies examining this phenomenon explored the intergenerational transfer of trauma-related traits that were shown in the offspring of Holocaust survivors. Children and grandchildren of survivors of the Holocaust came to share the trauma-based biochemistry of their biological parents and grandparents, without having experienced any of this trauma themselves (Yehuda & Seiver, 1997; Scharf, 2007, in Gindis, p. 45). These and further studies explain that stress and trauma in caregivers can result in negative epigenetic changes in children that can be passed down for generations if not resolved.

Studies suggest that experiences that change the epigenome early in life, when the specialised cells of organs (for example, the brain, heart, and kidneys) are first developing, can have a powerful impact on physical and mental health over the lifespan. The good news is that genes also respond well to supportive and nurturing experiences for young children in the earliest years when brain development is most rapid and there is ongoing potential for this throughout childhood, adolescence, and adulthood. The bad news is that genes are vulnerable to modification in response to complex trauma, relational harm, toxic stress, nutritional problems, and other negative aspects of a child's environment. Such harmful experiences very early in life, when the brain is developing most rapidly, can cause epigenetic changes that influence whether, when, and how genes release their instructions for building future capacity for health, skills, and resilience. If this is not resolved through experiencing other, more adaptive life circumstances that address these negative changes, there will be a risk that these modifications to the epigenome could be eventually transmitted intergenerationally.

This has huge implications for early childhood education and care and schooling. We now know from epigenetics that a trauma-aware response can help to resolve the impact of harm for children already sitting in classrooms or other education sites, which can also mitigate harm for their future children who will sit in future classrooms. If viewed through a societal lens, or even through social economics, epigenetics provides evidence that trauma-aware education can be understood as an ethical and efficient way to provide a 'mass dose' of the 'medicine' needed to resolve the current and future intergenerational impacts of child maltreatment, which has the potential to reduce the quite substantial personal, community, and societal costs associated with complex trauma.

Hyperarousal and Hypoarousal

Hyperarousal in learners can lead to the *fight* response and might involve behaviours such as fighting, punching, biting, hitting, and verbal aggression. It also can lead to the *flight* response and might involve behaviours such as running out of the classroom or school, climbing on roofs, or escaping to hiding spaces.

Hypoarousal can lead to the *freeze* response and this might involve behaviours such as learners covering their heads, moving their bodies into a position that makes them as small as they can, taking on a foetal position on the floor, hiding under desks or tables, or being very quiet and withdrawn. In serious cases, this can involve moderate to severe disassociation or learners even losing consciousness. Some students who freeze can 'go under the radar'. Their responses can be misinterpreted as merely being very shy or quiet. However, a young learner in a hypoarousal state may actually be experiencing a significant physiological event and is certainly deserving of our help, just as much as those learners who are experiencing fight or flight.

The Window of Tolerance

The Window of Tolerance is a concept or metaphor originally developed by Dan Seigel (1999) that helps describe the zone of arousal in which a person can function most effectively. It explains the zone (or window) in which people can receive, process, and integrate information and respond to the demands of everyday life without too much difficulty. The window has an upper limit that delineates where a person might be at risk of moving into a state of hyperarousal and a lower limit that defines the tipping point for moving to an experience of hypoarousal. Between these two limits is the window in which optimal functioning can occur.

This concept acknowledges that we all experience our emotional 'ups' and 'downs' and times when we feel more or less in control of our responses. However, if our experiences and responses are contained within the 'Window of Tolerance', the suggestion is that we will be able to function in an adaptive manner overall. This concept suggests that the distance between the upper and lower limits of the 'Windows of Tolerance' can vary for individuals, but it is accepted that the greater the distance between these limits, the better. Wider 'windows' provide individuals with more capacity for managing the emotional highs and lows associated with experience and make it less likely they will experience hyperarousal or hypoarousal. Alternatively, a narrow 'window' may lead to an individual being more likely to feel that emotions are intense and are less likely to be able to manage this effectively. Thus, they would be more likely to experience hyperarousal or hypoarousal and perhaps more often.

When a person goes into hyperarousal or hypoarousal, and is outside their 'Window of Tolerance', the brain stem becomes highly active, the body and brain go into survival mode, the pre-frontal cortex becomes less active, and it becomes harder to think clearly. Also, the body is flooded with stress hormones (including adrenalin and cortisol). It is important to remember that this profound neurobiological response is happening when trauma-impacted learners experience the fight, flight or freeze responses. Living with the outcomes of complex trauma can lead to a narrowing of the 'Window of Tolerance', so children and young people are more likely to experience hyperarousal or hypoarousal. However, they are generally more able to remain within their window when they feel safe and connected. Through repeated work with learners who have survived trauma, we help their emotional responses to be contained within their 'windows', more often and more effectively, with repeated practice. Learners might still experience emotional dysregulation, but over time, this should be less often and in a more contained manner that does less harm to themselves and others.

The Poly Vagal Theory

The Polyvagal Theory developed out of Stephen Porges' experiments with the **vagus nerve**. It explains the role of the various parts of this nerve in emotion regulation, social connection, and the fear response. 'Poly' in the title refers to 'many', and 'Vagal' refers to the vagus nerve. The vagus nerve has long axons and serves the Parasympathetic Nervous System (the calming part of the Autonomic Nervous System). It also balances the sympathetic or active part of the Aautonomic Nervous System. There are two main branches (and other smaller sub-branches) throughout the length of the vagus nerve. The two main branches are the dorsal branch and the ventral branch, and they work in different ways (Porges, 2011).

The dorsal vagus branch manages immobilisation and also recovery from immobilisation. It travels from the brain, down the back of the brain stem and branches out to the heart and lungs and parts of the body below the diaphragm, including the gut and organs. This branch has two sub-systems referred to as high tone and low tone. The high tone system activates in threatening situations by managing the immobilisation response (freeze, shock, shutdown, dissociation) as a protective mechanism to 'preserve life'. This can lead to a slowing of heartbeat, circulation, and respiration and can interrupt digestion. The low tone system helps in recovery from this state of immobilisation. It reverses the physiological reactions, increasing blood and oxygen supply throughout the body and to the gut, so digestion improves. It can cause an individual to feel restful and even sleepy, as systems can go through a process of repair.

The ventral vagus branch manages mobilisation. It travels from the brain down the front of the brain stem and then branches to the heart, lungs, and body parts above the diaphragm. This includes upper branches around the face, ears, and neck areas. This branch of the vagus nerve helps with gradual and nuanced reactivation of what is referred to as the 'social engagement system'. This causes the middle ear to filter out background noise, making it easier to hear the voices of others in the environment. Facial muscles become more active, enhancing the ability to make communicative facial expressions. The larynx loosens up, enhancing vocal tone and patterning so that sounds can be created that help communicate to others and are emotionally soothing to individuals. The activation of this part of the vagus nerve helps with reconnecting, re-engaging, and self-soothing, all important when individuals are recovering from a frightful event or circumstance.

The long axon of the ventral vagus nerve of young infants is not very myelinated, so initially, there is quite a slow transmission of electrical and chemical information along this nerve. As caregivers engage in social and attachment behaviours with their babies, the axon and branches of this nerve fire and activate more and more, leading to more myelination, a lowering of heart rate, self-soothing, and a gradually maturing 'social engagement system'.

Children and young people should not experience extreme sympathetic nervous system action or high tone dorsal vagal states for long periods. Indeed, this should only happen for a maximum of a few minutes. Sadly, learners who have experienced trauma can be in these states way too long and often. This can impact their physiological functioning and health, mental and emotional wellbeing, social connectedness and relationships, education, and recovery. For optimal health and functioning, these young learners need an active social engagement system (ventral vagus), good opportunities to rest, digest, and repair (dorsal low tone), a minimised sympathetic nervous system response (fight or flight), and minimised experiences leading to the freeze response (dorsal vagus high tone). In other words, we need to help these learners to practise staying within their 'Windows of Tolerance'.

It is important to remember that the perception of serious threat can trigger the dorsal vagal high tone response. Perceived safety can prevent this and can help with recovery. Perceived safety can lead to wanting proximity to others. Proximity to others can lead to bonding and relationships. Bonding and relationships can lead to helpful firing and reinforcement of neural networks and to recovery from the neurobiological impacts of trauma. A lack of perceived safety impacts all of this. So, perceived safety and social connectedness can be considered as biological and educational imperatives. When children and young people don't feel safe in education settings, their learning can be impaired and they present with behaviours (and faces) that repel others.

The Endocrine System and the HPA Axis

The Hypothalamic-Pituitary-Adrenal (HPA) Axis is mostly responsible for regulating bodily responses to acute and chronic stress. As suggested in its title, this axis involves three glands: the **hypothalamus,** the **pituitary gland,** and the **adrenal glands**. The hypothalamus and the pituitary gland are situated in the brain, near the brain stem, and the two adrenal glands are situated above each kidney.

When a person experiences a stressful event, the hypothalamus releases a hormone called corticotropin-releasing hormone (CRH). This CRH then triggers the release of another hormone from the pituitary gland, known as adrenocorticotropic hormone (ACTH). ACTH then enters the bloodstream and travels down to the two adrenal glands, which are each situated just above each kidney. The adrenal glands release the stress hormones, **adrenalin** and **cortisol** which are hormones that increase the body's capacity to respond to stressors.

In response to stress, levels of adrenalin rise relatively quickly. Increases in adrenalin can fasten your heart rate, elevate your blood pressure, and boost your energy supplies. In other words, this response is preparing your body for action to respond to a perceived stressor. However, levels of adrenalin also fall quickly, particularly when you realise that the perceived stressor is not as threatening as you first thought. So, it does not take very long for the effects of an adrenaline surge to wear off and a body to calm down.

However, cortisol levels rise and fall far more slowly. Surges in cortisol increase the availability of sugars (glucose) in the bloodstream, enhance the brain's use of glucose, and increase the availability of substances that repair tissues. Again, this is a natural response to stress and prepares the body to face a perceived stressor. It is important to understand however that cortisol does remain for longer in the brain and body, than adrenalin. When levels of cortisol become too great, this is detected by the hypothalamus and the hippocampus in the brain, and a *negative feedback process* occurs that shuts down the HPA stress response. Supplies of adrenaline and cortisol are then diminished, homeostasis or hormonal balance occurs, and the person who experienced the stressful event calms down.

Unfortunately, one of the impacts of living through complex trauma is impaired HPA Axis functioning. The toxic and chronic stress associated with trauma-impacted can involve intense reactions that frequently occur and last too long. The result is impaired functioning of the negative feedback loop which leads to an overexposure of the body and brain to high levels of the stress hormone, cortisol. Cortisol is a naturally occurring hormone and does have an important role to play, but when it is in the body and brain too much and too often, there can be detrimental outcomes.

Due to its role in the HPA Axis, this overexposure to cortisol can impact the hippocampus, the part of the brain that has a significant role in managing memory. High and persistent levels of cortisol can interfere with the function of neurotransmitters in the hippocampus, and this can impair the creation of new memories and access to existing ones. There are corticosteroid (cortisol) receptors all over the hippocampus so cortisol is readily attracted to this part of the brain. **Mineralocorticoid receptors** have a high affinity for cortisol and bind to cortisol even when a stress response isn't happening. This is needed for normal hippocampus function. However, **glucocorticoid receptors** have much less affinity for cortisol and these are usually only activated when levels are very high (during high stress). When these are activated, the neuronal formation of new memories is suppressed.

Too much cortisol in the brain too often, due to chronic and serious stress, can unfortunately cause long-term damage to cells within the hippocampus and therefore impact its structure. Some studies have shown that the hippocampus can even shrink in size! The combination of hippocampus shrinkage, nerve cell damage, and overactivation of glucocorticoid receptors, leads to an inability for the hippocampus to effectively form, store, and retrieve memories.

The Immune System

Cortisol also plays an important role in the body's immune response. A major component of immunity is the inflammatory response. **Cytokines** are the chemical messengers that link the brain and the **Immune System**. There are two main types: **pro-inflammatory cytokines** increase inflammation, and **anti-inflammatory cytokines** reduce inflammation. When faced with an immune threat (such as a bacteria or virus), the Immune System produces pro-inflammatory cytokines to destroy it, leading to inflammation. These cytokines act directly on the brain, leading to 'sickness behaviour' such as a loss of appetite, fatigue, irritability, or fever. This inflammation attacks the immune threat, thus protecting healthy cells and tissues. After the inflammation has done its job, the amount of anti-inflammatory cytokines increases and the amount of pro-inflammatory cytokines reduce. Inflammation then subsides. However, if the immune threat continues and continues, this inflammation process can start attacking healthy cells and tissues.

An overabundance of cortisol (due to chronic and toxic stress) can impact this immune response. High cortisol levels suppress immunity by reducing pro-inflammatory cytokines and increasing anti-inflammatory cytokines. This increases the chance of infection and damage to healthy cells and tissue. Research suggests that this interaction between the HPA Axis and the Immune System helps explain the long-term health impacts of Adverse Childhood Experiences (ACEs).

> The brain, endocrine, and immune systems share a common language of hormones, signalling molecules, receptors, and neurotransmitters, which facilitates communication across the network to maintain homeostatic balance. In addition, through interactions with the brain and neuroendocrine system, immune insults affect not only immune competence but also the building blocks of brain development, including neurogenesis and neural signalling. Early life adversities, including lack of nurturance and social support, poverty, and trauma, are translated into health and developmental outcomes via the neuroendocrine-immune network. Johnson, et al., (2013, p. 320).

Dissociation

Dissociation in humans is a defence mechanism that can stem from trauma, inner conflict, or other forms of stress. It can even be triggered by extreme boredom. Dissociation is understood on a continuum from mild to extreme in terms of its intensity and its effects.

Mild dissociation can occur from time to time for all of us. It is a normal phenomenon for both children and adults. Children might mildly dissociate when they experience fantasy worlds or imaginary friends or when they immerse themselves in an online game or activity. Adults might daydream, become immersed in a book, or 'lose time' as their thoughts are focused on something whilst driving. Mild dissociation can also occur due to experiencing a one-off terrifying or stressful event, but it is short-lived and has minimal effects on the person who experiences the event.

Moderate dissociation can occur when a person's experience continues to be terrifying, and they have no access to comfort or help to process the experience. This can lead to a numbing of emotions or body sensations. Sufferers may be able to block out strong emotions, body states, emotional needs, and even pain. They may act in an 'odd' manner, laughing when someone is hurt or becoming angry when things are going well. They may have a sense of being outside of themselves and, simultaneously, observing themselves (*depersonalisation*). They may feel that their situation or surroundings are not real (*derealisation*). Depersonalisation and derealisation can be triggered during a terrifying event. They can be retriggered when something happens that feels similar to the original event. For example, 'amnesia' or a loss of memory can occur during a terrifying event initially, extending to other situations that may feel similar over time. People can also 'lose time' during moderate dissociation.

Extreme dissociation can occur for a person in order for them to feel safe, and to separate their emotions, sensations, or experiences away from conscious awareness. Individuals can create separate parts of themselves (dissociate parts or dissociate self-states) to hold these emotions, sensations, and experiences. They also may not remember what occurs whilst in a dissociated state (dissociative amnesia). Victims, especially those who suffered sexual abuse, say that they felt like they were watching themselves from a third person's perspective, like watching a movie. Some victims have described dissociation as incredibly unpleasant, horrifying, and debilitating. In some cases, extreme dissociation can reoccur until the emotions related to the trauma are resolved.

Dissociation becomes serious in response to childhood trauma. Being psychologically present when experiencing a terrifying and possibly life-threatening event and feeling powerless can be incredibly painful as a child. Children or infants facing extreme and repeated threat without any safe support may not be able to escape physically, and so they escape psychologically. The child's psyche can self-protect by causing them to disconnect from what's happening to make it more tolerable to endure.

Dissociation can occur in children who experience direct violence (particularly physical or sexual abuse), witness violence (particularly to a family member or to a pet), experience the dramatic loss of a loved one, have to endure frightening or very painful medical conditions or procedures, or experience a terrifying natural or other disaster. Severe verbal abuse by caregivers (particularly during the middle-school years) has been shown to be a significant precursor of dissociation (Teicher et. al 2006).

Behavioural changes are the easiest symptoms of dissociation to notice in children. They can include a child acting younger or older than their chronological age, becoming aggressive when normally passive, presenting as unresponsive, and perhaps with a blank stare. Some might attempt to make their bodies small by curling up into a foetal position on the floor. Some might act protectively by placing their arms over their head or across their body or withdrawing into a corner of the room, under a table, or a blanket.

Emotional shifts can include the child rushing from one emotion to another, expressing emotions that may not fit situations (for example, laughing when observing someone hurt or something we deem as sad), or presenting as emotionally flat and 'without feelings'. You might also notice cognitive difficulties such as the child's capacity to complete a task or exhibit a skill might come and go without reason, or they may lack memory for past experiences or things just done. Children can also experience physical concerns for which there are no medical explanations (somatoform dissociation).

It is helpful to consider Poly Vagal Theory if you are trying to help a young learner who might experience dissociation when distressed. This theory suggests we need to provide ample time for the learner to calm. We need to give time for the dorsal vagus low tone to do its work of rest, digest, and repair. We can encourage slow breathing, with an emphasis on the exhale. This can stimulate receptors in the lungs that lead to the heart, enhancing blood and oxygen supply to the body. This type of breathing can also stimulate a release of oxytocin, a hormone and neurotransmitter associated with empathy, trust, and relationship-building. We can gradually re-spark the ventral vagus social engagement system by using a gentle voice with a wavering tone, a soft smile, and eye contact at appropriate times that communicates care and concern.

Memory

Being trauma-aware requires basic knowledge about the nature of memory to help with our understanding of 'traumatic memory' or memory of 'trauma'. Neuroscience explains that memory is not a singular process; instead, different types of memory are associated with neural networks stored in different areas of the brain. However, people's understandings of memory can often be limited to one type; the type that involves conscious recall.

Memory is a psychological phenomenon that works through five main processes; observation, encoding, storage, retrieval, and reaction. It commences with observation, defined as taking in information by engaging with the world via our senses (sight, hearing, taste, smell, touch). This information is then encoded, which involves an initial laying down of memory in the brain's neurology. The encoded content is then stored by the hippocampus in our short-term memory and (later) our long-term memory. Memory content can then be retrieved, both actively and passively, consciously and subconsciously. When memories are retrieved, we can experience physiological, cognitive, or emotional reactions, which can also be either conscious or subconscious. There are two main types of memory: explicit and implicit.

Explicit Memory

Explicit memory is the most commonly understood type as it involves the type of memory that we know about and can talk about. We use our explicit memory when recalling, recounting, or relaying stories or information. Explicit memory includes two subtypes: **declarative memory** (also referred to as semantic memory) and **episodic memory** (also referred to as autobiographical or narrative memory). Declarative memory is overt, conscious remembering. Episodic memory less conscious than declarative memory and involves the remembering of stories and events (episodes) from our life experience.

Implicit Memory

Implicit memory is mostly unconscious and can't be expressed in words. It is often experienced in the body and triggered by an experience. Implicit memory develops before explicit memory, as conscious recall depends on the development of the hippocampus in the second year of life. Implicit memories do not disappear when the hippocampus develops but are stored in different neural networks and can still manifest in later life. Implicit memory also includes two subtypes: **emotional memory** and **procedural memory**. Emotional memory highlights and encodes important experiences for immediate and later reference by overlaying them with emotional meaning. This type of memory connects us with what we are feeling, helps us communicate our feelings to others, and can be elicited by environmental cues such as smell, sight, sound, or touch. Procedural memory is the least conscious subtype and includes impulses, movements, and internal bodily sensations that assist us with how to perform actions and skills. These can include learned motor actions (like driving a car), emergency responses (such as jumping out of the way of an approaching car), or approach or avoidance tendencies (such as an innate aversion or attraction to people, things, or events) (Levine, 2015).

Traumatic events are often stored as implicit memories. Trauma increases the release of cortisol which limits the function of the hippocampus, which (in turn) disrupts the consolidation of explicit memory. Trauma blocks explicit processing and conscious recall and enhances implicit processing and sensory recall. The brain often does not encode traumatic memories as a narrative or story, so it can be challenging to recount them. Therefore, traumatised people may be unable to explain their experiences verbally, and some may be compelled to express or re-enact these unspoken experiences through behaviour. Remembering can come in the form of 'physical sensations, automatic responses and involuntary movements' (Ogden et al. 2006) or 'fragments of intense feelings, sensations, emotions, thoughts and sensory experiences' (van der Kolk, 2015). If recalling the content is likely to cause considerable distress, the brain may encode sensory 'warning signs' of the memory, which are associated with the perceived threat — — and this can trigger the fight, flight, or freeze response. So, rather than being stored as a narrative memory of the past, traumatic memory can be experienced as an immediate life threat (van der Kolk, 2015). Because they are implicit, these memories can be triggered by various situational cues such as anniversaries and birthdays, sensory experiences, and developmental milestones. Sometimes, when psychological 'warning signs' are activated via implicit memory, people who have lived through trauma can experience 'flashbacks'. Flashbacks are intrusive and unexpected memories from the past that seem to 'come out of nowhere' and feel like the experience is happening now. They are often associated with strong emotions and can include intrusive bodily sensations (Siegel, 2012).

Contrary to the myth that traumatic events are seldom forgotten, much trauma is not remembered until something happens to bring it to mind (Brewin, 2005). While our brains are wired to remember experiences important to survival, under some circumstances, survival may be assisted by 'forgetting'. Depending on the context and conditions, both remembering and 'forgetting' can be either healing and/or harmful. As children depend on adult caregivers, 'forgetting' traumatic experiences can have survival value in preserving the attachment bond (Freyd & Birrell, 2013). 'Disruptions in memory may be adaptive... if trauma and caregiving emanate from the same source' (Silberg, 2013: 12).

Executive Function

Executive function is processed mostly by the pre-frontal cortex in human brains (but also by the anterior cingulate, parietal cortex, and hippocampus). Executive function includes **working memory** (generally understood as the capacity to temporarily store and use information to assist with the execution of tasks), **inhibitory control** (the capacity to suppress impulses), and **mental flexibility** (the capacity to adapt behaviour and thinking in response to environmental stimuli). Effective learning, and the effective response to learning, are dependent on the brain having a well-developed and well-functioning capacity for executive function. *The Center on the Developing Child* at Harvard University (2011) uses the metaphor of an 'air traffic control system at a busy airport to manage the arrivals and departures of dozens of planes on multiple runways' to describe the complex capacity of executive function to 'focus, hold, and work with information in mind, filter distractions, and switch gears' (p. 1). The initial development of executive function occurs during the rapid neural development of the early years, and this is quite dramatically refined throughout adolescence and early adulthood and continues throughout life with some decline in proficiency during the older age.

The parts of the brain that mostly manage executive function have neural interconnections with the lower parts of the brain that process perceived threat and anxiety (e.g., the brain stem). As a result, executive function can be compromised when someone is in a state of emotional dysregulation and can be enhanced when one is feeling calm. When the brain stem and associated parts of the brain are 'buzzing' with neural activity due to emotional dysregulation, pre-frontal cortical activity slows down in response, making it far more difficult for an individual to focus and respond adequately to information. Think of times when you were highly anxious and how this may have impacted your capacity to learn, work, or respond to your environment in a thoughtful, calm, planned and/or effective manner. Often in such circumstances, our minds can become 'fuzzy', or we 'go blank', and we may not even remember details well after the event is well and truly over. Or we may be dealing with the neurophysiological impact of a 'fight' or a 'flight' response, which distracts us from being able to focus on the task at hand. Children and young people in learning environments who are experiencing emotional dysregulation may appear to be disengaged from learning tasks or deliberately refuse to do what they have been asked to do. However, it is likely that they are experiencing a temporary, cognitive inability to connect with the curriculum or to process learning, due to too much activity in the brain stem and the lack of activity in the pre-frontal cortex. Sadly, for learners living with the impacts of unresolved complex trauma, this impact on learning can be a regular and quite disabling experience that can leave them 'cognitively absent' for many lessons across (sometimes) years of their education.

Our trauma-aware work with these young learners should aim to calm the activity of the brain stem through purposeful activity to help with emotional regulation and therefore re-ignite activity in the pre-frontal cortex. When the pre-frontal cortex becomes active with electrical-chemical conversations between neurons, we tend to feel calm and focused. We tend to think more creatively, can problem-solve more effectively, and can respond to the task at hand in an effective manner. Over time, with repeated practice and support with emotional regulation, we can help our trauma-impacted learners to achieve just that! In the longer-term, executive function underlies a broad range of life skills, capabilities, and behaviours.

Oral Language

Oral language capacities develop most rapidly from birth and throughout the early years of life, but they continue to develop and refine throughout schooling. In most early parenting and caring contexts, language development occurs through early attachment experiences where caregiver and child interact with both verbal and non-verbal cues and responses (Cohen, 2011; Snow, 2009). The main area of the brain that develops rapidly during this time that manages language processing is the temporal lobe. This part of the brain includes **Broca's area** (which helps a child with speech and the fluency of their oral language) and **Wernicke's area** (which helps a child to understand oral and written language). However, these parts of the brain integrate with other parts of the brain, which combine in effect, to allow for effective receptive and expressive language to develop and function. Sadly, in the context of child maltreatment, including abuse and neglect, the development of these parts of the brain that manage oral language can suffer, which can have an ongoing impact on the capacity for learning, emotional regulation, and behaviour. This is because we use language to manage these and many other aspects of our life and functioning.

We know from investigations into young people involved with the youth justice system that these young 'offenders' can present with a range of complex needs, including mental health issues and language impairments. There is also evidence that many young offenders have lived through complex childhood trauma. Some literature refers to this as the 'maltreatment-offending association' (Cashmore, 2011; Hurren, Stewart, & Dennison, 2017; Malvaso, et al., 2017). This association finds that maltreated children are more likely to come into contact with the youth justice system than the general population.

An important body of research has examined how oral language capacities or impairments, can inform whether a young person who has lived through complex trauma, will end up in the youth justice system (Anderson, et al., 2016). Oral language is a skill that has particular significance in forensic settings, where the 'offender' must explain themselves and their actions to police, their appointed lawyers, and eventually to a judge and the court. A young person who has lived through complex trauma and whose language development has suffered as a result is at a considerable disadvantage through all these levels of the youth justice system. They are less likely to be able to string sentences together to explain themselves and their actions adequately, use language to help calm their emotions and connect effectively in a way that seems empathetic, apologetic, and thoughtful to their various audiences. They are also at risk of emotional dysregulation during any interrogatory processes during police interviews and court appearances, which is very likely to present them negatively to those who will be making decisions about responding to their 'offending'. Without an understanding of the impact of complex trauma on language development and use, the youth justice system will continue to contribute to the overwhelming number of adult inmates who live with language challenges or impairments.

We can easily extrapolate these findings from examinations of the intersection of oral language competence/impairments and youth justice and apply them to schooling. Young learners who are living with the outcomes of complex trauma, including a lack of capacity with oral language, may struggle to use language to settle conflict with others or to soothe their own emotions, to explain their behaviours and motivations for behaviours, and to negotiate any implications for their behaviours. As a result, they can resort to short, often confronting or aggressive statements and swearing, leading to them 'getting into further trouble' with school authorities. We cannot underestimate the importance of engaging the proactive intervention of speech-language therapists in schools and other contexts to provide the support needed to overcome the impacts on the parts of the brain that manage oral language due to child maltreatment. We also need to consider the impact of maltreatment on language development before we assume that trauma-impacted learners deliberately choose to use inappropriate language when responding to educators in emotion-charged contexts. We need to view this as a lack of capacity that requires repeated practice and support to be addressed, rather than viewing this as poor behaviour.

Sensory Issues

Growing awareness of the effects of trauma on the body and an increasing evidence base suggest that sensory-based interventions are very helpful in supporting those who have lived through complex trauma (Fraser, et al., 2017; McGreevy & Boland, 2020; Ogden et al., 2006; Ogden & Fisher, 2015; van der Kolk, 2015). Sensory-based interventions aim help to address sensory sensitivities in a manner that enable an individual to better adapt to their physical environment (Champagne, 2011) and have been used in occupational therapy with children and young people who struggle with behavioural issues and have lived through complex trauma (Fraser *et al.*, 2017; Koomar, 2009). Sensory processing is a term used to describe how the peripheral and central nervous systems process sensory information. It explains how incoming sensory signals from the environment or body lead to neuronal interactions in the brain, which lead to bodily and behavioural responses resulting from the input.

When you consider the neuroscience, it becomes clear that environmental (sensory) stimuli are received, processed, and responded to by the nervous system in ways that can be adaptive or maladaptive for certain people at certain times. The science also explains that trauma-impacted children and young people are at risk of maladaptive responses, which can lead to concerns with their schooling experience. You may also notice that there is quite a crossover between concerns faced by learners living with autism spectrum disorder (Beaney, 2021) and those who have lived through complex trauma. Therefore, there is also quite a bit of crossover with strategies that could be used to support both groups. Learners from both groups can struggle with some aspects of communication, relationships, emotional regulation, change and transitions, and sensory issues. It is actually quite helpful for educators to explore recommended strategies that assist learners living with autism spectrum disorder, for some really helpful ideas to support learners who have lived through trauma. Understanding and responding to sensory issues is an important first step. A trauma-aware approach to education can often include strategies to address any sensory sensitivities that learners might experience or strategies that include sensory activity to assist with the learner's emotional regulation.

You will notice that in several places in Chapter Five, there is mention of sensory strategies designed to help trauma-impacted learners to manage their sensory worlds and emotionally self-regulate. Ideally, we would gradually reduce the sensory sensitivities of young learners over time to allow their bodies to experience incremental increases in access to the sensory stimulation that is experienced and managed well by most learners. This needs to be done in a thoughtful and cautious manner that is informed by the individual needs of learners. However, in times of distress, it is important to address the sensory needs of dysregulated learners.

To assist trauma-impacted learners with sensory issues, it is helpful to know just a little about the Somatic Nervous System (please see earlier in this chapter for a brief introduction to this part of the nervous system) and the seven subcategories of this system to assist with understanding what is going on for young learners, and then to consider how we can respond to help. The Somatic Nervous System consists of:

- the auditory system (hearing),
- the tactile system (touch),
- the gustatory system (taste),
- the olfactory system (smell),
- the vestibular system (balance), and
- the proprioception system (body position).

Some learners are 'sensory seeking' or 'sensory avoidant' in one or more of these subsystems, which can lead to them responding to sensory input in ways that are not helpful for themselves, and sometimes for others around them within learning environments. If a learner is 'sensory seeking', they can need more than usual amounts of sensory stimulation in order to experience a homeostatic (balanced) sensory world. If a learner is 'sensory avoidant', they can become overwhelmed by even small amounts of sensory stimulation and need to have this reduced to cope with their sensory world. If learners' sensory needs (to increase or decrease sensory stimuli) are not met, the result often manifests in concerning emotional and behavioural responses.

In more serious cases where learners are truly struggling, it may be helpful to reach out to an Occupational Therapist to complete a sensory profile or assessment, to help educators to become aware of the challenges learners face, and some helpful strategies to support them (May-Benson & Teasdale, 2019). However, in most cases, some basic knowledge and some creative thinking, can truly help trauma-impacted learners with sensory sensitivities deal with their sensory worlds in a way that enhances their capacities for learning, emotional regulation, behaviour, and overall engagement with their environments.

Auditory processing occurs when the brain recognises and interprets sounds. The processing quality can depend on how well the brain understands, interprets, and responds to sounds. Learners who are sensory avoidant can become distracted or annoyed by sounds that are not usually noticed by others, such as the 'buzzing' of lights, the 'swooshing' of fans or the 'ticking' of clocks, or even quite distant sounds that are dismissed by most, but quite audible to them. They can frequently ask others to be quiet, which can come across as 'rude' or 'disrespectful' behaviour. They can be startled by noises that can trigger a fight, flight, or freeze response. They might cover their ears at certain times. Sensory-seeking learners might not respond readily and well to having their name called or to a request from a teacher and might require directions to be repeated. They might prefer that the volume of music, videos, etc. are turned up high. They might speak loudly, and they might make noise, just to hear noise. They might sometimes seem confused about the direction that sounds are coming from. Therefore, considering activities and responses that increase or decrease the amount of sound perceived by learners, might be helpful in assisting them with daily learning and engagement and/or during times of dysregulation.

The **tactile system** is one of the largest sensory systems in the body, and it plays an important role in the learner's ability to interact adequately with their environment. This system is responsible for recognising objects' qualities, such as their being hard, soft, sharp, dull, rough, or smooth. It also helps us to recognise variable experiences such as temperature, pressure, and texture. Sensory challenges in this area can lead to issues manipulating objects and interacting effectively with the environment. Sensory-seeking learners might seem unaware of touch unless it is intense touch. They might not respond to pain to the same degree as most learners. They might physically hurt others unintentionally and may not fully understand the impact of pain on others. They might not notice when their clothing is not sitting well on their bodies or when there is food on their faces. Learners who are sensory avoidant might touch objects and people frequently, which can annoy those who are being touched or whose possessions are being touched. They might seek 'messy' experiences such as playing in mud, food, or paint. They might rub or bite their skin or parts of their bodies. They may prefer to be barefoot, enjoying the connection between their feet and the ground. Therefore, considering activities and responses that increase or decrease their access to tactile experience perceived by learners might be helpful to assist them with daily learning and engagement and/or during times of dysregulation.

The **gustatory system** manages taste through chemosensors, sensory cells that transmit messages through nerves to the brain, where specific tastes are identified. Sensory-seeking learners may prefer foods with more intense flavours and enjoy licking, tasting, or chewing on inedible objects, their clothes, or parts of their bodies. Sensory avoidant learners might experience quite extreme food preferences, might only be interested in limited types of foods and brands of foods, and might be quite resistant to trying new foods. Some might prefer soft foods only, and some might struggle with swallowing some more textured foods. Therefore, activities and responses that increase or decrease the amount of flavour, texture, and temperature of food and drink might be helpful to assist them with daily learning and engagement and/or during times of dysregulation. Concerns with gustatory preferences can be more relevant for parents and carers than educators. However, educators might need to consider these preferences during food breaks or cooking activities, as examples. Some young learners with this type of sensory issue can benefit by having something to chew on during the day when they feel somewhat dysregulated.

The **olfactory system** deals with the sense of smell and is managed by receptors in the nose that send messages to the limbic system (and so smell can impact emotions) and then to the cortex for processing. These messages can combine with those from the gustatory system. Sensory-seeking learners need excessive amounts of smell information for this to register well for them. They might have trouble distinguishing between smells or fail to notice strong ones. They might overtly smell people or objects or use smell to interact with people or objects, which can be somewhat disconcerting for other learners. Sensory avoidant learners may react negatively to smells that don't usually bother others. They may speak about smells a lot, may refuse certain foods or drinks due to their smell, may be irritated by certain smells such as perfume or household cleaners, and may even refuse to go into a place or space, or to engage in an activity, due the smell involved for them.

The **vestibular system** is managed by parts of the inner ear, sending messages to the brain about body movement, head position, and the body's spatial orientation. It also is involved with motor functions that help with balance, keeping heads and bodies stable during movement, and maintaining posture. Sensory avoidant learners might avoid quick or jarring movements. They might avoid certain types of playground equipment, particularly those that rotate or spin or certain exercise or sporting activities. They may avoid elevators, escalators, and stairs. They might seem slow-moving at times as they focus on their balance and can prefer to hold onto stable surfaces such as walls or railings, or even people, during movement. They can seem overly cautious when moving around, easily be startled when knocked or bumped, and even experience motion sickness when moving too quickly. Others may brand these learners as unsociable, unphysical, or lacking courage. Sensory-seeking learners can be constantly moving as their bodies can crave intense and rapid movement. They may like to spin, jump on trampolines, skip, and run. They may find walking, or sitting or standing still, extremely challenging. If they have to sit, they might include rocking their bodies or rocking back and forth on their chairs. These learners can quite readily be branded as hyperactive, thrill-seekers, and perhaps disobedient due to their refusal to stay still in one place. Therefore, considering activities and responses that increase or decrease the number of certain types of movement perceived by learners might be helpful to assist them with daily learning and engagement and/or during times of dysregulation.

The **proprioceptive system** manages the process by which the body can vary muscle contraction in immediate response to incoming sensory information about forces that are external to the body. Sensory information is interpreted by the brain and sends messages to stretch receptors in muscles, which can help people to respond to external forces in a way that keeps them stable or upright. The proprioceptive system guides gross motor and fine motor skills. Sensory-seeking learners might love bumping, jumping, crashing or leaning into walls and other objects. They might enjoy stomping their feet when walking or they might kick the furniture of the learners in front of them in the classroom. They might enjoy giving and receiving strong hugs, wearing heavy clothing, or using weighted blankets. They might struggle with the grading of movements, misjudging how much pressure to use during activities such as playing, dressing, and writing. They might break toys and other objects without intending to do so. They can misjudge the weight of things, so they might pick up objects with too much force or slam doors instead of just shutting them. They can also be rough with other children and with animals. Sensory avoidant learners might dislike or become overwhelmed by touch and physical contact. They might keep their distance from other people, furniture, or objects. They might avoid tokens of physical affection, including hugs, pats on the back, 'high fives', etc. Both sensory seeking and sensory avoidant learners can appear clumsy. They may also experience writing and art activities challenges due to pushing too hard or too lightly on writing and art-making implements. They may also find life skills somewhat challenging, such as dressing themselves. Therefore, activities and responses that manage the amount of contact and pressure exerted on the bodies of learners might be helpful to assist them with daily learning and engagement and/or during times of dysregulation. It can also be important to support these learners to develop their capacities with a range of gross and fine motor skills.

Researchers and practitioners are now including an eighth sensory system that is referred to as 'interoception'. This system helps individuals to feel what is happening inside their bodies. It can help with the detection of a change of emotion or wellbeing. It can also help detect more physical stimuli and assist with signifying hunger and thirst, satiation after eating or drinking, body temperature, rates of heartbeat or breathing, sleepiness, the need to visit the toilet, and more.

It is important to know that all the sensory systems interact and hopefully integrate within the nervous systems and bodies of individuals. Most learners manage sensory stimuli from all systems in a very adaptive way and can manage their sensory world often without consciously considering it (Blanche, 2022). However, some learners may experience minor sensory preferences or aversions associated with various sensory systems, and others may experience more serious and debilitating concerns.

To help with learner emotional self-regulation, some more commonly used sensory stimuli prove soothing for most learners, and these are often incorporated in spaces and activities. Examples include soft music, light perfumes, fidget toys, colouring in activities, dimmed lighting, weighted blankets, stuffed toy animals, mindfulness apps, etc. These are certainly highly recommended within a trauma-aware response; however, it is important to also consider the learners who might find some of these more commonly used stimuli quite disconcerting. Simple adjustments in the types of sensory stimuli used with learners who have sensory sensitivities can be vital to help them stay in classrooms and continue to engage with their learning and relationships.

Resilience

Resilience after the experience of complex trauma is also known as post-traumatic growth (Tedeschi et al., 2018). Masten (2001) suggests that 'resilience refers to a class of phenomena characterised by good outcomes in spite of serious threats to adaptation or development' (p. 228). From a neuroscience perspective, resilience can be viewed as an outcome of how the child's brain, nervous system, and genes respond to environmental challenges and experiences throughout their development (see earlier explanations in this chapter) (Russo et al., 2012).

We aim to achieve resilience for young learners when we implement a trauma-aware approach to education. There is strong evidence from research examining developmental resilience that provides much hope and insight into what an effective, trauma-aware educational response can accomplish. Much of this evidence comes from research that shows that not all children who experience maltreatment develop long-term or life-long adverse outcomes (Masten, 2014). Indeed, many can grow to demonstrate an adaptive response that leads to what is commonly known as 'resilience'.

The Harvard Center on the Developing Child suggests that resilience eventuates from an interplay between internal predispositions and external experiences. They propose that a combination of warm, safe, and helpful relationships, support to develop skills, and positive life experiences can provide a strong foundation for resilience that can protect children from the developmental disruption associated with trauma. However, they emphasise that relationships are the main ingredient for developing this resilience. They also suggest that intervention early in life is best, when the brain is most plastic and malleable, but that it is never too late to build resilience in children and young people (National Scientific Council on the Developing Child, 2015).

Studies have explored the commonalities amongst young people who have lived through complex trauma and reveal that resilience is far more likely for those who engage effectively with one or more safe, positive relationships with warm and available adults throughout their years of development. Healthy caregiver relationships are clearly the driving force for overcoming the impacts of early trauma, so supporting the parenting or caring behaviour of primary caregivers is likely to have the most benefit. However, at-risk children and young people also need warm, available, and supportive adults outside their family who engender feelings of trust, belonging, and a sense that they matter.

Masten (2014) emphasises that it is vital that learners who have lived through complex childhood trauma have access to opportunities for growth in these areas at school. She views resilience as not coming from only rare and extraordinary internal qualities of particular individuals but rather a capacity available to all young people, including those who are trauma-impacted, if people and social systems support them through effective and caring relationships. Viewing resilience in this research-supported manner offers a far more optimistic prospect for doing something to effectively address the impacts of trauma, as opposed to believing that only some rather 'extraordinary' people have this capacity for resilience. Additional factors that promote higher levels of resilience in young people include a healthy belief in one's capability, developing capacities for executive function and self-regulation, and, interestingly, engagement in faith or cultural traditions (National Scientific Council on the Developing Child, 2015). It is worth considering how education providers can capitalise on these factors for trauma-impacted learners.

Sege and Harper Browne (2017) advocate for the balancing of positive life experiences for children to counteract the impact of adverse childhood experiences. They suggest there are four main categories of positive life experiences, including:

> ...nurturing, supportive relationships; living, developing, playing, and learning in safe, stable, protective, and equitable environments; having opportunities for constructive social engagement and connectedness; and learning social and emotional competencies' (p. 79).

A trauma-aware, whole-of-school/whole-of-service approach makes it more likely that quality relationships and other resilience-building supports will be available to trauma-impacted learners, year after year. A trauma-aware, whole-of-system approach will support schools/services to do just that.

Summary

It is hoped that this chapter becomes a resource for you and perhaps your colleagues who are educators so that you can have ready-reference to the aspects of science that are relevant for your discussions, advocacy, and response to responding to the concerns experienced by trauma-impacted young learners. Some understanding of the scientific explanations regarding the impact of trauma on the nervous system and brain, and the cells and structures with the nervous system and brain, are very helpful when facing some of the complex and sometimes quite perplexing behaviours and responses exhibited by learners who have lived through complex trauma.

Chapter 4

Behaviour Management (Behaviourism vs Neuroscience)

Considerations for Classroom Behaviour Management

Approaches to managing human behaviour are generally grounded in theories (beliefs and understandings about how humans behave, why they behave, and ways to manipulate, change, encourage, and discourage behaviour). These theories often draw from the behavioural sciences, such as psychology and sociology. The challenge for trauma-aware education is that the bulk of the more common approaches to 'behaviour management' in schools is mostly informed by Behaviourism and is not informed enough by neuroscience.

Behaviourism is grounded in an understanding of behaviour modification that developed from early studies into classical and operant conditioning by Pavlov (1846–1936), Watson (1878–1958), and Skinner (1904–1990) (Walker, 2018). Assumptions in school behaviour management that are informed by Behaviourism, include an understanding that all student behaviour can be explained as responses to environmental stimuli, all behaviour is learnt and therefore can be modified by actions by the educator, and by manipulating environmental stimuli, educators can achieve the behaviours that they want from their students and reduce or extinguish those that they do not want (Miltenberger, 2016).

Behaviourism informs many quite common behaviour management strategies in school. It is a common and regular practice for classroom teachers to establish and reinforce student behaviour expectations (or rules). To help students to meet these expectations, teachers set up practices and resources in the classroom. Some are designed to increase the likelihood that a preferred behaviour will be maintained or increased in frequency or intensity and therefore positive reinforcement (perceived reward) or negative reinforcement (withholding perceived punishment) are applied. Various types of positive reinforcers are used, and these can include those that are tangible (for example, stickers, vouchers, or certificates), those that are based on acknowledgement (for example, 'high fives', displaying students' work, or positive notes to parents or carers), or those that involve activity (for example, computer time, free time, or caring for the class pet). Negative reinforcers could include allowing students to have time away from a non-preferred activity or not have to complete homework (as examples).

Some strategies are designed to decrease the likelihood that a non-preferred behaviour will be maintained or increased in frequency or intensity, and therefore, punishments or the withholding of perceived rewards are applied. An example of a punishment would be requiring the student to write lines or pick up rubbish in the playground. An example of withholding a perceived reward would be not allowing the student to join in a social activity such as playtime during recess. It is, however, important to remember that to have a reinforcing effect on behaviour, the positive or negative reinforcer must be perceived by the student as positive or desired. To have an extinguishing effect on behaviour, the punisher or the withheld reward must be perceived by the student as negative and non-desired.

Students living with the outcomes of complex trauma, who already struggle with feeling safe, with relationships, and with emotional regulation, may indeed struggle with negotiating positive reinforcers, negative reinforcers, punishments, and the withholding of rewards, in a manner that results in desired behaviour change. They may have difficulty perceiving these things in the way that educators feel they should be perceived. This can prove very frustrating for educators who sometimes struggle with understanding why these strategies work so well for most students and yet consistently fail with a few. Often this type of frustration can lead to educators depending more and more on punishment and withholding perceived rewards. These consequences tend to become more serious and more often involve exclusion from class activity, from class, and even from school.

Behaviourist strategies can be applied individually to students but can also involve a social element. Group or whole-class reinforcement schedules might include a group reward if all students achieve certain pre-defined standards of behaviour. Examples could include special on-campus events, off-campus excursions, or token rewards for the whole class, such as vouchers or food items. Visual aids can help record group progress towards achieving awards, such as a jar of marbles that is gradually filled when students behave in desired ways, or charts or posters that identify whole class progress towards behaviour goals or that identify where individuals are contributing to whole-class progress.

These social reinforcement programs or schedules are often perceived as benign, but they can have a devastating impact on unresolved, trauma-impacted students. Not only may these students be dealing with the individual upheaval that results from them not managing individualised, behaviourist strategies effectively, but they also may need to deal with possible shame, humiliation, peer-condemnation, social exclusion, and persistent reminders of their 'failure', that can be associated with the social reinforcement processes.

Rather than applying the same processes that are working well with the majority of students to all students, classroom strategies should be designed that are protective of trauma-impacted students and that draw from trauma-aware theory and understandings. Strategies and approaches for behaviour management that draw from Behaviourism have a strong focus on the external worlds of the student. They can ignore the quite powerful impacts of the internal or bodily worlds of the student. A behaviourist approach would encourage manipulating the external environment for the student in a way that enhances the likelihood of desired behaviours and minimises the likelihood of undesired behaviours. However, behaviourist approaches may not acknowledge the significant impact of complex trauma on the internal bodies and brains of students that lead to behaviours of concern and also might disregard or overlook neuroscience-informed strategies that are more likely to positively impact these behaviours.

Trauma-impacted students certainly need experience with dealing with established classroom behaviour expectations, just like any child or adolescent. The difference for these young people is that they may need repeated opportunities to practise their developing skills to meet behaviour expectations and enhance their understandings related to them. Punishments or negative consequences are unlikely to help students develop these capacities. However, supportive, trauma-aware interventions can provide these repeated opportunities for growth, which in neuroscience terms, equates to repeated reinforcement of helpful and adaptive neural networks in the bodies and brains of students.

Considerations for Whole-School Behaviour Management

A whole-school approach to student support is often framed by a multi-tiered model that describes levels of intervention using a triangle-shaped template divided into three tiered sections. This model developed from the 'Response to Intervention' (RTI) process that commenced in the 1970s to better identify and respond to the needs of students with learning difficulties. Within RTI, Tier 1, or the primary or universal level, instruction is provided to meet the needs of all students. At Tier 2, or the secondary or targeted level, evidence-based interventions are provided to a smaller proportion of students who did not make satisfactory progress in response to Tier 1 processes. Finally, at Tier 3, or the tertiary or intensive level, individualised instruction is provided to a much smaller proportion of students who did not make enough progress in response to Tier 2 processes (Preston, et al., 2016).

A similar multi-tiered framework is increasingly being used to support students' positive behavioural success in schools, known as School Wide Positive Behaviour Support (SWPBS) and now is increasingly known as Positive Behaviour Intervention and Support (PBIS) or Positive Behaviour for Learning (PBL), or similar. This multi-tiered approach, which also draws from behaviourist methodologies, has proven to lead to positive outcomes for most schools and students and is now highly recommended and used in education contexts. Within the multi-tiered model, the lowest and largest section of the triangle (often coloured in green) is dedicated to proactive and preventative work done across the whole school to minimise the likelihood that undesired student behaviour will occur and to maximise the likelihood of desired behaviours across the school. The middle section of the triangle (often coloured in yellow or orange) refers to targeted interventions for a smaller proportion of students who might need extra help with maintaining desired behaviours. The apex of the triangle (often coloured in red) refers to interventions for those students who exhibit chronic and challenging behaviours and who require intensive support to address and overcome these behaviours. The premise of this model being used in schools is that the more proactive, whole-school work that is successfully done, the less targeted and intensive work that will be needed (Sugai, et al., 2000; Sugai & Horner, 2006).

Increasingly, the multi-tiered model for support has been used in school contexts to address concerns regarding the mental health and wellbeing of children and adolescents across areas including bullying (Nickerson, 2019), suicide prevention (Singer, et al., 2019), autism (Glasberg & LaRue, 2015; Thomeer et al., 2019), absenteeism (Kearney, 2016), and general mental health (Jones, et.al., 2017). Preston et al., (2016) suggest that schools have adopted these frameworks out of necessity as they have become the de facto providers of mental health support for students due to a lack of equitable and readily available access to traditional child and youth mental health services. There is a growing emphasis on incorporating this multi-tiered approach as a model for school psychology services (National Association of School Psychologists, 2016), trauma-aware school counselling practice in schools (Rawson, 2020), and general trauma-aware practice in schools (Berger, 2019; Chafouleas, et al., 2018).

As this multi-tiered system is now used to support both behaviour and mental health and wellbeing of school students, it seems logical that a single model (a single triangle) could be used to do both, and that this could incorporate activity to support trauma-impacted students. The concern is that there could be a clash between the behaviourism-informed approaches with a strong reward/consequence or reward/punishment focus and the neuroscience-informed approaches with a strong focus on addressing concerns with perceptions of safety, relationships, and emotional regulation. So, there needs to be discussion and negotiation of how both approaches can be maintained but that there is a differentiation of application according to individual student needs and circumstances. This is not a difficult process but rather involves an analysis of what is needed in each tier of support for trauma-impacted students, based on what is understood from evidence from research and science, and ensuring that this is included. It is also acknowledged that with appropriate and repeated trauma-aware support over time, students can build their capacities and then become more and more able to negotiate the behaviourism-informed strategies that are applied to their non-traumatised peers. This is truly an inclusive education approach!

Considerations for Intensive Behaviour Support

One highly recommended intervention for students requiring intensive behaviour support is the use of a Functional Behaviour Analysis. This approach to behaviour assessment and intervention draws from Applied Behaviour Analysis, which strongly focuses on analysing and responding to environmental stimuli that increase the likelihood of undesired behaviours and replacing them with stimuli that increase the likelihood of desired behaviours (Nohelty, 2021). This approach draws from an understanding that all human behaviour is driven by one or more functions — to either access or avoid something. Categories that people might be aiming to access or avoid include tangible 'things', activities, attention from people, or sensory stimulation. Functional Behaviour Analysis was originally designed to address the behavioural concerns of children and adults with developmental or intellectual disabilities but has since been conducted with people with other diagnoses and also with individuals without disabilities (Nohelty, 2021).

Functional Behaviour Analysis has become a highly recommended and sometimes mandated assessment and intervention process for students requiring Tier 3 behaviour support in schools. A school-based

Functional Behaviour Analysis can involve an intensive and thoughtful process of data collection from a range of sources, including the student, their family, and their educators, which is followed by data analysis to inform the development of an intensive intervention plan. The process aims to identify the function of the behaviour of concern and then to address this by manipulating elements in the student environment so that the function that drives their behaviour is still satisfied, but through behaviours deemed by the school to be more appropriate and adaptive. This process examines the life circumstances (or long-term triggers) that might be contributing to students' behaviours and any antecedents (or short-term triggers) that might occur prior to students' behaviours. The process also examines events or consequences that occur after the students' behaviours that might reinforce their behaviours. After analysis, a Functional Behaviour Analysis assessor devises, often with the support of a team, a plan of intervention that satisfies the function or functions of the behaviour, addresses the short-term and longer-term triggers, and replaces any consequences that reinforce the behaviour. Functional Behaviour Analysis is time and resource-intensive, and assessors require significant training and skill to do this well.

Although Functional Behaviour Analysis is a recommended Tier 3 intervention, there are some questions about the appropriateness of using Functional Behaviour Analysis with trauma-impacted students. This assessment and intervention planning process significantly focuses on manipulating environmental stimuli to achieve the intervention goals. As we know with trauma-impacted students, much of their behaviour is driven not by external stimuli but by internal, bodily forces. So, an intervention informed by a Functional Behaviour Analysis might address the environmental stimuli that can trigger emotional dysregulation for students to a degree, but without a stronger focus on the neuroscience that is explaining the behaviours, this approach may not be successful or successful enough, or successful for long enough. There is also an argument that all the time and effort taken to implement and respond to a Functional Behaviour Analysis for a trauma-impacted student might be better expended in developing a trauma-informed behaviour analysis and support plan that focuses on perceptions of safety, relationships, and emotional regulation.

Also, as Functional Behaviour Analysis requires intensive training and resources that might not be easily accessible to some schools, schools can sometimes devise alternative Tier 3 interventions. Without appropriate training and understanding of ways to respond to the chronic and challenging behaviours of students who have been identified as requiring Tier 3 interventions, educators and education leaders may resort to more punitive responses, particularly if they are drawing from behaviourist understandings that suggest that punishment or withdrawal of rewards or privileges should lead to behaviour improvement. This may not be helpful for various students and is certainly unlikely to address the behaviour and other concerns experienced by unresolved, trauma-impacted students.

Considerations for Crisis Management

This section will refer to crisis management as the processes put in place by schools to address significant behaviour outbursts by trauma-impacted students that involve behaviours deemed as unsafe for the students and those around them. Due to the long-term impacts of complex trauma on the bodies, brains, perceptions, and experiences of students, schools must be prepared for such outbursts. If trauma-aware supports are put in place, such crisis events will likely happen less often. However, all humans have 'bad days', which is certainly the case for children and young people who have lived through trauma. There will be days when certain experiences occur that will trigger a behaviour outburst. Circumstances that trigger outbursts are very much dependent on the individual student and could include examples such as a family argument before school or the night before or an experience of peer bullying in the playground. Sometimes severe emotional dysregulation can occur for trauma-impacted students if memory of past maltreatment is sparked by what would otherwise be considered as a benign learning activity (for example, one that explores family dynamics) or assessment task (for example, one that requires a presentation of autobiography). There will also be certain times when a student is less resilient and emotional dysregulation is more likely, such as when the usual class teacher is away on leave, or the student is not physically well. So, despite any wonderful progress that the student has made due to the supportive trauma-aware work that the school has put in place, schools should always be aware and should expect and prepare for the 'bad days'.

Also, it is worth considering how a school might respond to such behaviour outbursts, particularly when a trauma-impacted student is exhibiting progress in their emotional regulation and engagement with learning. In a trauma-aware context, punishing or excluding students for what occurs on these 'bad days' makes little logical sense. Indeed, from a trauma-aware perspective, these occurrences should be viewed as an opportunity for further learning and growth for the student, rather than an opportunity for discipline. Through trauma-aware crisis management, trauma-impacted students can learn important lessons about unconditional positive regard and develop their understanding that relationships can be repaired and rebuilt in a helpful and supportive manner. Remember, for many of these young people, adults who have been in their lives in roles of caring and support have left and not returned after 'bad days'. At school, there is a marvellous opportunity to change the worldview of these students by showing that despite what happened today, we will be here for them tomorrow.

It is worth examining the goals for crisis management at school. From a perspective of Behaviourism, these could be simply summarised as establishing a safe environment by containing the crisis event, stabilising the emotions and behaviours of the student, and then applying punitive or excluding sanctions to make it less likely that the student will behave similarly in the future. From a trauma-aware perspective, the first two goals do still apply. It is important that a safe environment for the student and others is achieved and that activity takes place to help calm the emotions and behaviours of the student. However, neuroscience would suggest that the third goal should be very different to that which involves sanctions. A trauma-aware approach would indicate that the third goal would be to return the student to an improved mental and emotional state, ready to attend school and re-engage in learning.

During severe dysregulation, the student's brain stem can be doing most of the work and may be focusing on perceived risk and survival. The frontal cortex may not be working well, so questioning the student or expecting them to engage in a logical discussion may not be helpful at this time. The hippocampus may be affected, impairing memory and recall. The amygdala may be working on overload so that the student may have little conscious control over their emotional responses. Stress hormones can be surging through the student's circulatory system, and the electro-chemical activity occurring in the brain is likely to be highly disorganised. Physical responses may be maladaptive and disturbing, and verbal expressions may be limited to silence, swearing, or illogical, incoherent, or threatening responses. Those who are in fight mode may become aggressive and destructive. Those who are in flight mode may try anything they can do to escape. Those who are in freeze mode may emotionally and psychologically dissociate. Some may curl up in a foetal position or hide behind or under furniture or objects. Some may present with behaviours from a much earlier developmental stage, such as hugging a toy or sucking a thumb.

At early signs of dysregulation, the student should be caringly encouraged to go to their safe space (see Chapter Five) and then given ample time to calm down. If they prove to be highly dysregulated, this calming process might take considerable time, and the fight, fight, freeze response might ensue until then. Also, the student may or may not make it to their safe space. If this is the case, it is not unusual for students to use 'bad language' and display physical outbursts; therefore, it is important that other students are removed to a safe environment, away from the dysregulated student.

When the initial crisis is subsiding and the student has started to calm down, it is important that they are left alone (with watchful eyes nearby) or that only those who have established rapport with the student engage at this time. Touching the student should be avoided unless people in attendance are sure that this will be helpful and that it is at the student's invitation. It is important for all involved to remember that the focus for this time is physiological repair. The student's body will need time to regulate the severely disorganised brain activity and the cocktail of hormones that have just been raging through their bodily systems. This time of repair may require long periods of silence. The student might cry. Some students might actually fall asleep. Do not interfere with this process, or you could risk re-igniting the stress response. Once the student has recovered, it is advisable for them to go home (as long as the home is a safe place) after a reassuring message from key support workers in the school that they will be welcomed back once they feel better. The school then needs to provide ample opportunity for staff debriefing if requested and wanted by individuals and groups, and then start planning for what comes next.

The Process of Co-Regulation

A trauma-aware perspective acknowledges that the experience of complex trauma leads to issues with emotional regulation, and there will be days when students will be more vulnerable to emotional dysregulation. This perspective also acknowledges that during severe dysregulation, the student is going through a significant physiological event that requires supportive co-regulation with supportive adults. This perspective also suggests that it is important to provide students and staff with the opportunity to repair and rebuild relationships after any highly dysregulating event.

It is important to understand and prepare for any co-regulation activity that might be required of you during a crisis event. Co-regulation is a process of helping, of you and the student working together to calm the neurobiological surges that are being experienced. Co-regulation work during a crisis event is not pleasant. It can even be quite upsetting or unnerving for any adult who is helping, so it is important that whoever does this work is as emotionally regulated as possible. If the adult wanting to help, finds that they cannot emotionally regulate, it is preferred that someone else steps in to do this important work. An emotionally regulated brain and body are needed to help co-regulate someone else's emotionally dysregulated brain and body! There are some techniques that can help with the co-regulation process and mostly, they involve how you use your voice and how you use your body language.

First, it is recommended that you use a quiet and calm tone of voice. Perhaps try deepening your tone and speaking more slowly. When we are emotionally dysregulating, we tend to speak more quickly, and the tone of our voice can become higher. It is recommended you do the reverse of this by deepening your tone and slowing your pace. You don't have to speak all the time as periods of silence are often helpful too. You might even feel that you sound quite boring when you do this, and that is completely fine. For this process, you need only to contribute sounds and language that are calming and regulating. The words you use are also important. Perhaps you can remind your student that they are not alone and that you are there to help. Perhaps you can remind them that the two of you have practised this previously to prepare for any bad days, and now you are going to do what you have practised. Perhaps you can remind them that it is okay to take the time they need to feel better and that you will be there when they are ready. Importantly, you can remind them that they are safe with you and safe in the space that you both are in.

Second, your facial expression and body language are important. Aim to have a benign facial expression as you don't want to look frightened, shocked, or even too happy. Try for a calm and caring expression. Vary your eye contact so that you are sometimes looking at the student and sometimes providing them with time when they are not being overtly watched. Aim for relaxed body language and open gestures. You might want to avoid crossing your arms or legs and instead place your hands in your lap, for example. Where you place yourself in the space is also important. You need to ensure you are not blocking any exit for the student, such as the door to a room, as this could cause them to feel trapped and could also place you in an unsafe situation if the student wants to leave quickly. Avoid touching the student unless you are sure they are now regulated, and it is by their invitation. Restrain from doing anything that might interfere with the calming and repair process or that could re-ignite the stress response.

During co-regulation, it is helpful to use your cognitive scripts (see Chapter Five) to help with your emotional regulation. Keep telling yourself silently the words and phrases that help you to keep calm and remind you of the importance of helping trauma-impacted students. Remind yourself that you are not dealing with deliberate and defiant behaviours but rather intense physiological and neurobiological surges. Remind yourself how sad and unfortunate it is that this student has lived through trauma and that they have to face such 'bad days' at school.

Ideally, you would not restrain a severely dysregulated student. However, sometimes the safety risks are so serious that this cannot be avoided. Damage to property is always unfortunate, but this should not be the guiding consideration for implementing physical restraint, as restraint can actually lead to the calming response taking longer and being more difficult. It is strongly recommended that personnel at your school are trained in non-violent, safe, and supportive ways to temporarily restrain a student. Techniques for restraint can be different for different-sized students or varying contexts, so accessing thorough and professional training for this activity is important. Restraint should always be considered a last resort response, as the process of restraint may increase the challenges in rebuilding and repairing relationships with your trauma-impacted student. It is also important to acknowledge here that some education sites or education systems have policies that exclude restraint as an option for intervention.

Suspension and Time Away from School

Disrupting attachments is always harmful to trauma-impacted students as often their lives have been full of times when important relationships discontinue. So, avoiding the disruption of attachments is an important goal for trauma-aware work in schools. However, if disruptions cannot be avoided, minimising the harm of disrupting attachments is the next objective. Sometimes, it is deemed necessary for a student to spend some time, or days, away from the school after a crisis event. This might be to help the trauma-impacted student to have time to recover, or it might be to help school personnel and other students time to recover. It might also be deemed important for the school to have time when the trauma-impacted student is absent to develop processes in preparation for their ongoing support on return.

So, if time away from school is going to happen, it is important to consider how the harm of disrupting attachments can be minimised. First, it is important to minimise the number of days that the student is away from school, so consider the needs of your school and then balance these with what might be the least number of days that your student should be separated from relationships at school. The younger the child, the less time they should be away from school; ideally, very young children should be away from school for no longer than a day. Also, you need to consider whether the student has a safe place to be when they are not at school. Second, it is important to consider what occurs during the student's time away from school. Are there times and places where someone from their school who has an established, supportive relationship with the student could connect with them? This could be via phone calls, emails, texts, or meeting in person. So, consider ways to minimise the harm of disrupting attachments by embedding relational activity.

Unfortunately, the time a trauma-impacted student spends away from school is often termed a 'suspension'. This term certainly has a punitive connotation, which is not helpful when you are trying to communicate unconditional positive regard to the student and you are aiming to rebuild and repair relationships on their return. It is acknowledged that many education systems dictate that terms such as 'suspension' must be used. However, if this is the case for your school and your student, relational work is even more important. The student needs to hear clearly that you do not view this time as a punishment but rather as a time of repair and support. Ideally, schools should have the freedom not to use the term 'suspension' to label these periods of time away from school.

Re-Entry Meetings

Re-entry meetings are a common strategy for the first day a student returns to school after a period of suspension. These meetings can vary in design from those that are quite structured and strict to those that are quite supportive. The more structured and strict types could include a meeting in the office of a representative of school leadership such as the principal or their delegate, that is attended by the student and sometimes by a family member or support person. The meeting could include a review of the behaviours of concern and could outline the behaviour expectations for the future, and could aim to have the student agree that they will do their best to meet the behaviour expectations. Some students can even be required to view and sign a document outlining this agreement during these meetings. The more supportive versions of these meetings might still be held in the office of a school leader but might not be as focused on gaining student agreement for improved behaviour, but rather might focus more on the supports that will be available to the student. Despite the design of these meetings, they can be quite a stressful event for a trauma-impacted student as they are usually the first event they face after a period of disrupted attachment, and they are usually in a space that is stress-inducing for the student. Unfortunately, these meetings can sometimes end up with students becoming so overwhelmed that further unpleasant behaviours occur, and, in some cases, this can lead to another suspension or worse!

From a trauma-aware perspective, it is worth considering alternatives to re-entry meetings that still achieve the same objectives but use less stress-inducing strategies that focus on rebuilding and repairing relationships and helping returning students feel safe on their first day back at school. As an example, the student's mentor (see Chapter Five) could meet with the student whilst they are off campus during the suspension to work through the elements of the re-entry plan in a supportive, non-anxiety-provoking manner. Then, on the first day back at school, the student could check in with their mentor as usual, and the mentor can be provided with the time needed to assist the student in re-engaging with the classroom context in the most supportive way.

Exclusion from School

Despite all these recommendations, we know that schools are complex communities driven by a multitude of dynamics and pressures, and, for a variety of reasons, trauma-impacted students do sometimes end up being excluded from school. If this is deemed unavoidable, schools should (again) consider ways to minimise the harm of any disruption of attachments. Many of these students have experienced quite concerning disruption to attachments throughout their young lives due to people who are living with or supporting them going away and not returning. For some, this can include parents or carers and a variety of child and adolescent support personnel. Some adolescents in government care placements have experienced years of time-limited attachments with adults who are paid (as a job) to be with them. Some young people have not experienced the type of committed, long-term family attachments that so many of us take for granted.

For these students, exclusion can present a further serious disruption to key relationships that have been developed at their schools, and it is important that consideration is given as to how this harm can be minimised (Bomber, 2009). Perhaps, the student should be given the opportunity to say 'goodbye' and hear 'goodbye' from school personnel and students with whom they have developed relationships, before they leave. Perhaps communication between the student and key adults from the school should continue for a time after the student moves to a new school, so that the disruption to relationships is not as severe. Perhaps personnel who have been involved with support planning for the student could share their learnings and recommendations with support personnel at the new school. Although these may not be common school responses following exclusion, it is always worth discussing what could be done to minimise harm to disrupted attachments (Bomber, 2009).

Behaviour Management Policy

After school personnel are trained in trauma-aware education principles, it is valuable to review whole-school policy, particularly in the area of behaviour management, to interrogate what aspects of the policy are aligned with a trauma-aware approach to student support and what aspects might hinder this approach. It is also helpful to explore which elements are informed by Behaviourism and might need to be modified or added to, to be inclusive of trauma-impacted students. It is helpful if you think of a trauma-impacted student at your school and apply aspects of your current school policy to them and their circumstances. Question whether applying the policy will lead to greater inclusion and opportunity to address the impacts of trauma for this student or whether it has the capacity for excluding and potentially doing more harm to this student. It is helpful to gather a team or committee of trauma-aware staff members to review the policy and to present the school leadership with some recommendations. Policy review does not need to result in the exclusion of content that works well for most students. However, it might need to result in some recommendations for additional content or modified content so that it is inclusive of trauma-impacted students.

School policies (particularly those that focus on student behaviour) are very powerful documents. The structure of these documents and the wording within these documents can have a significant impact on decisions made about individual students. Policies can be conceived as social constructions. They start with several people discussing their constructed beliefs about many issues, including what school behaviour management is, what approach or theory behaviour management should be drawing from, what behaviour expectations are, what the cut off lines between acceptable and non-acceptable behaviour are, or what should be done when unacceptable behaviour occurs. Individually constructed beliefs about these issues then become consensus, or a group or socially constructed set of beliefs. These sets of beliefs are then documented into a policy and implemented. This process of consensus can happen at an education system level, resulting in education systems (such as education departments) developing policy templates for schools to use to frame their response to student behaviour. These templates might also include recommended sections of text or recommended wording. This template can then be further developed by educators at individual schools who come to a consensus about what other content is needed. What can result is a socially constructed policy that draws from socially constructed beliefs from a variety of sources.

A good example of this is a school behaviour management policy section that refers to 'consequences' or what should happen if a student exhibits what is deemed as behavioural breaches or if behaviour concerns arise. How the consequence section is structured, what is included or excluded in this section, and how this section is worded are vital. These aspects of the consequence section can lead to school processes being either inclusive and helpful or excluding and harmful for trauma-impacted students.

Although becoming less frequent, some schools might refer to a 'levels' approach for framing how they manage consequences. This approach often includes a table or list that outlines increasing levels of behaviour concerns and aligns these with increasingly serious sanctions or consequences. So, a policy might identify students' self-managing or positive behaviours as 'level one', slight misbehaviour as 'level two', more serious behaviour as 'level three', very serious behaviour as 'level four', and extremely serious behaviour as 'level five'. Aligning with this might be information outlining the consequences that are associated with each level of behaviour. So, a 'level one' consequence might include an individual or group reward, 'level two' might state that students no longer receive the 'level one' reward, 'level three' might include some punitive responses, 'level four' might include more serious responses and might include suspension from school, and 'level five' might include even more serious responses and might refer to permanent exclusion from school as an option. Unfortunately, the significant emotional dysregulation that can be experienced at various times by trauma-impacted students can result in behaviour deemed as deserving the 'higher level' consequences that often involve punitive and excluding responses, neither of which are likely to minimise future behaviour concerns or address the influence of complex trauma on the education experience of students. Indeed, these consequences are more likely to do further harm by making school feel unsafe, disrupting attachments, and by removing the support that they need to develop their capacities for emotional regulation.

One way to minimise the impact of a level system is to ensure that each 'level' of consequence includes a range of responses that also include supportive interventions. Then, as people meet to discuss what the response to certain behaviours should be, they have a range of responses from which to choose and are not limited only to only punitive responses dictated by a small number of words on a page of a policy document. This approach should also be embedded in policies that don't use a level system but rather incorporate other means to frame responses to student behaviour. An additional protective measure is to replace the use of the word 'will' with the word 'may' when discussing consequences. So, instead of documenting that a particular consequence 'will' be applied to address a particular type of behaviour, the wording should be that this consequence 'may' be applied. A truly inclusive approach would ensure that there is a range of responses that can be individually applied to students and that no consequence is mandated.

This more inclusive approach is also enhanced by including a section in the policy that overtly refers to the 'individual circumstances' of students and the principal's right to consider these circumstances as decisions about consequences are made. It is understandable that school personnel, other students, students' families, or community members present during a behaviour crisis or hear of the event after the crisis, can be concerned. If they are not trauma-aware, the adults in the school community can become very protective of the impact on other students and can express the expectation that the school takes serious steps to apply punitive consequences to the student of concern. Including a section in the school policy referring to 'individual circumstances' can help to divert community discussions from expectations for the application of sanctions to more empathetic discussions about inclusive support for children and young people who experience disadvantage or harm. However, it is important that efforts are taken during such discussions to not reveal confidential information about the student of concern or their family or carergivers without their appropriate and informed consent.

Another consideration is to check whether your policy refers to practices that have been in place for a long time and have not been assessed as to whether or not they are appropriate to apply to trauma-impacted students. For example, it might be worth exploring if your policy suggests that if a suspension of a certain number of days proves unsuccessful in addressing a student's behaviour, then increasingly longer suspensions should be applied. This is quite a common approach in many schools, and yet, from a trauma-aware perspective, increasing the length of time that attachments are disrupted can increase the likelihood of more serious behaviour and other concerns for the student. Another example would be to check any stipulations regarding re-entry meetings (as discussed previously) or, if your school utilises a multi-tiered system of support framework, to explore whether Tier 3 interventions are more focused on punitive responses rather than intensive support processes. By interrogating whole-school policy in this way, it is more likely that school personnel will be able to discuss and negotiate options for individual students rather than having responses driven by more 'zero tolerance' or mandated statements from a policy document.

Case Management and Individual Support Planning

It is recommended that an informed case management process is used to comprehensively oversee support for trauma-impacted students who need intensive intervention. Often, the team-based case management processes that are already in place for students with needs in areas such as disability, learning, or behaviour will be adequate. However, it is vital that team members are aware of the neurobiological impacts of living with the outcomes of complex trauma and that their support planning has a focus on supporting students to develop their capacities for feeling safe at school, for relationships, and for emotional regulation, and for recovering from severe dysregulation.

It is important to avoid case management and planning processes that draw from Behaviourism when supporting trauma-impacted students. This type of planning mostly involves setting measurable and time-limited goals for student progress and planning for activities to help students to meet these goals. For example, a plan might suggest that a student will increase their in-seat behaviours by 20% by the end of the first term of the school year or that a student will decrease calling out without permission during class time by 50% by the end of week six, or that a student will increase their attendance at school by at least 80% by the end of semester. Plans also tend to refer to the manipulation of environmental antecedents that occur before concerning behaviours and reinforcing consequences that occur after concerning behaviours. This type of planning can certainly be helpful for many students. However, it may be less successful with students who have experienced complex trauma due to an emphasis on the 'external', or the dynamics in the student's environment that can be adjusted, and a lack of emphasis on the 'internal', or the bodily forces that are driving the behaviour.

Trauma-aware support plans should instead draw mostly from an understanding of neuroscience to develop interventions. They will have an emphasis on the three main foci of trauma-aware education: perceptions of safety, relationships, and emotional regulation. Many recommended strategies that can be used to address these foci are discussed in Chapter Five. The focus of these strategies will not be on reinforcing or extinguishing behaviours, but rather on developing and strengthening helpful neural pathways and networks to enhance education and life outcomes for students. Providing repeated opportunities over time for students to practise their developing skills in the areas of feeling safe, relating to others, and regulating their emotions is important to help students' bodies and brains connect with others and the curriculum functionally throughout their schooling years. However, challenging the way the brain works does take time, consistency, and repetition, and the pace at which this occurs is very different for different students. So, it is important that planning is individualised and does not include strict time frames for goal achievement. Also, rather than focusing on quantifiable measurements of improvement, perhaps more qualitative explanations of progress could be more helpful. Also, when planning for student support, it is helpful to include planning that is proactive, reactive, and reparative.

Support plans should include a section dedicated to documenting proactive measures (see Chapter Five) that are designed to minimise the likelihood of concerns arising. Establishing support relationships for the student is proactive, and this could include a key mentor relationship that is accessed daily. Plans should identify whom the student should go to and where they should go if they need assistance. Proactive planning might include information on what the student might do or say when they are experiencing increasing stress levels so that school personnel are forewarned that they need help. Plans can identify a 'safe space' that has been organised for the student to retreat to when they are feeling emotionally aroused and could detail how the student will be supported to negotiate using the space, what they need to do to access the space, and what they will do when in the space and with whom. It is also helpful to document anxiety reduction techniques that the student is comfortable using and explain how they will be supported to engage in these techniques. The case management team might also include other strategies and activities in their support planning that are designed to prevent concerns for their trauma-impacted students.

Reactive measures also need to be planned so that on any day when severe emotional and behavioural dysregulation occurs, every staff member mentioned in the plan knows what they should do and when and how they should do it. Planning documentation could articulate what is likely to happen physiologically as the student experiences dysregulation and what types of behaviours might be expected. It is helpful to engage the help of the student's mentor at this time to assist with emotional co-regulation, so identifying this in the plan can be helpful. It is also important that risk mitigation processes are documented, such as moving the students' classmates to a designated safe area that is away from the dysregulated student.

The reparative work to be done after any crisis has subsided is a very important part of the support plan. Neuropsychology would tell us that the most important response to such a crisis event in a child or young person includes repairing and rebuilding relationships. It would suggest that punitive or excluding consequences could further exacerbate the relational and emotional concerns of the student. It would also suggest that the crisis event should be viewed as an opportunity for learning and growth rather than an opportunity for punishment. So, this section of the support plan would articulate what will be done after the student has calmed down and over the following days. If it is decided the student should spend some time away from school, the plan will describe the steps that will be taken to mitigate the harm of any disrupted attachments during this absence and also how the student will be supported on their return to school.

Summary

A trauma-aware approach to education in schools must take into consideration how the behaviours of students are understood and responded to by the adults working with them. This approach does involve a paradigm shift away from more traditional, behaviourist methodologies that have informed much of what is done in schools for many years. Many strategies that are informed by Behaviourism do work relatively well for many learners but can 'fall flat' when applied to trauma-impacted learners and indeed, can do more harm than good. After educators have a general understanding of the impact of trauma and what a trauma-aware response might entail for a school, it is important that time and effort are expended to interrogate behaviour management policy and process. This step is vital to remove worrying barriers to providing a comprehensive and successful trauma-aware response to student support. These learnings are important for both education sites and education systems.

Chapter 5

Trauma-Aware Strategies (Safety, Relationships, Emotional Regulation)

Much of what is written in this chapter will seem to have a school focus. However, the strategies discussed are very applicable to the early childhood education context and various alternative education contexts. They will just need to be modified according to the age and stage of development of the child and the circumstances of the education site context.

There are three main focus areas for trauma-aware education. First, students need help to perceive that they are safe in the various environments within the education site and with the various relationships within the education site. Second, students need help developing the skills to engage adaptively in relationships with adults and peers. Third, students will need help to develop their capacities for emotional self-regulation. The strategies and approaches discussed in this chapter address one or more of these foci and draw from an understanding of the neurobiological impact of trauma and the potential for trauma-aware practice to remediate this impact. This chapter will discuss some examples of strategies and approaches, but creative educators do develop additional or different strategies and should certainly be encouraged to do so. However, there are two important things to remember when trying something different. Does this strategy focus on perceptions of safety, relationships, and/or emotional regulation, and does this strategy draw from neuroscience understandings and not behaviourist methodologies? Keeping these two things in mind will ensure that your ideas adequately and appropriately address the needs of trauma-impacted students in a manner that is far more likely to be successful.

The Mentor, Check In and Check Out

A mentor (or you can use a different term) is someone at your workplace who is an additional and key relationship for a trauma-impacted student, who is relationally available and warm and who is perceived by the student as safe and supportive. Of course, in very small schools or early childhood services, there may not be a lot of choice as to who can provide the mentor service. However, ideally, this should be someone different to staff members who already have a substantial amount of responsibility for and contact with the student (for example, not the classroom teacher in a primary school). The role is designed to provide a relational 'secure base' and 'safe haven' for the student and to make coming to the education site, and being at the education site, feel safe and supportive. The mentor offers 'unconditional positive regard', so no matter what the student does or says, the mentor is unconditionally there for them and always expects and encourages progress.

First thing each day, the student 'checks in' with the mentor. As the mentor relationship is increasingly perceived as helpful and unconditional by the learner, it is more likely that the student's experience of arriving at the education site each morning will feel safer and safer. On arrival, the mentor can assess whether the student has all they require to engage in their learning that day and can check whether the learner is emotionally regulated enough to enter the first class of the day in a stable manner. The mentor might check, for example, that the student has eaten breakfast, has food for the day, has the books, pens, or pencils they need, or was able to do their homework the night before. The mentor might develop communication systems with the student's classroom teacher or teachers to inform them of any concerns and recommendations to alleviate or avert any future difficulties. This could be done, for example, by using communication cards or mobile phone texts, or emails. The mentor might allow a dysregulated student some extra time in their company to assist with their emotional regulation before leaving for class. So, an important outcome of the mentoring strategy is the increased likelihood that the student will enter their first class of the day in a regulated state, and to minimise the likelihood of disruption to the work of the teacher and the learning of the other students. Starting the day well is always beneficial!

Toward the end of the day, the student may be released from class a little early to visit the mentor to check out. This is a brief but predictable visit during which the mentor chats with the learner in a positive and encouraging manner about their day, even if there have been concerns that day. The mentor might remind the student that they know they are trying hard and how pleased they are that they attended that day. The mentor might finish the chat with a reminder that they are really looking forward to seeing the student the following day. By ending the day like this and by making these simple statements, the mentor strategy can make returning to the education site the following day feel safer for the student, enhancing the likelihood that, more and more, the student will arrive back at the site in an emotionally regulated state.

There may be times when a young student might need to check in and check out more often during the day. For example, this might be needed when a trauma-impacted student is new to a school or if they have returned to a school after a period of absence. It might also be needed if a young student has been experiencing difficult life circumstances outside of school hours or days. So, under some circumstances, it might be helpful to have students check in or check out before or after lunch breaks or during other times during the day, with the goal of helping them manage their emotional regulation during a time when this is difficult for them. However, this way of working is certainly very resource intensive, and it is important to gently move students back to checking in and out only before and after school as soon as reasonably possible.

Safe Spaces

This strategy requires you to work with young students to help them find a place in which they feel safe, where they can go when they have the need to emotionally regulate or to prevent emotional dysregulation from happening. Initially, you might help the student to practice going to their safe space when they are feeling emotionally calm and regulated, so that going to their safe space feels more and more usual to them and therefore becomes more achievable for when they are experiencing dysregulation. You might also work with the student to help them to recognise how they feel, or what symptoms they might experience, when they are beginning to dysregulate or when they are quite dysregulated. They can then compare this to how they might present or feel when they are emotionally calm. This can help them to recognise when they need to access the safe space and when they should return to class. The type of space provided can differ according to the individual circumstances and age of the student and the education site facilities and available resources. You will need to problem-solve the circumstances of your workplace to come up with the best space option for an individual student. Some schools have a 'chill out' corner in the classroom or a 'chill out' room at the school. In some schools with significant numbers of students exhibiting challenging behaviour, they may have 'chill out' rooms for dysregulated staff members (see Chapter Eight). This needs to be managed thoughtfully but can be very helpful, as emotionally regulated educators are needed to help emotionally dysregulated students. This strategy will initially need you to provide your student with practice and support to access the space appropriately. Once this strategy is soundly in place, students tend to need the safe space less and less as their perceptions of safety and unconditional support are enhanced.

Emotional Regulation Strategies

Emotional regulation strategies work nicely with the 'safe space' strategy. This is when you help your student to practice their preferred self-regulation strategy or strategies when in their safe space. In some cases, as students get better and better at using their strategies, they can use them in their usual classrooms to help them remain calm enough so they don't need to move to their safe space. The first step with this strategy is to work with the student to discover what strategies they might prefer or which ones might be more effective. Some examples of strategies include regulated breathing, counting, colouring, listening to music, being wrapped in a weighted blanket, sitting under a table or in a segregated part of a room, running, bouncing a ball, talking it through, being quiet, wearing noise reducing headphones, or using mindfulness apps. Some sites have spaces that incorporate calming sensory stimuli, such as small water fountains, pleasant aromas, fidget toys, or soft music.

Once the mentor strategy, the safe space strategy, and emotional regulation strategies are effectively in place, relatively soon you should see a reduction in the frequency of emotional dysregulation of the student and therefore fewer behavioural outbursts and experiences of hyperarousal and hypoarousal (fight, flight, freeze). Students still might experience quite intensive dysregulation at times, but this should become less and less frequent. In other words, you will be helping your student to stay within their 'Window of Tolerance' more often and more effectively. So, although these strategies are not focused on managing learner behaviour or their engagement with learning or with improving their learning outcomes, due to their impact on emotional regulation, they can have a positive impact on both behaviour and on learning.

Check Curriculum and Assessment Triggers

For learners in some family or caregiver contexts, certain learning activities or assessment tasks may trigger emotional responses that can lead to behavioural and engagement difficulties for those who have lived through trauma. It is important that educators become critically aware of potentially harmful aspects of the curriculum and assessment for learners who have lived through adversity and become courageous enough to modify activities to mitigate harm (Sempowicz et al., 2018).

As a starting point, family diversity necessitates being cautious in how we approach learning activities about the family dynamic, but this is even more important for learners with trauma histories. There are learners in classrooms who have been abandoned, neglected, or abused by family members. There are those who were adopted and no little of the detail of the biological family. There are those who have lived in multiple foster placements or who are living in residential care. There are those who are homeless and/or living in poverty. There are those who take on most of the care for their caregiver who is physically or mentally unwell, or who is addicted to substances. The list goes on! For these learners, engaging in a task that explores 'the family' can be quite triggering (Sempowicz et al., 2018).

There are other areas of the curriculum of which we need to be thoughtful and cautious. This could include activities that require reflections on life events. One example could involve asking learners to explore and document timelines of their lives that identify events of importance during particular years. For learners who have lived through adversity, the events that might be prominent could be those they prefer not to recall or share. Also, their 'timelines' might look very different to those of their non-traumatised peers. Assessment tasks that require this type of reflection can also include autobiographies that are presented either as written tasks or as oral presentations to the class. Asking a trauma survivor who has lived through complex and harmful family dynamics to do this just seems cruel and unnecessary. Even asking young children who have a problematic home environment to write about 'what they did over the school holidays' or to 'bring in a photo of themselves as a baby' could be problematic for some. Certain areas of the science curriculum or health curriculum might also need to be approached carefully with some students. Activities that explore family and genetic traits could be difficult for trauma-surviving learners who now live with foster or adoptive caregivers. Activities that explore human sexuality and reproduction might prove very challenging for those young learners who have lived through sexual abuse (Sempowicz et al., 2018).

I will share some examples that illustrate just how harmful engagement in curriculum and assessment practices (that seemed quite benign on the surface) can be for trauma-impacted learners. I was told of a child who was usually quiet in class who reacted in an aggressive manner after being asked by a relief teacher (the regular teacher was absent that day) to draw a diagram of his bedroom at home to scale. Due to the aggressive outburst, the child was 'sent to the office' to face the serious consequences of this behaviour, as outlined in the school behaviour policy. It was discovered that this child was living in a tent with his mother and siblings due to being homeless and 'on the run' from the father who had perpetrated very serious domestic violence. He was terrified most days after leaving school that his father would find and harm the family. Asking this child to draw a diagram of his non-existent bedroom triggered the emotional dysregulation that led to a sympathetic nervous system (fight, flight) response that was quite reasonable under the circumstances. He did not have his trusted and known teacher available to assist with his regulation, so he hit and he ran. Another example is a high school student who was asked to produce a written autobiography that was to be summarised in an oral presentation to the class as a summative assessment task. The assessment criteria required in-depth description of life events and life context that was creatively and clearly expressed and communicated. This student was living in a residential care facility after experiencing complex trauma and had been through numerous foster placements. She refused to engage in the assessment task and therefore was failed. Whilst her peers were preparing and presenting their oral assessment pieces, she was at 'home', experiencing severe anxiety, refusing to eat, and engaging in self-injury.

National curriculums articulate learning standards, content areas, and recommended activity and assessment which is very good and helpful for educators. Most of what is recommended will do no harm to most learners. However, rather than just implementing recommended activity for all learners, it is worth interrogating some learning activities and assessment tasks for elements that could prove retraumatising for trauma-impacted learners. Educators are creative, thoughtful, learner-focused professionals who must uphold their rights to modify learning and assessment activity so that it 'does no harm' to any of the learners in their class, including those living with the outcomes of complex trauma. Reasonable adjustments to activity and assessment are vital if we are to provide equitable access to learning and achievement for all learners.

Pick Your Battles

Sometimes it is just not worth going into battle with an emotionally dysregulated student over some issues. Sometimes, it is just better to wait. Remember that you will not have access to the learner's pre-frontal cortex during these difficult times because their brainstem and the amygdala in the limbic system are overactive. You do need access to the student's higher cognitive functions if you are going to have any impact on their current or future behaviours. If you confront a student during times of dysregulation, you are likely to become dysregulated yourself, and you are unlikely to achieve the behaviour outcomes you were hoping to achieve. These situations can quickly become more complex and confronting, and when this occurs, the student will likely end up being the recipient of a significant punitive response (such as detention, suspension, or exclusion). This is what we want to avoid, as this can have ongoing negative impacts on relationships and perceptions of safety. So, sometimes just not worth going into battle over some issues!

Some examples of issues that might not be worth battling over whilst you are working in a trauma-aware manner with some students might include not wearing their uniform in the manner outlined by school policy, not completing homework or assessment tasks on time, not agreeing to perform an oral or public task, not working well with a particular peer or group or group of peers, or refusing to pick up rubbish in the playground when asked to do so. There are always behaviour or performance standards that are established as whole-school or classroom expectations for all students, which is a great practice. However, with a trauma-aware approach, we acknowledge that there will be times and contexts when our trauma-impacted students may not meet these expectations or where they will need support to repeatedly practise the new skills to meet these expectations, without feeling threatened, unsafe, or rejected.

Allowing some trauma-impacted students to 'get away with' some undesired behaviours does concern educators due to what is referred to as the 'fear of contagion'. Contagion can occur when classmates observe that different behavioural expectations are being applied to a particular student, and they therefore 'push the boundaries' to see if they can also 'get away with' similar behaviours. Educators also worry that having different behaviour expectations for one student is 'unfair' to others.

Educators must realise that inclusive education requires a differentiated approach to allow equitable access to education by various students from various backgrounds. Sometimes it can be more challenging to be comfortable with differentiating behaviour expectations compared to (for example) differentiating teaching and learning strategies. It might also be somewhat uncomfortable differentiating behaviour expectations for trauma-impacted students compared to (for example) students who have diagnosed and clearly observable disabilities. However, as neuroscience has clearly explained the impact of child maltreatment on the functioning of bodies and brains, we understand how important it is to implement strategies to help reduce the likelihood of emotional dysregulation, and 'choosing your battles' is one important example of this.

Educators can implement strategies to mitigate 'contagion' by letting other students know that although a different behaviour expectation is in place for one student, this does not change the expectations for all. This could be done through individual or group discussions with particular students who need to hear this and have it explained to them. Or in some situations, a class meeting might be beneficial. However, to prevent embarrassment for the trauma-impacted student, it might be appropriate to hold such a meeting when they are not in the room. It is important that the personal circumstances of the trauma-impacted student are not shared during discussions or meetings with other students, but educators can explain that the student under discussion needs some extra help, practice, and support to feel happy and calm and therefore, for a time, different behaviour expectations might be in place. It needs to be communicated clearly that the usual behaviour expectations are still firmly in place for the class, despite the more flexible approach being adopted for your student of concern.

Non-Verbal Messages

Rather than always talking, sometimes it is more effective to use non-verbal strategies to help your student communicate something of importance to you or for you to communicate something of importance to your student. You need to negotiate with your student what strategy will work for you both, so developing a trusting and non-conditional relationship with your student comes first. You then agree on a non-verbal cue that the two of you will use to communicate quickly and well. There are numerous options depending on the age and preferences of the student, such as using cards, objects, your proximity, touching the student's desk, or hand signals. Knowing that the strategy is in place can help your student with their emotional regulation, as they can give you a message quickly and easily without having to speak, minimising the likelihood that they will have to wait longer periods for a response, or that they might be embarrassed in front of their peers. Receiving non-verbal messages from you throughout the day reminds them that you are thinking of them and that you care and are there to help. Using non-verbals is quick, relational, and doesn't stop the teacher from teaching. Examples might include when you need to remind a student that an activity is coming to an end and that they need to prepare to transition to something new or when a student needs to let you know that they are feeling uneasy and need some help. It is important that you don't use many different non-verbal cues with your student but rather minimise these to just those that are most important for your student to remain regulated and engaged in their learning.

Exploring Exceptions

Some more traditional ways of analysing and addressing behaviour concerns require us to focus on when, where, and how the behaviour occurs. However, there is value in 'flipping this' and instead adopting the solution-focused strategy of exploring exceptions when analysing and responding to concerning behaviours of trauma-impacted students. This strategy comes from Solution-Focused Brief Therapy that was initially developed Steve de Shazer (1940-2005), and Insoo Kim Berg (1934-2007) in the late 1970s (Berg & Steiner, 2003). Solution-Focused Brief Therapy is a goal-directed approach to therapy that draws from positive psychology principles and focuses on solutions rather than on the problems experienced by people seeking therapy. There are a range of questioning and other techniques used within Solution-Focused Brief Therapy that is quite easily and appropriately applied in the school context (Bannink, 2015; Milner & Bateman, 2011). It is not suggested that you should 'do therapy' when you use these techniques at school (unless you are a school counsellor or psychologist). Rather, these are easily implemented and often quite enjoyable strategies that help to explore options and solutions for students in a positive and encouraging way.

The technique of exploring exceptions suggests that rather than always examining contexts where challenging behaviour is evident, we should examine contexts where the behaviour is absent or less likely to occur. It proposes that we ponder what the circumstances or conditions are that lead to the behaviour not occurring or being less likely to occur, and then work with the student to create similar circumstances or conditions in broader contexts, so that the likelihood of the behaviour being exhibited overall is minimised. So, this might be as simple as asking questions like, 'Why does he not play up during music classes?' or 'Why is she so calm in Mr Smith's class?' or 'Why are Wednesdays easier for this student?' or 'Why is first break more challenging for this student compared to second break?'. It is beyond the scope of this book to write about solution-focused strategies in detail, but if you are interested, it is recommended you explore some books or resources that are dedicated to this. They can be helpful with many students but are certainly helpful when working with trauma-impacted students.

Relational Rewards

It is important to capitalise on any moment you can throughout the school day to work on relationships and emotional regulation. It is also important to utilise relational rewards rather than non-relational rewards when you are aiming to encourage your trauma-impacted student's efforts. So, rather than providing a tangible reward or token reward (for example, stickers or spending time using an iPad), provide time with people who can offer a positive and engaging experience for the student. This is not to 'reinforce' behaviours, which is a behaviourist concept, but rather a way to work on reinforcing networks in the parts of the brain that manage emotions and relationships.

A Better Way to Use Detention

If your school chooses to use detention as a consequence for misbehaviour, rather than placing a student in an isolating situation, provide a relational detention experience. In a space that is deemed safe by the student, provide an adult who will help the student process any harm that was done, in a constructive way. Capitalise on this opportunity to develop pathways in the brain associated with relationships and empathy and to help the student practise newly developing skills for relating.

Use Inclusive Education Strategies

You can use strategies that work with students who live with Autism Spectrum Disorder (for example) because both groups of students can present with similar concerns and challenges regarding perceptions of safety, relationships, and emotional regulation. Both groups can have difficulty managing unpredictable occurrences, change and transitions, and certain sensory stimuli. Both can experience challenges with communication, dealing with their social worlds, and calming themselves after an escalation of emotions. It is a good idea to chat with special (inclusion) educators and ask them about the strategies that they use to help students who live with Autism Spectrum Disorder. Consider which of these might benefit your student living with the outcomes of complex trauma. Some examples of strategies that might be helpful include using visual timetables to help students know what the day will entail and when transitions will occur, using clocks or timers to help students know how much time is left before a transition or change, or providing sensory support aids to help students to seek or avoid sensory stimuli to reduce their anxiety. Also, you might consider staffing or placement arrangements for days when the usual class teachers are absent to help avoid students becoming anxious with the presence of a yet unknown relief teacher.

So, for both groups of students, working on relationships is important, but there might be some differences between each group that might need to be further understood. Many, but not all, students living with Autism Spectrum Disorder can be less interested in the work we do to help them with relationships and social skill development. We still may include activity to help students develop capacities for these areas, but for some of these students, this may not be something that they are passionate about or even keen to do. In comparison, many students living with the outcomes of complex trauma can be relationally thirsty, and their behaviours can be driven towards gaining access to relationships. Unfortunately, they may not be very good at this, and they may tend to harm or sabotage relationships, despite their really wanting to engage in relationships. Knowing this should inform how we work with these students.

Cognitive Scripts

When relational sabotage occurs, a very helpful strategy is for educators to use cognitive scripts. Cognitive scripts can help you self-regulate when a student's behaviour 'pushes your emotional buttons'. Cognitive scripts are simply words or phrases that you can repeat again and again to yourself, silently in your thoughts. This strategy is drawn from a therapeutic approach known as Cognitive Behaviour Therapy (CBT) which emerged in the 1960s, firstly by psychiatrist, Aaron Beck (Weishaar, 1992; Wills, 2021). CBT suggests that what we tell ourselves (our self-talk or thoughts) can influence what we feel (our emotions), and this can then influence our behaviour (what we do).

A very usual response to relational sabotage is an overwhelming feeling that I call the 'How dare you!' response. Relational sabotage by a trauma-impacted student can leave you feeling hurt, betrayed, or attacked, particularly if you have invested much time, energy, and emotion into developing the relationship. When this occurs, your self-talk may become quite negative (for example, 'How dare you do this to me after all the effort I have put into helping you!'). You may not actually say the words that you are thinking, but you will certainly think them, and this can then impact your emotions (you dysregulate), which can then impact your behaviours (withdrawing from the relationship with the student). However, by practising and purposefully using cognitive scripts that help you to emotionally regulate (for example, 'I don't like what you are doing right now but I really like you!', or 'I know you are sabotaging this relationship because it is important to you!'), you should be less likely to experience the negative impact of sabotaging behaviours. Sometimes, it is helpful to just remind yourself of how unfair and sad it is that the student had to live through the type of harm that now leads them to behave in the way they are behaving. Or perhaps you could remind yourself not to take what is happening personally, as the behaviours are due to the student living with the impacts of complex trauma.

Remember, this sabotaging behaviour happens because child victims of complex trauma can have a lot of difficulty believing that people truly like or love them. For some of these children, all the evidence in their short lives has led them to believe that adults can't be trusted and that they are not being truthful when they express kindness and care. So, for these children, when a relationship is beginning to feel safe and warm, they can tend to test that relationship through sabotaging behaviours. These students can expect you to fail and reject them. So, it is important to practise using your cognitive scripts so that they come to you more easily during times of relational sabotage. The more you work on your thoughts, the more this will influence your emotions, and the more this will influence your behaviours, so you can get back in and do the work your student needs you to do! Using cognitive scrips can have a powerful and helpful influence, making it more likely that you will want to continue engaging in a helping relationship with your students, despite their behavioural presentations.

Look for the Gold!

Finding the 'gold' is a simple but effective strategy that helps educators increasingly value relationships with their trauma-impacted students, despite the concerns that they might experience or express. This strategy can involve seeking out something wonderful about the students, which may not come easily at first, as often the wonderful things are buried beneath the observable behaviours and repeated challenges. So, sometimes educators need to be reminded to 'dig' and 'keep digging' until they 'find the gold'! You could, perhaps, explore students' talents or skills (for example, dance, art, construction, jokes), or you could explore favourable attributes of students (for example, kindness to animals or younger children). It is important to keep digging until the gold is found because once it has been found, relationships between educators and students can be enhanced.

Model and Coach

This strategy involves a process for teaching students social behaviours and allowing them to practice newly developing skills for social interaction and emotional self-regulation. It is important that educators understand that social engagement can be stress-inducing for trauma-impacted students, so this process provides the means to gradually enhance the student's social engagement with less and less emotional discord. You can use the model and coach approach for students of all ages and many social contexts where students engage with peers at school. For example, this approach could be used for a student who needs help working in groups, a young child who needs support playing with peers in the playground safely, or an adolescent student who needs help to engage adaptively with team sports.

This strategy involves a series of scaffolded steps. First, the educator models the behaviour that they are hoping for the trauma-impacted student to develop whilst the student observes (for example, safely working in class with a group, playing in the playground, or kicking the soccer ball with friends). After this, the educator and student spend time together discussing what happened and what was learned, and how this is helpful. Second, the student engages in social interaction with teacher support as needed. You can expect that the student may not exhibit the desired behaviours well in the early stages of this process. There may be a need to repeat the first and second stages several times, allowing the student to practise their newly developing skills. After each try, the educator and student spend time together discussing what happened, what was learned, and how it is helpful. The third step is to provide more independent opportunities for the student to engage in social activity, remembering that at times they might still need support. When using this strategy, it is important to remember that each time you provide the supported opportunity for students to engage in social activities at school, important neural pathways in the brain are being reinforced, which will contribute to longer-term gains for future social experiences. However, some trauma-impacted students may need lots of opportunities to repeatedly practise and be encouraged to try again if they 'fail' at times. Any 'failures' should not be viewed as times that need punishment or discipline, but rather as evidence that they need more support and more practice.

Whole Class Lessons

It is recommended that each year level in school is provided with scaffolded learning about areas of student wellbeing that are informed by neuroscience. All students can benefit from understanding how their brains, and parts of their brains, work during emotional regulation and dysregulation and how this might impact their behaviours, feelings, and learning. All students can benefit from knowing ways that they can self-regulate their emotions and behaviours. Educators can explain these things using video, drawings, models, puzzles, animations, and also just by discussing. Providing this learning to all students is helpful but allowing access to this learning for trauma-impacted students is vital. Trauma-impacted students may need more intensive support to develop their understandings and skills for emotional and behavioural regulation but knowing that all their classmates also have access to this information can take some of the stigma away about their needs and circumstances.

It is also recommended that schools adopt a common vocabulary that both students and educators can use to refer to the parts of the brain, emotional dysregulation, and regulation. For example, a school might refer to the pre-frontal cortex as the 'thinking or clever brain', the limbic system as the 'upset or emotional brain', and the brain stem as the 'stormy or wild brain'. What vocabulary is used can be informed by the ages and developmental stages of students. Older teenagers, for example, might prefer to use anatomical terms rather that than the metaphorical terms preferred by younger students.

Brain Breaks

Brain breaks are shifts in planned learning activity that activate different networks of the brain to revitalise the learning and engagement of all students. For students' brains to work efficiently, neurochemical messages need to be sent from sensory receptors (what they hear, see, touch, read, imagine, and experience), through to the amygdala (emotional filter), to be processed by the pre-frontal cortex, and then to move to the memory storage regions of the brain. When a student experiences high anxiety, activity in the amygdala changes so that rather than it filtering experience, it stops the processing of experience, and will not allow the process of learning to reach the pre-frontal cortex and to be sustained in memory.

By switching neural activity to differing brain networks, brain breaks can allow original areas of the brain to rest and revitalise, enhancing mood, attention, and memory (Willis, 2006; 2007; 2009). Importantly, brain breaks can allow the brain regions of trauma-impacted students that might be impacted by the stress of high-intensity activity or long periods of engagement, to rest and repair before emotional dysregulation occurs, which can help to re-engage pre-frontal cortical activity. Due to how brain breaks can affect neural activity, incorporating them throughout the school day can help lift students' mood and enhance motivation for engagement and learning. Depending on the type of brain break used, they can calm or energise students. A calming brain break (such as students quietly and slowly tracing around the outside of one hand with a finger from their opposite hand, whilst breathing rhythmically) can settle overactivity in the amygdala. Short bursts of physical activity during an energising brain break can increase blood flow and oxygen supply to the brain and the availability of mood-enhancing neurochemicals such as dopamine and serotonin.

The type of brain break used is limited only by the imagination of the educator. Examples could include activities involving laughing, moving, listening to music, singing with movements, interacting with peers, reading aloud from an engaging text, jumping rope, tossing a beach ball while students ask and answer study questions, or asking students to move to imitate a biological, physical, or mathematical process. Brain breaks should take place before student fatigue, boredom, distraction, and inattention set in. Depending on students' age and developmental stages, the frequency and the types of brain breaks can vary. Brain breaks do not have to interfere with the flow of learning if this is not deemed appropriate. Rather, educators can simply ask students to stretch or stand, turn around, and sit back down. It is also helpful for educators to 'train' their students to understand that when the brain break is over, it is straight back to work!

Mindfulness

Mindfulness can be explained as a mental state of being fully aware of yourself and your surroundings, without any judgement. It is a time of quiet contemplation, focusing on the present moment and welcoming and experiencing your environment through your senses. The practice dates back thousands of years and has its roots in Eastern religions such as Buddhism and Hinduism. In the West, mindfulness has more of a secular history, but people worldwide practise it as either part of their religion or in a non-religious manner.

Increasingly, mindfulness has been the focus of studies in psychology to examine the potential of the practice to enhance overall wellbeing. In the field of positive psychology, there is evidence to suggest that it can be used to address stress, anxiety, depression, and even chronic pain. Studies have shown that the practice can improve emotional self-regulation, self-compassion, and reduce negative mindsets and patterns of thinking (Joss, et.al., 2019; Seigel, 2007). Other research suggests using mindfulness can positively impact the body's immune response, stress reactivity, and overall physical wellbeing (Farb, et al., 2007; Vibe et al., 2017).

Neuroscientists have used brain scanning technologies to explore how the brain changes when people practise mindfulness, with many of these studies focusing on people who have lived through child maltreatment (Joss & Teicher, 2021). Findings suggest that areas of the brain may change in structure and function in response to regular mindfulness practice. The amygdala can become less reactive, so the capacity for emotional regulation is enhanced (Joss, et al., 2021; Kral et al., 2018). The hippocampus can become thicker, enhancing memory and learning capacity (Joss, et al., 2020). Studies show that mindfulness can lead to enhanced immune function, and increased production of the enzyme telomerase (that maintains and repairs the ends of our chromosomes) and can strengthen and thicken the insula (Farb et al., 2007; Murakami, et al., 2012; Siegel, 2007).

So, evidence suggests that practising mindfulness techniques at school could be helpful in allowing children and young people develop skills for emotional self-regulation and therefore an increased capacity to engage in their learning. Through these techniques, they can learn to be fully present in the 'now' without being overwhelmed by thoughts, feelings, and sometimes memories from the past (Broderick, 2019; Cozolino, 2013; Jennings, 2015; Yeigh, 2020). However, it is recommended that these techniques be used at school only as a tool to help students with their emotional self-regulation. Educators should not use these techniques as a tool for therapy for trauma-impacted students. Conducting therapy is for highly trained specialists and should not be within the purview of educators. Remember, we must avoid at all costs any potential to retraumatise these young students.

The Assistance of Animals

Animals (particularly mammals, and even more particularly horses and dogs) have been instrumental in supporting human beings in therapeutic ways for a long time. Since the 1960s, trained assistance or therapy dogs have been increasingly used in places like hospitals and care facilities, residential care settings, and prison-based populations, and now are also increasingly being used in schools (Gee et al., 2021; Hoagwood et al., 2017; Muela et al., 2017; Villafaina-Dominguez et al., 2020). Aside from research findings that celebrate the benefits of including animals in therapeutic contexts, there is strong evidence that animal-assisted support is helpful with children living with disabilities (Dimolareva, 2020) There is emerging evidence that engagement with dogs can offer children aspects of secure attachment that were previously associated with human-to-human interactions (Hawkins, 2022; Karl et al., 2020). Also, animal-assisted therapy has been shown to reduce symptoms of post-traumatic stress disorder for people (and children) living with this concern (Hediger, 2021; Mims & Waddell, 2016). Engaging children who have experienced sexual abuse with various approaches to therapy can be quite challenging, but when this is complemented with animal-assisted therapy, engagement in therapy and therapeutic outcomes can be enhanced. One Australian study found that canine-assisted therapy for child victims of maltreatment was greatly preferred by caregivers in comparison to more traditional approaches (Dravsnik, et al., 2018).

Research findings mostly suggest positive and encouraging impacts for trauma-impacted learners and learners who live with disability if they engage with equine or canine therapies or support. As canine support is an easier on-campus option for schools, this support intervention is being incorporated more and more (Brelsford et al., 2017; Kropp & Shupp, 2017). As well-trained school dogs can provide consistent and unambiguous responses to the emotions and behaviours of trauma-impacted children and young people, they can contribute a calming effect to the daily experiences of these young learners during the hours that they are at school. Activities including children grooming, talking to, or engaging in some way with a dog can assist with their capacities for emotional self-regulation and enhance their self-perceptions (Dravsnik, et al., 2018; Signal, et al., 2017).

Assistance, service, or therapy dogs in schools need to be highly trained animals that perform tasks to support learners with particular needs, whether that be to help with their reading, their motor skills, or (in the case of trauma-impacted learners) their emotional regulation and engagement in learning. The contribution of these animals can be considered as a reasonable adjustment for a student to enhance their schooling experience. There are (and should be) strict standards to support the safety and wellbeing of learners and school personnel and also the safety and wellbeing of the dogs. It is highly recommended and very helpful if education systems have policies to guide the use and support of animals on campus.

Dogs working in schools need to meet standards of health, hygiene, and behaviour appropriate for use in a public place. In most instances, the school's principal will need to approve the use of canine-assisted work and ensure that standards are met. Dog owners/handlers need to provide evidence of animal registration, current vaccination, temperament, training, and skills appropriate for a school context. Ideally, risk assessment and management plans should be completed before canine-assisted work commences. Consideration might need to be given to any concerns regarding student allergies and phobias, or fears regarding dogs. There also needs to be planning for the animal's wellbeing, including providing times and places for rest (and 'toileting') away from learners, food and water, comfort, and exercise. Just as with learners, schools should have a duty of care to look after the safety and wellbeing of these incredibly valuable animals. So, sometimes there is an amount of preparation and paperwork required before commencing canine-assisted work in schools. Still, with the right animal in the right context, the benefits for trauma-impacted students (and others) can be immense.

Summary

This chapter has discussed some strategies that can be incorporated into a trauma-aware response in schools, early childhood education, and care settings. Some are highly recommended and some are quite optional. However, educators should not view this chapter's contents as limiting their ability to design and implement other creative, thoughtful, and trauma-informed strategies. Importantly, as you consider strategies to include in your support planning for learners, it is vital that you choose those that are most likely to meet the support needs of the individual, trauma-impacted children or young people with whom you work. It is also critical that strategies are used to address the three foci of a trauma-aware response: perceptions of safety, relationships, and emotional regulation. It is hoped that providing a collection of strategies in this chapter will enhance discussions amongst learners as to how best this can be done.

Chapter 6

The Complex Intersection Between Trauma and Disability

There remain many questions in the education sector about how complex trauma intersects or interrelates with disability. Does disability lead to trauma, or does trauma leads to disability, or do both apply? Are children living with disability more prone to experiencing trauma, and if so, why? Can our 'usual' trauma-aware practices in education sites be used with learners with disability, or should we be doing something different? (Jackson, et al., 2015; McNally, 2021). This chapter will explore this intersection by firstly looking at the current legal and policy context, issues with diagnosis, and the known prevalence of people (and children) who live with both the outcomes of maltreatment and disability. Then the topic of universal screening in schools will be discussed by examining the pros and cons of using a universal screening approach to identify trauma-impacted learners in a similar way that many education sites and systems identify learners who live with disability. A complex intersection indeed, but one that needs further attention and response from the education sector.

Legislation and Models of Disability

In Australia, the national Disability Discrimination Act (DDA, 1992) is the legislation that refers to discriminatory and equitable responses and provisions for people living with disability. This Act defines disability as:

- 'total or partial loss of the person's bodily or mental functions; or
- total or partial loss of a part of the body; or
- the presence in the body of organisms causing disease or illness; or
- the presence in the body of organisms capable of causing disease or illness; or
- the malfunction, malformation, or disfigurement of a part of the person's body; or
- a disorder or malfunction that results in the person learning differently from a person without the disorder or malfunction; or
- a disorder, illness or disease that affects a person's thought processes, perception of reality, emotions or judgment or that results in disturbed behaviour; and includes a disability that:
- presently exists; or
- previously existed but no longer exists; or may exist in the future; or
- is imputed to a person'.

This piece of federal legislation outlines conditions where it is illegal to directly or indirectly discriminate against a person living with disability. There are also Disability Acts specific to states and territories in Australia that refer more closely to the impact of any disability and entitlement to services. As in many parts of the world, education sites and systems in Australia are required to align their processes with national disability legislation and disability and education legislation for their state or territory, which is complex but important work.

In recent years, there has been a move away from models of disability that pathologise the person and emphasise deficiency towards increased recognition of the potential of people with disabilities and their inherent rights to equitable access to services and provisions. There is greater awareness of how the environment influences the experience of disability, with the potential for the systems within the environment to be either enabling or disabling. There is also a greater understanding and acceptance that people living with disability are not a homogenous group but rather a diverse group of people with many other characteristics, including their age, culture, gender, and life experiences (including possible experience of trauma). There is also growing acceptance that people's experience of disability should not define them.

Some ' conditions ' are certainly disabling yet are not quite understood or accepted as disabling by the general public, or in some circumstances, by education sites and systems. In general, physical, sensory, or intellectual impairments or those that result from genetic disorders or brain injury, are generally clearly understood, diagnosed, and interpreted as areas of disability that require adjustments in the environment to remove or remediate conditions that disable. Disabling conditions resulting from children being considered 'neurodiverse', such as Autism Spectrum Disorder or Attention Deficit Disorder, can sometimes be less clearly understood, diagnosed, and interpreted. Unfortunately, disabling conditions related to the impact of complex childhood trauma can be far less clearly understood and interpreted and certainly there are complexities with diagnosis. For example, experiencing chronic emotional dysregulation that results from living with unresolved complex childhood trauma can certainly disable but may not be viewed as a disabling condition. Chronic emotional dysregulation by young learners can be misinterpreted as 'poor choices', 'deliberate behaviours', 'poor attitudes', or similar, and this understanding can drive disciplinary responses that can exacerbate rather than remediate concerns. There is also a significant amount of uncertainty regarding when trauma amounts to a disability under the legislation. This leads to inconsistencies in how these young learners are identified and supported. This is a growing and important area for discussion and action.

What is precisely identified in legislation and how it is interpreted has an influential impact on education policy and practice.

Problems with Diagnosis of Complex Trauma 'Disorders'

The Diagnostic and Statistical Manual of Mental Disorders (DSM) is a resource published by the American Psychiatric Association that is used by healthcare professionals in much of the world as the authoritative guide to diagnosing mental disorders. It was originally published in 1952, and at the time of writing this book, the most current edition is the fifth (DSM-5), published in 2013. Prior to the fifth edition, there was reference to a disorder associated with the relational harm experienced by children. *Reactive Attachment Disorder* referred to a disorder suffered by children who had experienced 'disorganised attachment' and who exhibited either or both inhibited (internalising) behaviours and disinhibited (externalising) behaviours. The fifth edition expanded this category of disorder into two. *Reactive Attachment Disorder* now refers to a stressor-related disorder that can only be caused by social neglect during childhood (meaning a lack of adequate caregiving) with internalising, withdrawn behaviours and depressive symptoms. *Disinhibited Social Engagement Disorder* is the newer diagnosis that refers to an emotional disorder associated with a lack of adequate caregiving that begins during childhood and presents with externalising behaviour and a lack of inhibition, particularly with unfamiliar adults (American Psychiatric Association, 2013).

When the revisions began for the new DSM-5, Dr Bessel van der Kolk and colleagues sought to include *Developmental Trauma Disorder* as a new diagnostic category (van der Kolk et al., 2009). Dr van der Kolk is a psychiatrist, researcher, and educator who specialises in post-traumatic stress. He proposes that there are serious concerns in studying and treating some psychiatric disorders when childhood maltreatment and early life stress are not considered. He suggests that maltreated and non-maltreated individuals with the same primary DSM-5 diagnosis (including Bipolar Disorder, Attention Deficit Hyperactivity Disorder, Post Traumatic Stress Disorder, Oppositional Defiance Disorder, Conduct Disorder, Phobic Anxiety, and others) can differ clinically, neurobiologically, and genetically. Dr van der Kolk, estimates that millions of children in the United States alone have been diagnosed with Bipolar Disorder or Attention Deficit Hyperactivity Disorder and, as a result, have been prescribed large doses of medication. He professes that oftentimes, the cause of the problems experienced by these children was disrupted attachment and untreated emotional abuse and neglect (D'Andrea et al., 2021; Ford et al., 2022; van der Kolk, 2005).

Dr van der Kolk organised a task force to conduct, collect, and present research from clinical studies that could help make their case for developing this new category of *Developmental Trauma Disorder* for the DSM-5. After much discussion and controversy, the DSM Committee rejected this proposal, suggesting that the range of symptoms covered in the proposed criteria was too broad and the new disorder was not well enough supported by research. There was also the concern that including this new category of disorder may complicate or even supersede many established categories of disorder in the DSM. This could require rethinking many diagnoses used in research and clinical practice and could require huge changes in the way that mental health professionals are trained, paid, supervised, and licensed. Textbooks may need to be rewritten, insurance coverages would have to be updated, and mental health practitioners already in the field would have to change how they practice and could require additional training. Dr van der Kolk believes it will take a massive public crusade against child maltreatment to alter the political realities that are blocking this change.

Dr van der Kolk would suggest that vast numbers of children and people under psychiatric care and with a range of psychiatric diagnoses are actually living with the outcomes of childhood trauma. He suggests that rather than focusing on the symptoms that contribute to particular diagnoses, we should be enquiring into what happened to these people as children that led to them developing these symptoms and treating them accordingly. He suggests that we are ignoring the social conditions that contribute to the concerns experienced by children and the potential to remedy these conditions, and rather are over-depending (or only depending) on the prescription of medications to treat them. He sees this as a serious public health issue and one that a trauma-aware response can address. It is important that these children and young people come to know that they are not 'broken' but rather they have developed survival responses to help them manage very concerning and harmful experiences. They now need help to modify their neurobiology so that they can live more happy, healthy, and productive lives.

Prevalence of the Intersection

To start to explore this intersection, we first need to examine some prevalence data. At the time of writing this book, the *Australian Royal Commission into Violence Abuse Neglect and Exploitation of People with Disability* was still in process. The Commission found that (for people over the age of 15 years), 64% of people with disability report experiencing physical violence, sexual violence, intimate partner violence, and/or emotional abuse compared to 45% of people without disability. This Commission also found that over a 12-month period, people with disability were 1.8 times more likely to experience physical violence, 2.2 times more likely to experience sexual violence, 2.6 times more likely to experience intimate partner violence, and 1.9 times more likely to experience emotional abuse, when compared to the population without disability (Centre of Research Excellence in Disability and Health, 2021). It is important to recognise that these data do not include children under the age of 15.

Studies examining this prevalence with children uncover equally (if not more) concerning findings and that the worrying numbers of children who live both with disability and experience trauma are a global concern. For example, a study in Israel reported that the likelihood of children living with disability experiencing child maltreatment was 6.2 higher than for children without disability and that the more severe the level of disability, the greater the likelihood that maltreatment would occur (Karni-Visel, et al., 2020). An examination of substantiated child maltreatment cases in Canada revealed that one in ten of these children (11.3%) were identified as living with an intellectual disorder and suggested that maltreated children with disability face additional challenges necessitating an urgent response in prevention and early intervention programs (Dion, et al., 2018). An American study showed that compared to other maltreated youth, children living with Autism

Spectrum Disorder and/or Intellectual Disability are at risk for more frequent and complex experiences of maltreatment (McDonnell, et al., 2019). A study in Finland suggests that hearing impairment, physical disability, and mental health problems increased the likelihood of polyvictimisation (experiencing more than one type of maltreatment) for children (Seppälä, 2021). An international systematic review exploring research on the prevalence of maltreatment for children living with disability found only minimal studies and none from Australia but was able to estimate an international, pooled average of 27% of children and adolescents who live with disability who also live with violence and maltreatment (Jones, 2012).

There is some (but not yet enough) research in Australia examining this prevalence for children. A study in Western Australia found that 10.4% of children born between 1990 and 2010 lived with disability, but a disproportionate number (29%) of children with substantiated child protection lived with disability (Maclean, et al. 2017). In 2012, Robinson suggested that abuse and neglect of children and young people living with disability is a longstanding and pervasive social problem in Australia yet studies examining this concern were scarce. A report by the Victorian Ombudsman (2010) suggested that children and young people with a disability are likely to be among the most vulnerable group of children and young people 'in care', and that they are over-represented in the Out-of-Home-Care population. However, this intersection between disability and trauma in children does remain under-reported.

Maltreatment is likely to be under-reported for various reasons. This could be due to children or young people lacking the support to make a complaint or not feeling they would be believed, or their not having the words to name the harm they are experiencing, or their feeling intimidated and fearful due to being reliant on an abuser who also provides their daily personal support. Also, some caregivers and professionals may have a limited understanding of trauma and trauma-related symptoms and therefore may attribute trauma-related behaviour to the disability alone. In addition, the detection of maltreatment might be hampered when professionals face difficulties in distinguishing between accidental injuries that result from impairment, and abuse-related injuries.

Research regarding the experience of these children and young people is also very difficult due to methodological challenges. This includes sample selection, which involves identifying young participants and gaining their permission (or that of their caregivers) to participate in research. It is also challenging to gain ethical clearance to research such a young and vulnerable group that lives with disability and also has experienced maltreatment. It is challenging to design studies that are ethical and effective, and that allow for rigorous research without doing any harm to participants or their caregivers. Also, there are inconsistent definitions across various institutions and geographic areas regarding disability and trauma which can complicate data collection and analysis (Jones et al., 2012; Leeb et al., 2012). These research challenges probably contribute to the fact that what research is done is more likely to be done with adults. Despite these significant limitations that may hamper what we currently know, there is consensus across many nations that child abuse should be prevented and that children with disabilities are especially vulnerable (Frederick et al., 2019; Paddy et al., 2021).

Children and young people who live with disability can be more vulnerable to trauma for a number of reasons. This can include reasons directly associated with their disability, including their potential to be manipulated, their relative exposure to perpetrators of harm, their dependence on others, difficulties with processing information, and other cognitive challenges. There are also social reasons, such as people with disability living more often in poverty or in a home that lacks resources, or their lacking social relationships and support. There are also comorbidities that can occur with disability, such as medical, physical, mental health, or behavioural concerns, that can lead to disruptions in attachment and add to the stress within the homes of these children and young people, increasing the likelihood of harm at the hands of their distressed and overwhelmed carergivers (Keesler 2014). For some children and young people, trauma can result from restraint and seclusion; teasing, bullying, rejection, and exploitation by peers; or repeated and invasive medical procedures.

However, knowing that there are far too many children and young people living with disability who also experience complex trauma, and that living with disability can place children and young people at additional risk of harm, doesn't fully answer the regularly asked questions about which of the two 'conditions' (disability or trauma) comes first. Does living with disability make it more likely that a child will be maltreated or does the experience of maltreatment make it more likely that disability will occur? I believe that the evidence suggests that the answer is both. For some, such as the children who were raised in orphanages in Romania who were discussed in Chapter Two, trauma led to disability, or increased disability. For some, being born with a disabling condition or becoming disabled due to accident or illness, can leave children at increased risk of maltreatment. Importantly, to understand this intersection for individual children, we need to consider their circumstances and not make assumptions about whether trauma led to disability or disability led to trauma. Also, it is vital that we approach this topic respectfully and overtly acknowledge that many children and young people who live with disability are clearly not suffering maltreatment but are being cared for exceptionally well.

Even more important than knowing what led to what, is how we respond to this in schools and early childhood education and care. Keesler (2014) strongly advocates for the integration of trauma-informed care within all organisations that support people living with intellectual and developmental disability, whether or not complex trauma is part of their experience. A narrative review by Berger et al., (2021) found that trauma-informed school interventions clearly overlap with those designed to support students living with Autism, and therefore a combined framework would be highly recommended for children with Autism who have lived through maltreatment. The question for educators to consider, is if a trauma-aware response is recommended for learners who have lived through maltreatment, why would it not be appropriate for those who have lived through maltreatment, who also live with disability?

A trauma-aware response focuses on helping learners feel safe, connect and bond with others, and develop their emotional regulation skills. These three areas are vitally important for any child or young person who has lived through trauma and are even more important if they also live with disability. Learners may need to be supported to view their education site, classrooms, and educators as 'safe havens'. They may require help to find places to go, people to help, and activities to do to help them feel safe when they feel unsafe. Despite their disability 'type', these young learners may need support to develop relationships with others. Attachments are vital for any developing child, but they might need to be negotiated and managed somewhat differently for some learners. It is a sad myth that some learners (for example, those living with Autism), do not need or want relationships with others. These learners may also need support with developing their capacities for emotional regulation. They may need help to know ways to regulate and ways to practice regulating. They may need support to have and to use words to help them understand regulation and dysregulation. They may need help to access places and activities that help with regulation. They could need access to individually appropriate sensory interventions to help with regulation. They may also need help to keep themselves and their peers safe during dysregulation, and they definitely need to know that they are still liked and will still be cared for, even if they do dysregulate.

Educators might benefit from understanding developmental considerations that help to explain the behaviours of learners who live with both disability and the experience of trauma. To assist with this, the following is drawn from helpful research and resources from the National Child Traumatic Stress Network (https://www.nctsn.org/).

- During early childhood, the ability of very young children to communicate verbally may be limited by both age and disability. Children may have more difficulty calming down after becoming frightened. They may withdraw or become less responsive in an attempt to communicate that they are fearful or are feeling unsafe. Developmental gains are at times more fragile for young children living with disabilities, and sometimes they can regress with skill development when feeling unsafe (such as toileting). Young children living with disabilities may experience and express more negative affect, have more trouble interacting with peers, may become more aggressive, may develop new fears, and may be more behaviourally or emotionally dysregulated (especially infants). There is an unfortunate and inaccurate myth that young children do not experience trauma because they are too young to understand or remember. Adults who believe this may be introducing a type of bias that may be heightened even further for a child living with disability. This bias in thinking can impact the delivery of trauma-aware responses, that are so important for these young children

- During middle childhood, children can experience attention problems related to experiencing intrusive thoughts or interruptions with sleep. They can become preoccupied with frightening moments from their experiences of trauma and can develop intense and specific new fears to the extent that they avoid previously enjoyed activities. Some may become withdrawn at times and experience developmentally 'immature', tantrum-like behaviour at other times. Some can lose developmental gains they achieved years ago. Some may experience challenges with peer relationships and become quite vulnerable to teasing, bullying, and purposeful isolation from other children.

- During adolescence, young students may experience a decreased motivation for learning and may feel that learning and planning for the future are annoying and difficult. Some may experience an increased dependence on their caregivers as their worlds become increasingly challenging to negotiate. Some can become demoralised and depressed or can become angry and aggressive. Their perceptions of feeling 'different' to other students can become stronger, and this can exacerbate their worries about feeling less accepted by peers.

As some learners who live with disability may have difficulty in areas such as cognitive processing, reasoning, problem-solving, coping skills, language, or communication, there is an increased likelihood that they will communicate their needs through their behaviour. Also, the more severe the disability, the more likely they will use behaviour rather than verbal communication to express their needs. Some behavioural indicators can include developmental regression, social withdrawal or isolation, reduced self-care, increased disorganised and dysregulated behaviour, aggression, and self-injury. All of these circumstances and presentations become even more worrying if learners have also experienced maltreatment. So, despite the area of disability, or the behavioural presentations of learners, a trauma-aware response that focuses on perceptions of safety, relationships, and emotional regulation, is highly recommended.

These learners' best hope is for educators to create or recreate safe, interpersonal environments that are sufficiently healing to counteract any trauma that has been experienced. It is complicated, as for learners living with disabilities, their circumstances too frequently increase their exposure to adverse events and disability can affect their abilities to self-soothe or participate actively in healing interventions. Also, disentangling the impact of trauma, disability, mental health needs, and behavioural expression is not easy. However, when viewing all this through the lens of trauma-aware thinking and practice, it is really not that complicated. The goal of a trauma-aware response to supporting learners living with disability is to focus on safety, relationships, and emotional regulation. It involves creating a 'secure base' and 'safe haven' for learners that is characterised by sustained and available relationships with a small number of key adults who are perceived as attuned, comforting, and trustworthy.

What about Universal Screening for Trauma?

Education systems commonly apply screening processes using measures to identify students living with defined disabilities. These screening processes help with the allocation of resources, funding, services, and supports to education sites. They also help guide recommended adjustments to delivering education services to individual learners. However, depending on the education system, these screening processes may adopt differing definitions of disability and types of disability, and some 'types' of disability might be included or excluded. For example, some might include categories similar to 'emotional or behavioural disorders' or 'learning disorders', whereas others might exclude such categories. Also, funding and support provision can vary according to how data is collected and analysed, the amounts of resources available to systems, and any algorithms used to distribute these resources.

Due to the growing recognition of the prevalence and impact of childhood trauma, there is increasing discussion and debate regarding whether there should be universal screening for trauma in public health systems and in schools so that trauma-impacted children and young people have access to supports and resources needed to improve their access to and experience of their education. There are important reasons why screening might be helpful to education sites and to trauma-impacted learners. However, there are also serious cautions about adopting this approach, and these need to be considered before a systemic approach to screening, data collection, and resource distribution is adopted on a large scale (Afifi, 2018: Dube, 2018: McLennan, et al., 2020). It is worth considering the pros and cons as education systems ponder whether to implement universal screening.

Arguments to support the use of universal screening

It is accepted that positive outcomes for learners who experience challenges accessing their education may be achieved through early identification and intervention. Early screening can help identify at-risk students who were previously unknown to site personnel, whose needs were not clearly evident, or those not receiving services who need services (Eklund & Dowdy, 2014). Universal screening within and across education sites could also help with the acknowledgment of the need for increased support for sites servicing trauma-impacted learners and, indeed, an increased allocation of funding and support available to these sites. As the prevalence of childhood trauma becomes more known and understood, it is timely to consider systemic funding and support to address this area of need that has previously gone unnoticed or under-noticed.

Universal screening for complex trauma is increasingly being implemented in health, mental health, and other social services contexts and is helpful in identifying how childhood trauma can contribute towards and often complicate, the physical and psychological concerns of clients and patients receiving these services. It also provides the opportunity for these services to adopt trauma-aware frameworks and processes to support clients and treat patients. Understandably, people working within these services would encourage the adoption of trauma-aware frameworks and processes in education sites where their clients and patients attend. It is understandable also that they could advocate for universal trauma screening in education sites and systems. For example, Dr Nadine Burke Harris is a highly regarded paediatrician and the Surgeon General of California who is well known for raising awareness of the impacts of adverse childhood experiences and toxic stress. She strongly advocates for universal screening in schools to enhance early identification and remediation of trauma. She suggests that this will help educators understand the needs and behaviours of learners from a trauma perspective and for education sites and systems to adopt trauma-aware frameworks of support. She proposes that this could be an effective way to address an urgent public health crisis associated with the long-term health and mental health impacts of adverse childhood experiences (Nelson, et al., 2020; Oh et al., 2018).

Arguments against the use of universal screening

In their systematic review examining trauma screening measures for children and adolescents, Eklund, et al., (2018) and Ford, et al., (2019) found that there is very limited research on the efficacy of using trauma screening tools in education sites and a dearth of studies examining best practice for universal screening techniques for identifying trauma-impacted learners. They suggest that caution is advised as there is minimal psychometric evidence to support the use of these measures in education sites.

Current processes to identify learners living with disability that is associated with mental health or behavioural concerns usually derive from diagnostic procedures performed by health practitioners that align with the Diagnostic and Statistical Manual of Mental Disorders, Fifth Edition (DSM-5). For example, a learner exhibiting symptomology associated with Autistic Spectrum Disorder could be evaluated by a paediatrician, and a letter of diagnosis (or similar) could be provided to an education site which would be considered as evidence to include the learner in their disability data collection procedures. However, as no DSM-5 diagnosis currently exists that can account for the cluster of symptoms that children with trauma histories can experience, this process is not clearly available to trauma-impacted learners (D'Andrea et al., 2012). Sometimes, these learners could be encapsulated within categories such as 'emotional or behavioural disorders' or similar, but in many sites and systems, no such categories exist. So, education sites would need to consider what other tools they would use to screen for trauma-impacted learners.

An initial and relatively simple way to capture the prevalence of trauma-impacted learners within a site is to investigate the learners who are receiving child protection services. These data are often easily available and ideally all education sites should already be aware of these learners and be responding to their needs. However, reducing identification of trauma-impacted learners to just this group, would be inadequate and inappropriate as there are additional (and sometimes many more) learners who have lived through trauma, and perhaps are still living through trauma, who have not been formally identified and who are not associated with child protection services. Additional screening for trauma or adverse childhood experiences is likely to yield more thorough, accurate information, but this presents education sites and systems with ethical, logistical, and budgetary challenges.

Very importantly, participation in universal screening processes could be confusing and disturbing to non-traumatised learners and potentially re-traumatising and stigmatising to those who have lived through adverse childhood experiences. This impact could be exacerbated if data collection measures are delivered by untrained and trauma-unaware adults. If not managed with great sensitivity and if not embedded in solid confidentiality processes, quite private information about the life experiences of learners could become known to other learners and adults in the education community.

Additional concerns, as with most forms of screening, relate to the site's ability to respond to the concerns of individuals identified through the screening process. Screening proves very unhelpful if there are not the resources, responses, and adult capabilities available to address the concerns raised through the screening process. Also, an over-dependence on the screening of individuals by schools could replace or prevent the creation of a trauma-sensitive, whole-school environment for all learners.

There are some relatively brief trauma screening tools that have emerged from clinical settings, and research supports their psychometric properties. Most incorporate checklists, rating scales, or individual interviews that inquire into the adverse life experiences of learners or the impacts of these experiences on their current lives and functioning (Gonzalez et al., 2016; Woodbridge et al., 2016). However, without careful monitoring and governance, well-meaning education sites and systems may choose to adapt published screening tools or develop their own screening tools, which could be problematic if these lack clinical efficacy and have the potential for inadequate or inaccurate assessment. Ecklund and Rossen (2016) warn that some education sites may opt to not ask the questions to which they are not prepared to know the answers. One example of this was identified in a study by Gonzalez et al. (2016) when school administrators requested that screening tools omit questions regarding child sexual abuse.

Some institutions suggest that using the Adverse Childhood Experience (ACE) list of 10 items of adversity (or similar), is quick and helpful to screen for trauma-impacted individuals (Felitti et al., 1998). However, there are certainly some concerns with reducing screening to just this element of ACE measurement. Despite overall agreement that ACEs can have a significant impact on life and health, it is also suggested that ACEs do not clearly account for the positive events in a child's social world that may promote better health and protect against the negative effects of adversity and maltreatment (Dubowitz et al., 2019; McEwen & Gregerson, 2019). Also, it has been noted that just measuring the number of ACEs experienced during childhood does not adequately capture the chronicity and severity of each adverse experience but rather just gives each an equal weighting, which can misrepresent just how much these experiences can impact individuals (Crandall et al., 2021; Holden et al., 2020).

Due to the sensitive nature of inquiring into trauma histories and experiences, initial caregiver consent for participation in screening is paramount but also presents challenges. Dependant on policy guidelines and site procedures, education sites can use either active or passive consent processes. Active consent requires permission from the caregiver for their child to 'opt-in' to the screening process. Passive consent suggests that consent is implied unless a caregiver actively 'opts out' of the screening process. This latter option would be far less likely in education sites as it would contravene many commonly held assumptions about caregiver consent when working with minors, and as it could be viewed as less ethical, particularly in communities with high illiteracy rates or number of non-English speaking families or families where English is not their first language.

However, in studies of universal screening for trauma in schools, Gonzalez et al. (2016) and Woodbridge et al., (2016) found that less than half of caregivers gave active consent for their child to participate in screening. Caregiver consent rates can be impacted by self-selection bias. This can occur when caregivers become less likely to or refuse to, issue consent because they are knowingly the source of harm to their child or children. In cases where children are living in harmful home environments, the knowledge that universal screening will be occurring at their child's or children's education site could place these young learners at greater risk as caregiver anxieties and harmful responses are triggered in response. Or this could lead to caregivers providing false information or their insisting that their children do the same. Another response could be that caregivers remove their child or children from the education site that is implementing the screening. This can create a serious barrier to accurate and helpful data collection during screening.

If consent is secured, screening tools used by education sites can collect data from learners, their caregivers, and/or their teachers. When administering screening tools to learners, it is important to ensure that processes consider their comprehension of survey items or interview questions. This may include the need to make developmentally appropriate modifications such as using verbal rather than written items, clarifying the meaning of terms for learners, or using visual aids (Gonzalez et al., 2016). Accurate identification of trauma-impacted learners and the challenges that they face relies upon both learner understanding of screening items and administrator adherence to appropriate standardisation procedures for making high-stakes decisions (Eklund & Rossen, 2016). In some studies, caregivers and children tend to not demonstrate high agreement when reporting on a child's experiences with adversity and trauma (Shemesh et al., 2005; Stover et al., 2010) and for the same reasons discussed above regarding consent, there is a risk of false information being obtained from some caregivers. As teachers spend the most time with learners during the day, they may arguably provide important and informed information during a screening process. However, this could be impaired if teachers do not know about or understand trauma-related symptoms, reactions, and behaviours or if they are unaware of learner's adverse experiences outside of their time at the education site.

Prevalence, time, and cost of universal screening

Universal screening that is thorough and designed to capture accurate and helpful data on the numbers and needs of trauma-impacted learners in education sites and systems is likely to take much time, to be logistically challenging to implement and govern, and to be expensive. This process must consider not just the screening but also the planning required for how to address the results of the screening. Due to known prevalence data and a growing understanding that known data can be considered a significant underestimate of actual cases of trauma-impacted children and young people, there is a strong argument that we already know trauma-impacted learners will be enrolled at most education sites. This begs the question, why implement a time and cost-heavy process of screening when (as an alternative) these funds and human resources could be used to embed trauma-aware frameworks of practice in all education sites? This could benefit all learners and all educators and could reduce or remove altogether the potential for learners becoming retraumatised and stigmatised through screening processes. After all, screening just identifies. It does not remediate. It might just be more cost and time effective to use resources to support sites with quality staff training and support (Baweja et al., 2016; Chafouleas, et al., 2010).

A 'middle-of-the-road' approach?

As there are quite substantial and valid concerns associated with universal screening in education sites and systems, there is an argument for a 'middle-of-the-road' approach. The most effective approaches are those that exist within an overall site environment that incorporates trauma-aware practices consistently and sustainably throughout the entire school or early childhood community without resorting to screening.

However, some (but not universal) screening at the hands of qualified and skilled administrators could be helpful and could support an overall, whole-of-site approach. Trained and qualified mental health practitioners, such as psychologists or counsellors, can use clinically evaluated and endorsed screening and assessment tools to identify learners living with the outcomes of trauma and the more specific challenges that they might face in an education context. Importantly, they can do this in a way that is protective of individual learners and can use these data to contribute to trauma-aware support planning for learners or groups of learners.

Summary

Our understanding of the intersection between complex trauma and disability is growing, but it is still under-researched and is sometimes perceived as confusing or is misunderstood. Educators in education sites and education systems continue to question the dynamics of this intersection and query how they should respond. There remain challenges with the formal diagnosis of developmental, complex trauma, and there remain questions regarding whether living with the outcomes of this type of trauma should be considered disabling. There are also questions regarding whether universal screening processes should be used to identify trauma-impacted learners in a similar way that learners living with disability are screened. These conversations need to continue to ensure that learners who live with the intersection between trauma and disability are adequately, ethically, and equitably cared for and educated. There is definitely enough evidence to show that the prevalence of maltreated learners who live with disability is substantial, and a trauma-aware response is justified for this cohort of children and young people.

Chapter 7

Trauma-Aware Early Childhood Education and Care

Much of the rapid neural development from birth and throughout early childhood occurs as a response to interactions with caregivers (Arden, 2019; Hughes & Baylin, 2012). The experience of complex trauma during early childhood is particularly concerning as neural growth during the early years is very rapid. This early development provides a vital foundation for ongoing neural development and behaviour, functioning, and achievement during the schooling years and in later life (Chu & Lieberman, 2010; De Bellis & Zisk, 2014; Jimenez et al., 2016). Due to the brain being exceptionally malleable or changeable during this time, the incorporation of trauma-aware ways of supporting, educating, and caring for infants and young children has great potential for early intervention and reparation of the harm of trauma. This understanding has huge implications for early childhood education and care!

Some infants and young children have already experienced (in their very short lives) physical, emotional, or relational abuse or neglect. Some have lived in homes experiencing domestic violence and coercive control, and some have been removed from the homes of their biological parents and placed in foster care or kinship care. The greatest proportion of children in Australia who live in out-of-home-care placements due to child protection concerns are under the age of one year and rates remain very high throughout the early years (Australian Institute of Health and Welfare, 2021).

Children taken into out-of-home care may suffer from a disruption in attachments and, despite being in a safer home context, may still be grieving the loss of their parent or parents and perhaps other family members (Whitters, 2020). Of the approximately 46,000 children living in an out-of-home-care placement due to child protection concerns in Australia in 2020, 20% were living with grandparents (Australian Institute of Health and Welfare, 2021). Of course, it is wonderful that these children are still living with family. However, sometimes caring for their young grandchildren, after raising their own children who exhibit somewhat challenging or harmful behaviours, can be quite difficult for older caregivers. This is even more challenging if their grandchildren exhibit some of the behaviour outcomes from living through trauma at such a young age.

Many trauma-impacted infants and young children access early childhood education and care (Bartlett & Smith, 2019). Therefore trauma-aware knowledge and practice in these services becomes even more vital knowing that most of the children who have been moved from the care of their biological parents are very young, and young children are more likely to express their grief and distress through emotions and behaviours, rather than words. The overarching focus of any trauma-aware work in early childhood settings should be to help children feel safe and unconditionally cared for. Children need to know that safe and caring adults are unconditionally and readily available to meet their physical and emotional needs and, once this is done, assist with their learning needs (Neitzel, 2020). Children need to feel safe in environments and safe in relationships. This may not come easily for young ones who have lived through complex trauma.

Play and Brain Development

From the early months of life, interactive games (like peek-a-boo) delight both children and adults by stimulating the neurobiology that underpins attachment, including the Mirror Neuron System. Early childhood practitioners have a wonderful opportunity to provide regular and predictable stimulation of the Mirror Neuron Systems of all children through their interactions with them and by reading and responding to children's social cues (verbal utterances, facial expressions, voices, and behaviours). However, educators have an additional opportunity to embed purposeful and trauma-aware activity to enhance mirror neuron development for trauma-impacted children, who might not have had enough of this activity in their young lives thus far (Ryan et al., 2017). This is most effectively done through play (Gil & Terr, 2010). However, for children (and actually for many animals), play only occurs in the absence of danger, when food is available, and when the physical and social environments are conducive to wellbeing. Providing an early childhood education and care context that feels unconditionally and consistently safe for children is a vital first step.

Playful behaviour is organised within parts of the brain (such as the basal ganglia, the cerebellum, and other subcortical regions) that manage sensory, motor, and emotional reactions that lead to behaviour. The frequency of play correlates with the size of the cerebellum (the movement centre of the brain) in children, so the greater access to safe and supportive play, the more robust the cerebellum. Play allows children to respond well to environmental and sensory stimuli and to practice and improve inhibitory motor control whilst also building important executive networks in the pre-frontal cortex. Play enhances procedural memory (managed by the hippocampus) when children engage in ordering and sequencing activities to achieve play goals. Play is reinforced within networks through the activation of neurochemicals such as dopamine (which provides a sense of reward and accomplishment), endorphins and serotonin (which help children to feel happy and motivated), and hormones such as oxytocin (which helps with bonding and attachment). Physical play is eventually reshaped into verbal play as children grow, further developing the organisation and integration of many brain structures while motivating their interest and excitement about language, remembering, and learning. Imaginative play allows children to connect mental and physical behaviour as they explore ideas, solutions, and relationships. Play helps develop healthy social communication skills and serves many important roles in social learning and understanding roles within groups. Play also provides the opportunity for skill development through acquiring and practising new skills (Arden, 2019; Cozolino, 2013; Porges & Furman, 2011; Yogman et al., 2018).

Whilst all this marvellous activity occurs, children consistently read and respond to social cues and information. This is the vital activity required for the development of a healthy Mirror Neuron System. The healthier the system, the better the child's capacity for effective, empathetic, caring, and responsive relationships as they grow older (Howard, 2020). Adults are vital in providing children's access to effective play during the early years.

Secure Base and Safe Haven

Early childhood educators also have a wonderful opportunity to become a secondary source (after their immediate caregivers) for 'secure base' and 'safe haven' activity for traumatised children (Dolby, 2017; Powell et al., 2014). As the 'secure base', educators can regularly engage in activity that helps build up children's confidence and capacity to physically separate from them and engage in their 'play' environments with other children, which is imperative for their cognitive and social development. By pointing, explaining, modelling, encouraging, and joining in the play, early childhood practitioners use their bodies and voices to help children to engage with their environment and with other children and to play. As the 'safe haven', educators can welcome children back into their physical presence when they become emotionally dysregulated. They can then use their own physicality (body, arms, face, voice) to help co-regulate the emotions of children who are frightened, hurt, sad, angry, unwell, or in other ways dysregulated. Interpersonal neurobiology suggests that repeated practice with emotional co-regulation through 'safe haven' activity during the early years enhances important neural development and will develop children's skills for later emotional self-regulation, which is vital for them as they enter and then journey through the schooling years (Cozolino, 2013).

Serve and Return

The *Harvard Center on the Developing Child* (2019) use the tennis analogy of 'serve and return' to help explain the role of adults when engaging with and playing with young children. They suggest that a caring environment rich in back-and-forth, relationally responsive activity provides a foundation for healthy and functional brain architecture. They also suggest that a lack of this type of activity can present a serious threat to the development and wellbeing of young children. They encourage adults to take purposeful notice when a child is communicating their interests and needs (the 'serve') and to purposefully acknowledge and respond to this with their own behaviours and words (the 'return'). They encourage adults to clearly name whatever the child is focussed on to provide language for children to use as they negotiate their environments. This also provides a clear message to children that adults understand them and are engaged in what they are experiencing. The *Harvard Center on the Developing Child* (2019) also encourage adults to take turns with children as they engage in mutual activity and to patiently give children enough time to form their responses. They encourage adults to become purposefully aware of when children want to stop, start, or change an activity and allow them to take the lead (*Harvard Center on the Developing Child*, https://developingchild.harvard.edu).

Investing in Early Brain Development

The more we understand the intricacies of the development and functioning of the human brain and the impact of complex trauma on brain development, the more we are to recognise the value of early intervention. Early childhood practitioners are well placed to help address the harm of early childhood trauma through informed and purposeful practice that is known to repair and reinforce neural pathways during the rapid neural development that occurs during infancy and early childhood. For some children who have lived through complex trauma, an early childhood education and care environment might be their only source of activity and approaches that can help to address the impacts of the harm they have experienced (Asmussen et al., 2019; Loomis, 2018).

This type of activity is fantastic for all children! However, it is so important, and can even be life-changing, for some of our most vulnerable and victimised infants and young children.

Our education systems, providers, and our governing institutions must recognise that investing well in trauma-aware practice within early childhood education and care may actually reduce or remediate many of the longer-term concerns experienced by children left with unresolved trauma. This could also reduce the costs associated with managing the behavioural and learning concerns of learners throughout their schooling and, indeed, the significant ongoing costs of unresolved trauma in the adult population (see Chapter One) (Forsman & Jackisch, 2021). However, without training to help educators understand the impact of trauma and training in how they can best respond to trauma-impacted children, early childhood educators may be under-prepared and under-resourced for this important work. Also, thoughtful and realistic practitioner-to-child ratios are vital so that educators have the time and opportunity to meet individual children's safety, relational, and emotional needs.

Summary

To respond in trauma-aware ways in early childhood education and care takes consistent effort by informed practitioners to manage their own patience, emotions, and behaviours, so that they can do the regular and repeated work to enhance early brain development and children's capacities for relationships and emotional regulation. Ideally, this requires adequate and thoughtful investment into staff training, staffing ratios, and staff wellbeing. It is never too late to adopt a trauma-aware approach to the education and care of victims of complex trauma. The earlier children access trauma-aware interventions, the better! Although all areas of trauma-aware education are vitally important, investing in ways to address the early impacts of complex trauma on very young and rapidly developing bodies and brains through trauma-aware early childhood education and care, is indeed a smart and proactive use of our systemic efforts and our systemic dollars.

Chapter 8

Trauma-Aware Staff Support: Looking after our Educators

Although an under-researched area, a trauma-aware approach to supporting the wellbeing of educators, is a growing area of interest. A trauma-aware approach to education in schools and early childhood settings should strongly focus on protecting and nurturing educators' personal and professional wellbeing. After all, the relational healing afforded to trauma-impacted learners depends on the relational capacities of educators working with these learners. Also, a healthy, resilient, functioning adult nervous system is needed to co-regulate a learner's dysregulated nervous system. So, looking after the wellbeing of educators is a vital consideration for an effective trauma-aware education response.

A Team Approach

A trauma-aware education response would emphasise that all staff share responsibility for all learners. This approach emphasises teamwork and suggests that staff should support and encourage each other, particularly on tough days, and that it is never an individual staff member's 'fault' for the behaviours and responses of their trauma-impacted students. This approach would value providing ongoing access to quality staff learning to build staff knowledge and skill in trauma-aware education, which can, in turn, enhance personal and professional wellbeing. Also, mentorship, particularly for early career educators, is greatly encouraged.

It is recommended that education sites embed processes to support staff members when they find themselves in the difficult situation of not being able to manage their emotional regulation. These moments should not be viewed by colleagues and supervisors as evidence of failure or weakness, but rather as part of being a human being working with trauma-impacted learners. Even very resilient and effective educators can experience a difficult day or moment where they would benefit from a planned and effective response for their support. One example of a school response is a system (perhaps using mobile phone texting) that signifies that an educator needs the quick support of someone to take over in their classroom while they remove themselves and take the necessary time and activity for self-regulation. Another example is to provide a space at the school or service that is dedicated to educators needing this support; for example, a small and relatively private room could be set up with the types of sensory supports that are helpful for self-regulation (dim lighting, soft music, etc.). Different sites can develop different strategies for this type of support, dependent on their site context. Rather than viewing these supports as excessive and resource-consuming, they should be viewed as an investment into staff wellbeing and resilience. They are ways to avoid the potential escalation of relational and emotional harm that can occur when forcing dysregulated staff members and learners to remain together, which can, in itself, become very time and resource-intensive. These supports can also provide an emotional 'safety net' for educators, and just knowing they exist can be reassuring and calming.

Another helpful support is to embed ready access to peer, supervisor, or counsellor support or debriefing as needed for educators who have been through a challenging experience with a trauma-impacted learner. However, if a challenging event has impacted a number of staff members, it is important to consider individual needs when responding rather than insisting on a group debriefing. Some people might respond well to this type of group support. Others might prefer and might respond more effectively to other means to process the experience (for example, time with loved ones, time with nature, or a coffee with a friend or colleague). It is also important to remember that school and service leaders and counsellors can also be impacted by highly emotive events and may require unconditional and non-judgemental, collegial understanding and support.

The 'secure base' and 'safe haven' concepts initiated by Bowlby (1958) and later developed by Powell et al., (2014) are useful to consider when planning for staff wellbeing support. Educators need their workplace to be a 'secure base' and for it to provide a 'safe haven' as they require. As a 'secure base', the education site provides what is needed for educators to build the fortitude and skill to do their work educating and supporting trauma-impacted learners. Staff members need to feel valued for the work they do and to be trained, empowered, and resourced to do it. However, when things go wrong, staff members need a 'safe haven'. They need to know where to go and who to go to when things aren't going well. They need to be aware of any supports available and feel confident in accessing these supports, knowing that this will be unconditional and that there will not be any judgement from others.

A trauma-aware approach would also encourage the purposeful embedding of enjoyable and social activities into the working week. Purposeful and regular events and processes that focus on enjoyment can enhance staff wellbeing and a sense of collective purpose and provide a 'stress release' for busy educators. Education sites should acknowledge and celebrate their successes and progress in their efforts to deliver trauma-aware education and the individual and group efforts of educators. These types of planned activities can be considered as investments into the mental wellbeing of a precious and vital workforce so that even though they may face challenging times, they should continue to thrive both personally and professionally.

Vicarious Trauma

It is important to acknowledge that sometimes the wellbeing of educators who work with trauma-impacted learners can suffer. This needs to be addressed. The notion that 'there is a cost to caring' (Figley, 2013, p.1) underlies the phenomenon of vicarious trauma, also referred to as secondary traumatic stress or compassion fatigue. Authors, researchers, and clinicians can differ in how they define and how they use and work with these terms. However, for the purposes of this book, I will refer to the term 'vicarious trauma' and the reader can assume it to be synonymous with 'secondary traumatic stress' and 'compassion fatigue'. Vicarious trauma is therefore defined as a transformation in the helper's (educator's) inner sense of identity, purpose, and efficacy that results from repeatedly using controlled empathy when listening to or seeing evidence of clients' (learners') stories of trauma.

Vicarious trauma is different to what is referred to as 'burnout'. Burnout refers to emotional exhaustion and reduced personal accomplishment that results from circumstances where a worker feels that the demands of their job outweigh their perceived resources to do their job. Rather, vicarious trauma is what happens to your cognitive, physical, psychological, emotional, and spiritual health when you listen to traumatic stories day after day or respond to situations resulting from a person's experience of trauma while having to control your reactions. This is a particular issue with people working in human services, mostly because they view their work as more than just a job, but more so as part of who they are. This can lead to vulnerability in workers who work with high-risk populations and encounter multiple exposures to children and adults who have experienced or continue to experience traumatic events.

The bulk of research examining vicarious trauma focus on human services and a variety of 'helping professions' (Holland, 2022), but very little examines the experiences of educators in schools and early childhood services (Caringi et al., 2015). For educators, vicarious trauma can result from their over-connecting with the traumatic and disturbing life events of young learners. Vicarious trauma tends to be a process that evolves over time, and the impacts of this type of trauma can be cumulative. Although being impacted by the hurtful experiences of children and young people can be considered as empathetic and perhaps a relatively 'normal' reaction, vicarious trauma can 'sneak up on you' and, if not managed carefully, can have quite a significant impact on your functioning as an educator and on your wellbeing.

The Adverse Childhood Experience (ACE) Study (see Chapter Two) that explored the childhood origins that contribute to many health, mental health, and social problems across the world also explained the concerning prevalence of ACEs. This, and other findings from prevalence studies, suggest that there will be many great educators in schools and early childhood education programs, who will also be survivors of complex trauma, and this may be known or unknown by their supervisors and colleagues. Despite evidence of incredible resilience and achievements in their lives, these educators can be vulnerable to having unwanted and difficult emotions and memories triggered during challenging interactions with trauma-impacted learners. If their experiences are not managed carefully, some of these educators may become vulnerable to vicarious trauma (Caringi, 2015). These talented and admirable people are deserving of a trauma-aware response that both protects and supports their wellbeing. A whole-staff approach to staff wellbeing will ensure that they receive the required support without their having to necessarily reveal or discuss their own experiences of childhood trauma.

Vicarious trauma can become a worrying concern for educators who find it difficult to stop thinking about, and ruminating on, the trauma that learners in their care have experienced. They may find it very difficult to shake the impact of these thoughts (Rothschild & Rand, 2006). Some indicators of vicarious trauma that can be specific to educators include a perceived lack of control, feelings of failure, a resistance to relating to and bonding with students and colleagues, a feeling of disconnection from their workplaces, leaving or considering leaving their job or career, and a significant decrease in motivation. In addition, anxiety and other serious mental health impacts can be experienced.

Vicarious trauma necessitates a response, and the response needs to be thoughtful and individually appropriate. There are recommended initial strategies for self-care and recovery from vicarious trauma that can be considered. These include those that are bio-behavioural (for example, enhanced nutrition, health, sleep, exercise), positive self-expression (for example, art, cooking, writing, sport), spiritual connectedness (for example, connections to faith, church, nature), altruistic activity (for example, philanthropic or volunteer activities), and social connectedness (for example, spending time with friends and family, social gatherings, and activities). There is also activity that is ill-advised. This includes escapist strategies that allow you to shut down and dismiss your thoughts and feelings (for example, drinking, shopping, excessive sleeping, gambling, and video games). It is also important to acknowledge that in some rare cases, sufferers can develop clinical symptoms (for example, prolonged sleeplessness, anxiety, isolation, depression, and disordered thoughts) and may require professional, therapeutic, or medical help. So for most, self-care strategies can be helpful, but for others, extra help may be needed. No one should feel judged for taking the responsible and prudent step of seeking extra help.

Siegel (2012) explores the concept of vicarious trauma and ways to address this concern, from a neurobiological perspective. He suggests that 'compassion circuits' in the brain link up areas such as mirror neuron circuitry, limbic circuitry, and the pre-frontal cortex that help manage the human experience of compassion and empathy. When the brain of the helper/educator is functioning in an integrated and healthy manner, these deeply relational capacities are helpful for both the person experiencing them and for those with whom they are connecting, even if this includes a trauma-impacted child or young person. However, when the brain of the helper/educator is functioning in a non-integrated and unmanaged manner, dealing with trauma-impacted others can lead to vicarious trauma. Siegal suggests that self-talk and thinking patterns are critical to whether a person might develop vicarious trauma or will become resilient to this.

Siegal (2012) explains that it is important that workers and educators become aware of how they are processing the trauma suffered by those they are aiming to help. Studies from neuroscience show that, if a person consistently over-connects or over-empathises with the traumatic circumstances of another person, to the extent that they are thinking 'I wonder what it would be like if that was me?', they may become more prone to vicarious trauma. This is due to this type of thinking leading to circuitry firing up in the brain, similar to that which fires up during primary trauma (that which is directly experienced). Siegal recommends a purposeful change in thinking (self-talk) to address this. He suggests that thinking similar to, 'I wonder what that would have been like for them?' can shift neural activity to what he refers to as the 'compassion circuits' in the brain. Although it may still be quite upsetting to think about the trauma suffered by another, the brain can process it more adaptively and protectively, which can reduce the possibility of vicarious trauma. As with any purposeful change in thinking patterns, this move to more adaptive and helpful thinking and self-talk can take repeated practice but is certainly worth the effort.

Vicarious Trauma and Supervisors

Supervisors or managers of education sites can become a central point for trauma suffered and manifested by both learners and staff, which may impact their emotional and mental wellbeing if not managed carefully. It is recommended that a supervisor should not take on the role of a therapist, and if it is identified that a therapist is needed for someone on staff, the supervisor should outsource or refer on wherever possible, perhaps through an employee assistance program or a psychologist or counsellor. Despite this, the supervisor can still remain a collegial support to staff members who may be symptomatic of vicarious trauma, as needed and if deemed appropriate.

Education leaders can become overwhelmed by feelings of accountability and responsibility, have a heightened awareness of resource and systemic factors, and become wedged between organisational demands and the personal needs of their staff and learners. They may also have to deal with some direct verbal or even physical 'assaults' from emotionally dysregulated learners or their caregivers. Also, having to deal repeatedly with crisis responses from learners, staff, and caregivers can be very time-consuming and can lead to less time being available for other work considerations, which are likely to have to move to after-work hours or on weekends. Not great for personal and professional wellbeing!

School or service leaders should be aware of the possibility and evidence of vicarious trauma in their site workforce and be available to provide sound and supportive supervision and respond in a protective manner if circumstances become complex. However, it is helpful for education sites to acknowledge that supervision and support do not always have to be through the supervisor and to share this load across the staff of the site is important. Ideally, a team or workgroup culture should include a system of peer support, whereby educators have a collegial support network to which they refer, and only if still needed, do they refer to the supervisor. Also, it is helpful and recommended to embed a support mechanism that is available to supervisors, that is confidential and comes from a no-shame perspective. All of these considerations for supervisors could also be applied to the school counsellor, who may also regularly be listening and responding to the trauma experiences of others.

Responding to Vicarious Trauma

To respond to vicarious trauma, it is important to debunk the myth that emotions have no place in the work environment. It needs to be acknowledged that working with trauma-impacted children and young people can be emotionally taxing at times. Educators need to understand what vicarious trauma is and what it looks like and feels like in self and others. They need to know about the neuroscience underpinning their own emotional regulation and dysregulation and to purposefully investigate and use strategies to enhance emotional regulation that best work for them. All of this can be discussed as a whole staff.

Educators need to reach out to and support colleagues who are seemingly not coping. Some educators just need some extra opportunities to process trauma, and this is best done by connecting with trusted others (Essary et al., 2020). Education sites need to adopt a no-shame approach to supporting each other, emphasising the shared responsibility for the wellbeing of both staff and students. Perhaps more formal strategies could be embedded if needed and could include vicarious trauma awareness programs, discussion groups, debriefings, peer supervision groups, and perhaps leave-of-absence provisions.

Research of Vicarious Trauma

Although research examining vicarious trauma in educators is limited (yet growing), findings suggest that embedding trauma-aware education within education sites can help! Findings are certainly showing that, due to the potential benefits of trauma-aware education for educator wellbeing and retention, this topic is deserving of far more research attention. A few studies are summarised below.

A study by Christian-Brandt et al., (2020) explored traumatic stress in 224 teachers in underserved elementary schools in the United States after the second year of implementing trauma-aware education at their sites. Findings suggest that a trauma-aware education approach helped to bolster teachers' positive feelings and self-efficacy related to helping students and mitigated chronic exhaustion, cynicism, low self-efficacy, and decisions to leave the profession. So, it is suggested that providing trauma-aware training and support for educators, which includes techniques and activities to prevent and address vicarious trauma, can greatly reduce staff wellbeing concerns in this area.

In their study of 205 school personnel working within a trauma-aware framework, Sprang & Garcia (2022) found that the increased use of trauma-informed practice can reduce the secondary traumatic stress levels of educators. They mention that some educators may be enhancing their own wellbeing and resilience by incorporating the same trauma-informed care principles to themselves that they are using with learners. However, these researchers highlight that informed and specific support is still needed for those educators exhibiting significant and persistent wellbeing concerns. If this is not done well, these educators can become resistant to implementing trauma-informed practice which could potentially impact the overall success of implementation across the school.

Other studies reinforce the growing need for education sites and systems to work from a trauma-aware perspective, to address the needs of the people working with trauma-impacted learners. For example, Gultom et al., (2022) report that characteristics of various trauma in educators have understandably increased since the global pandemic, including physical and emotional exhaustion, feelings of being overwhelmed, reduced efficacy and empathy, and increased mental anguish. Also, a study of 299 educators found that an educator's experience of vicarious trauma reduced the likelihood that they would engage in mandatory reporting of child maltreatment, a role that positions them as vital in prevention, detection, and intervention of harm done to children (Hupe & Stevenson, 2019). These are recent and worrying findings that again reinforce the importance of addressing vicarious trauma in educators.

> Without trauma-specific training, teachers fail to recognise trauma's symptoms and lack the resources to reverse its course. When teachers come to believe that there is nothing they can do to effect changes in children's behaviours, they give up trying. (Craig, 2016, p. 89)

Prevention is Better than Cure: Initial Teacher Education

Prevention is always the preferred option for addressing the concern of vicarious trauma in educators, Studies show that the implementation of trauma-aware education in education sites can reduce the prevalence and impact of vicarious trauma for education personnel, a logical and preventative means to address this even earlier is to include trauma-aware education content in initial teacher education programs. One Australian study found that the perceived knowledge, self-efficacy, and resilience of pre-service teachers related to their working with trauma-affected students, dramatically increased after completing university-delivered learning on trauma-aware education, and this increase was maintained into their early careers (L'Estrange & Howard, 2022). Findings such as these suggest that this preventative approach could limit concerns before they start for early career educators.

As well as learning about trauma-aware education in general, trainee educators could learn about and discuss issues associated with vicarious trauma during their higher-education preparation. They could become aware of self-care and other means to manage vicarious trauma and school or service-based strategies that can develop their resilience to vicarious trauma and their capacities for compassion satisfaction (the pleasure derived from helping others) (Essary et al., 2020). Unlike higher education coursework within social services disciplines, there is a significant lack of research literature on this topic informing initial teacher education programs, and the inclusion of trauma-aware education content, in general, is quite sporadic across universities. This needs to change if we are to adequately address the issues of complex trauma for learners and vicarious trauma in educators and to reduce educator attrition rates (DuBois & Mistretta, 2020; Skaalvik & Skaalvik, 2011, 2015; You & Conley, 2015).

Summary

Valuing and upholding the personal and professional wellbeing of the education workforce is a vital component of a trauma-aware approach in education sites and systems. To educate, support, and care for trauma-impacted children and young people, we need to educate, support, and care for the education workforce. A team approach is recommended in schools and early childhood services whereby all educators are responsible for all learners and where collegial networks provide unconditional and non-judgemental support. Early research suggests that workforce knowledge and skill in implementing trauma-aware education can mitigate concerns regarding staff wellbeing, including the possibility of vicarious trauma for individuals. However, it remains important to take informed and considered steps to help workmates who might be experiencing difficult times, and this can include education leaders. It is becoming increasingly clear that a proactive approach to embedding trauma-aware education within initial teacher education programs may just be the effective investment into the personal and professional wellbeing of the future education workforce, which is becoming increasingly needed.

Chapter 9

Leading Trauma-Aware Education

If you aspire to or already lead or work in trauma-aware education, then this section of this book is for you. However, leadership can mean many things to many people. You could be a leader of a school, early childhood service, education system, or part of an education system. You could be a classroom teacher wanting to enhance your own practice whilst mentoring others, or you might be keen to contribute to or lead a whole school approach. You could teach within or lead aspects of early childhood education and care. You could be a teacher aide who aspires to lead the professional development of other teacher aides, or you might be someone designing courses to qualify teacher aides. You could be a school-based counsellor, psychologist, occupational therapist, speech-language pathologist, police officer, or nurse keen to progress a trauma-aware education response for your young clients or to support or provide training for their education sites. You could work for an organisation supporting young people with mental health or child protection concerns, and you are keen to collaborate with schools to progress this work. You could be a university academic leading or aspiring to lead curriculum development in trauma-aware education for pre-service teachers or post-graduate educators. There are many professionals within many professions, each of whom has diverse 'spheres of influence' to uphold and progress trauma-aware education.

It is important to note, that much of what I write in this chapter is aspirational, as research in the area of trauma-aware leadership (particularly in education), is still in its infancy. However, there are helpful considerations that draw from our understanding of the impact of trauma on children and young people and their experiences of education that can inform our understanding of how we should be leading this important area of education practice and reform. The US Substance *Substance Abuse and Mental Health Services Administration* (SAMHSA, 2014) summarise trauma-aware work into four areas of activity, that are very relevant for working with survivors of trauma and are just as relevant for leading trauma-aware practice and reform. They focus on 'realising', 'recognising', 'responding', and 'resisting re-traumatisation'. I will summarise these as SAMSHA's four R's.

> A program, organisation, or system that is trauma-informed **realises** the widespread impact of trauma and understands potential paths for recovery; **recognises** the signs and symptoms of trauma in clients, families, staff, and others involved with the system; and **responds** by fully integrating knowledge about trauma into policies, procedures, and practices, and seeks to actively **resist re-traumatisation** (SAMHSA, 2014, p. 9).

So, leadership in trauma-aware education is certainly about applying SAMHSA's four R's as they relate to the work within an education practice or organisation. We need to realise the impact of trauma on learners, recognise the signs and symptoms, respond in by incorporating trauma-aware thinking, knowledge, skill, policy, and activity, and do all we can to prevent traumatisation of young learners by addressing practices and approaches that could potentially do more harm.

However, SAMSHA's four R's can apply equally to how we should be leading people in a trauma-aware manner. We need to realise that many people with whom we work and those who we lead have experienced or are still experiencing various types of trauma and impacts on their personal and professional wellbeing. We also need to recognise the signs and symptoms when colleagues are not managing well or seem to be exhibiting concerning signs that their mental wellbeing is suffering. We need to respond by leading and supporting colleagues in a trauma-aware manner. We need to be courageous enough to critique and resist any policies or organisational processes that can potentially re-traumatise individuals or groups.

So, both these aspects (leading the work and leading the people) need to be considered by leaders in trauma-aware education. In this chapter, three examples of leading trauma-aware work will be discussed; leading in education systems, leading in education sites, and leading as a school counsellor. Then the focus will shift to understanding what it means to lead people, in a trauma-aware manner.

Leaders in Education Systems

Since the early 2000s, there has been an ever-increasing awareness in Australia and internationally of the need for systemic, organisational support for children and young people who have experienced complex trauma (Quadara & Hunter, 2016). As a result, system-wide initiatives have consistently increased in areas such as child protection, health and mental health, youth justice, and more recently, education. It is becoming increasingly common to read references to 'trauma-informed' work in policy and guideline documents designed to guide practice in human services and education. However, it is worth mentioning that consistent and effective systemic implementation and oversite of trauma-aware education is likely to be challenging, as there are multifarious complexities inherent in, and specific to, education systems (Howard, 2019). However, these complexities do not negate the importance and value of working towards systemic support for trauma-aware education and the ever-increasing need for educators and other interested parties to advocate for this goal to be realised.

Complexities and Opportunities

One complexity is that education systems are diverse in structure and purpose and can vary greatly in how they are resourced and managed. These systems can include those that oversee the implementation of education policy and practice within national, state, regional, local, and other jurisdictional classifications. Some systems oversee work done in alternative education provision, religion-based education, education for learners living with disability, education for learners from particular cultures, rural and remote education, distance education, and home-delivered education. Some systems focus on the early years, primary or elementary schooling, or secondary or high school education. There are also multiple education systems that focus on the delivery of pre-service and post-graduate education for educators. So, each of these system 'types' would have systemic considerations specific to their structure, purpose, and processes. Therefore, embedding trauma-aware education would need to align with these contextual considerations.

Another complexity is that education systems are often large organisations, encompassing regularly changing leadership roles that oversee regularly changing areas of responsibility. These organisations often oversee and manage competing agendas and priorities that also regularly change. Ensuring that all new and ongoing personnel within systems are trauma-aware will be challenging but is not impossible. For trauma-aware education to gain the respect and interest of people in influential positions within these systems, there will be the need for considerable, consistent, evidence-based, and resilient advocacy from trauma-aware workers within education systems and those busy leading and delivering education in schools, early childhood services, and higher education facilities. Also, embedding mandatory learning regarding trauma-aware education for any new and ongoing system leaders could diminish some of these complexities. Trauma awareness at a systemic level can take time (Quadara & Hunter, 2016), but this could be minimised by lessening the impact of systemic leadership change. Ideally, systemic trauma-aware education should be quarantined from the impacts of political and leadership change (Howard et al., 2022).

Embedding trauma-aware education at a systemic level should also take account of the cultural and geographic diversity represented in the education sites within systems, as well as the varying needs of sites and communities. For example, in Australia, it is vital that such an approach should be developed in consultation with Australia's First Nations Peoples (Aboriginal or Torres Strait Islander Peoples) to ensure the cultural strength and appropriateness of any approach or provisions for First Nations learners (Atkinson, 2013). These cultural leaders understand the impacts of historical and intergenerational trauma on their peoples, including their children and young people. They are best to advise how this should inform a trauma-aware approach to education. So, depending on where in the world you are delivering education services and what cultures are represented within the site populations and communities you serve, discussions should be held with cultural leaders to help with the thoughtful design of trauma-aware education for your system. Culturally appropriate, trauma-informed approaches to services are certainly growing in importance in many societies across the world.

Education systems are also likely responsible for adhering to education and other law relevant to their geographic areas and systems. Elements of education system law and policy can be either a facilitator or significant barrier to trauma-aware education. Therefore, education system leaders should peruse (or even scrutinise) law and policy (particularly in the area of how learner behaviours are managed) and advocate for review as required. This can require 'big' conversations with people with great authority, and trauma-aware system leaders should courageously grasp opportunities to contribute to these discussions.

> The research base on the negative impacts of unresolved trauma and overwhelming stress on the brain and body is now solid. Its findings mandate a changed approach to service delivery of all kinds. The provision of law and delivery of justice comprise critical terrain to which trauma-informed principles should be applied (Kezelman & Stavropoulos, 2016, p. 20).

Advocacy

Another important element of the role of trauma-aware education system leaders is advocacy. Ideally, in the not-too-distant future, information about the impact of complex trauma and the ways that a trauma-aware education approach can help will become easily and broadly available to all education systems. However, despite the increased interest and activity regarding trauma-aware education, there remain many education system leaders who have not yet had access to this information. Therefore, we continue to have a very real need for those education system leaders who are trauma-aware, to advocate for this approach to their colleagues and supervisors. This advocacy could be supported through organising presentations regarding trauma-aware education at key events such as committee meetings, training, forums, and conferences and by engaging in and sharing ongoing research findings from university colleagues.

This can then lead to advocacy for the equitable access of all education site leaders to the evidence for trauma-aware education and the value of this approach. Education system leaders who are trauma-aware can advocate for the resourcing of training or learning provisions for the education sites within their jurisdiction. This resourcing could initially focus on ensuring education site leaders become trauma-aware, which may involve embedding learning into orientation processes (also known as induction or onboarding) for new site leaders, and ongoing professional learning for all site leaders. Ongoing learning could involve formal (in-person or online) training, providing resources or required readings, participating in peer discussions, or embedding learning within systemic supervision practices (as examples).

In addition to education site leaders being supported, trauma-aware education system leaders could join with site leaders to advocate for and support the provision of systemic learning for all personnel in education sites under their authority or professional reach. How this is done will vary from system to system, but ideally will involve the development of policy and funding frameworks to provide equitable access to learning in all sites and for all educators. These frameworks could consider the development of leadership teams to oversee the implementation of policy requirements and recommended best practice across the system.

Building a Staff Leadership Framework

Trauma-aware leaders in education systems should recognise the importance of investing in and building leadership structures throughout systems. By investing in the development of dedicated roles for trauma-aware leaders, the likelihood of this work becoming sustainable within their organisations can become realised. So, rather than repeatedly funding external providers to provide training and support to sites, the system itself can develop and sustain these services. Initially, dedicated leadership roles can be established at the system level, and these roles can then focus on developing and training a range of leaders to support education sites. By thinking and acting in this way, education system leaders hold the potential to drive positive impact consistently over time, across many education sites and for many educators and learners (Howard et al., 2022; QUT & Australian Childhood Foundation, 2021). This could also proactively influence the longer-term and very concerning economic costs to systems and governments of large-scale, unresolved trauma (see chapter one).

Collaboration

Ideally, a whole-of-government response that recognises and supports trauma-aware education would be the most effective and helpful foundation for long-term, consistent, widely available, and effective systemic trauma-aware education. Ideally, collaborations between government and non-government agencies supporting children, youth, and families should be explored and enhanced to develop cost-sharing and cost-saving frameworks. After all, often these groups are working to support the 'same kids'. In addition, collaborations between education systems and universities and other tertiary training programs should be explored to help with pre-service and post-graduate training provision, resource development, program evaluation, and further research (QUT & Australian Childhood Foundation, 2021).

Leaders of Education Sites

Research has clearly shown that leaders of schools and early childhood education services who are unaware of the impacts of complex childhood trauma on children and young people are far less likely to support trauma-aware thinking and processes within their sites or governing organisations. Thus, a lack of trauma awareness among education leaders can be considered one of the major barriers to the implementation of this work. There are many dedicated teachers (and others) within schools, early childhood education and care, and other education settings who are now aware of the impact of complex trauma on learner development and the experience of learning and education. These educators are working diligently to address this within their professional spheres of influence. However, when these practitioners work in settings where leaders are trauma-unaware, their jobs can be challenging for many reasons, including the feeling of being unsupported, the need to repeatedly justify their approaches to behaviour management and learner support, and the need for their ongoing advocacy for growth in trauma-awareness throughout the workplace or practice. Alternatively, leaders who grasp the theory-informed and science-informed evidence-base for trauma-aware education are far more likely to recognise the necessity and benefits of this approach and to support recommended practice and educational and policy reform in this area. Therefore, they can become one of the greatest facilitators of this work. In the growing number of schools and early childhood education services where the leadership is trauma-aware and whole-site trauma-aware practice is developing as a collaborative and shared effort by all personnel, not only is student support enhanced, but so too is the personal and professional wellbeing of educators.

Design of Service Delivery
Trauma-aware education site leaders need to initially consider how to structure the delivery of trauma-aware practice throughout their site. Depending on the site context, perhaps one or more people can be given designated roles to champion this work and take on the responsibility for staff capacity building, policy review, case management processes, or staff support. This, of course, is easier and more achievable if education systems are trauma-aware and are providing systemic staff allocations or supports.

Site leaders need to acknowledge that a whole-of-site approach to trauma-aware education is best and therefore support processes that provide all their staff members with access to quality learning about what complex trauma is, how it can impact child and adolescent development and the experience of education, and how a trauma-aware approach can help. If dedicated roles in developing and delivering training are not possible within current staff allocations, perhaps site leaders can source systemic services or external organisations to provide these services. Alternatively, site leaders can themselves provide access to readings and online resources for their staff and lead discussions with them over time about important aspects of trauma-aware education.

Policy Review

Site leaders should be willing to scrutinise and review site policy, particularly in the area of learner behaviour management, to ensure service delivery is trauma-aware and responsive. To gain the willingness and motivation of the whole staff for this work, it is recommended that this is only done after staff have accessed adequate learning regarding the impacts of complex trauma and trauma-aware education. It is advisable that policy review is a staff-led process, where the informed voices of individuals contribute to the critical analysis of policy and ideas for reform.

Collaborations

Rather than 'soldiering on alone', perhaps site leaders could benefit by collaborating with other site leaders. This could lead to benefits such as sharing ideas and resources and providing and receiving mentoring. Perhaps collaborating sites could even share personnel to lead trauma-aware education training and support across their sites. Interesting models could include collaborations between secondary or high schools and the various primary or elementary schools that feed into these schools, or primary or elementary schools and the early childhood services that feed into these schools. This could allow for thoughtful and supported transitions of trauma-impacted young learners into their next education contexts. There also could be benefits from collaborating with external support organisations and specialists to share ideas and source some quality staff training and consultancy regarding trauma-aware education.

The School Counsellor

Despite the diversity of their roles, it is clear that school counsellors have much capacity for leadership in trauma-aware education and should be valued and supported to do this work. Some authors recommend that trauma-aware activities led by school counsellors should be encompassed within a multi-tiered framework to align with other whole-school practices. This could include proactive, universal, whole-of-site staff training and processes (Tier 1), targeted supports and interventions (Tier 2), and intensive interventions for individual learners (Tier 3) (Berger, 2019; Berger & Samuel 2020; Ormiston et al., 2020: Rawson, 2021; Reinbergs & Feffer, 2018).

However, often the trauma-aware work of school counsellors can focus mostly on supporting individual learners or educators. Due to their specialised knowledge and training, they can often provide therapeutic support to enhance the mental health and wellbeing, and academic engagement of learners (Allison & Ferreira, 2017; O'Gorman, 2018) or can support learners within their family context (Berger & Samuel, 2020; Costa, 2017; O'Gorman, 2018). It is not unusual for school counsellors to support the wellbeing and school functioning of learners in the child protection system who live in out-of-home care (Martinez, et al., 2020). Also, school counsellors may be involved in work to support the personal, professional, and mental wellbeing of their school colleagues who are working with the trauma-impacted learner (Berger & Samuel, 2020; DuBois & Mistretta, 2020). School counsellors can also collaborate with support organisations and community groups to enhance trauma-aware support of students at their schools (Howard, et al., 2021).

School counsellors can also lead broader activity in trauma-aware education. Counsellors can provide group or whole-school training for their colleagues about the neuroscience of trauma. Their work can also involve the co-development of student support plans with educators, coordination of case management processes, and debriefing sessions with school personnel after challenging events involving student behaviour. They can support the development, review, and implementation of site policies and practices and advocate for the support and inclusion of students with trauma-related needs, particularly with regard to the ways that student behaviour management processes are considered or applied (Howard, et al., 2021; Rawson, 2021).

However, school counsellors cannot lead or do all the work mentioned above all of the time. Indeed, the work in which individual counsellors are involved often must be prioritised, and this can be influenced by a number of factors. This can include directives by site leaders and education systems, which can be helpful if directives encourage trauma-aware work and not helpful if they do not (Berger, Martin, et al., 2020). Also, the capacity for counsellors to engage in this work can be influenced by the amount of time and resources available and whether they have access to supportive peer, professional, and clinical supervision and adequate and ongoing training. Also, their work can be heavily influenced by whether there is adequate, shared responsibility for the trauma-aware work implemented at the site so that they do not become overloaded with responsibility (Balch & Balch, 2019; Howard, et al., 2021). Also, it is important that school counsellors are given support to engage in purposeful and planned strategies for self-care to ensure that they have the stamina and resiliency to lead this important work (Berger & Samuel, 2020; DuBois & Mistretta, 2020; Parker & Henfield, 2012, Tang, 2020).

Spheres of Influence

So far, this chapter has discussed systemic leadership, site leadership, and the school counsellor's role. These are some obvious areas of leadership that can support the delivery of trauma-aware education. However, leadership in this important body of work comes in all shapes and sizes, and each area of leadership contributes in important ways to the trauma-aware support and education of children and young people who deserve our unconditional and unreserved efforts to address the impacts of maltreatment they suffered at the hands of those who should be loving, nurturing, and protecting them. A helpful way to frame this is for educators to consider their 'spheres of influence'.

For example, one of my 'spheres of influence' has been to inform how pre-service teacher education can include important learnings regarding trauma-aware education. In my role as an academic in a faculty overseeing education, I have been able to draw from research findings to develop a curriculum for university students. I have been able to advocate for this learning to become mandatory within initial teacher education programs at my university, and I have been able to advocate for other universities to consider doing the same thing.

As part of my university role, I am often listening to the stories of a broad array of educators who have developed their own 'leadership space' by considering their 'spheres of influence' in trauma-aware education. I love hearing these stories as they are so diverse yet so very important. Some have developed impressive classroom practices to support the learners in their care and have been able to share this practice with colleagues to grow trauma-aware understandings and responses across their sites. Some have focussed on helping their site leaders to become trauma-aware, as they realised that this could be one of the more influential ways to progress trauma-aware education at their sites. Some site leaders have focussed on helping their system leaders to become trauma-aware, as they realised that this could be one of the more influential ways to progress trauma-aware education throughout their system. Some have taken leadership roles in case management processes for their sites, ensuring that processes draw from a neuroscience perspective rather than behaviourist methodologies. Some have led processes for policy reform at their sites or systems. Some have applied their learnings to how children and young people who live with disability are supported within their sites or systems. Some have developed training for teachers, teacher aides, and others within their sites. Some have focussed on how trauma-aware alternative education systems can better support trauma-impacted learners who are removed (voluntarily or involuntarily) from mainstream education.

Outside of the education site space, there have been other inspirational stories. Some have developed trauma-aware implementation plans for their child, adolescent, or family support organisations so that they are better prepared and resourced to enhance the educational experience for their clients. Often this includes the admirable offer to provide staff training in trauma-aware processes to education site personnel. Some of this work has come from leaders in areas such as (but not limited to) supporting learners from refugee, immigrant, or First Nations backgrounds, supporting learners from military families, supporting learners who have lived through online exploitation, and supporting young learners who might be pregnant or parenting. Some have focussed on providing helpful messages for adults who have survived complex trauma and are now working in important fields supporting trauma-impacted children and adolescents, including education. These valued messages (understandably and thankfully) often come from trauma survivors themselves.

Leading People in a Trauma-Aware Manner

Leading in trauma-aware education necessitates that you acknowledge your own capacities for leadership including any challenges you might face and the challenges faced by those people you are leading. This would include acknowledging that some of your colleagues may be living through the impact of various types of trauma (including complex childhood trauma). A trauma-aware approach to leadership would therefore emphasise that both you, as a leader, and those you are leading, need perceived safety and dependable support, which would include physical, emotional, social, moral, and cultural elements (Perry & Jackson, 2018). Much of this was discussed in chapter eight of this book. The next part of this chapter will focus on the recommended capacities and other considerations for those who are leading trauma-aware education work, within their spheres of influence.

It starts with you and your nervous system!

First, it is helpful for leaders to understand their work from an interpersonal neurobiology perspective (Cozolino, 2014). As a leader, you will be guiding and encouraging the thinking and actions of others. So, your nervous system will be engaging and interacting with the nervous systems of your various colleagues, sometimes individually and sometimes in groups. So optimal functioning of your nervous system is the goal so that you can engage with the nervous systems of others in a supportive and productive manner.

> Trauma-informed leaders can recognise trauma-related behaviours and acknowledge how their own unresolved traumatic events and experiences may influence how they lead (Emerick, 2022).

Leaders are certainly not immune to stressors and pressures that can arise as part of their work. Indeed, many education leaders, particularly those servicing disadvantaged and trauma-impacted communities, are themselves crisis fatigued, and this has certainly been exacerbated recently by the impacts of the global pandemic (Stokes & Brunzell, 2020). Therefore, just as it is important when engaging with young learners, it is important that trauma-aware leaders establish the means to manage their emotional regulation so that their leadership capacities are optimal for growing the capacities of others.

So, it is highly recommended that leaders take purposeful steps (both proactive and reactive) to manage their emotional regulation. They need to understand that they are very likely to experience difficult days and moments when their emotional regulation is not at its best. During these times, they need to be careful with interactions with colleagues. Also, as emotional dysregulation (such as that associated with anger, fear, sadness, perception of threat, time pressure, family concerns, etc.) can impair pre-frontal cortical functioning, it is not a great time to make important decisions that will lead to important actions. There may be the need to take time to review decisions. Trauma-aware leaders should feel confident and justified, and certainly not embarrassed, to review decisions after their emotions have settled.

Personal and professional concerns faced by leaders can become exacerbated if their role leads to them being somewhat isolated from engaging with others and being supported by others. In some cases, isolation can increase a sense of threat and reduce the capacity to think and solve problems. So, purposeful activity to establish and maintain a network of supportive others is very important. The myth that strong leaders need to maintain relational distance from their workers is quite a damaging one that can impact work and personal relationships, and that can have mental health implications for both leaders and those being led. This myth can be grounded on the belief in a particular leadership style that emphasises the need for leaders to control or manage the behaviours of their workers to maximise outcomes. There is quite a similarity in this way of thinking to a behaviourist approach to the managing behaviours of young learners or the 'boss management' style denounced by William Glasser (1992). A trauma-aware approach to leadership would challenge this way of thinking and therefore would not view colleagues through this lens but would rather value the individual human beings who are being led and support their ongoing development and their personal and professional wellbeing. In his discussion of leadership styles, William Glasser referred to this non-preferred style as 'boss management'. Although his work is now quite dated, Glasser's argument for replacing 'boss management' with an approach that he labelled as 'lead management' is still very valid and does align nicely with a trauma-aware approach. 'Lead management' proposes that leaders encourage, guide, and learn alongside those they lead (Glasser, 1992; Wubbolding, 2007). Perhaps it is helpful to think of leaders with whom you have worked during your career who adopted more of a 'boss management' or a 'lead management' approach. Consider how you worked for these people and how you felt during your time working for these people. Consider which approach more closely aligns with a trauma-aware paradigm.

Then, You Can Lead Others

> A trauma-informed leader should be aware of the prevalence of developmental adversity and traumatic experiences that can impact the lives of anyone in an organisation. Leaders are responsible for ensuring that practitioners are safe and supported to prevent or reduce vicarious trauma and burnout (Perry & Jackson, 2018, p.146).

To lead others in trauma-aware education, it helps if you are informed and intrigued by human behaviour. You need to become a keen observer of the behaviour of both the learners and the educators at your workplace. You need to be a listener and a protector of the stories that learners and staff share with you regarding their experiences and understandings. It helps if you consider yourself a lifelong learner who desires to continue to develop knowledge and skill in trauma-aware education and who distributes this learning generously to those being led. You should feel comfortable letting people know that you don't 'know it all' and that sometimes you will need to collaborate with people within and external to your workplace to grow your understanding, and the understandings of the workplace. You also need to be a confident advocate of trauma-aware education to your staff, professional peers, and supervisors. Leading in a trauma-aware manner also suggests that leaders should identify and mitigate any policy, practices, systems, or mindsets within a workplace that may lead to staff experiencing unnecessary stress responses or even vicarious trauma (Greig et al., 2021). Much of this is discussed in chapter eight.

> Today's leaders need to lead with a trauma-informed and a do-no-harm lens to identify stress responses occurring in the workplace when they see them and know how to respond in a way that doesn't unintentionally cause further harm (Emerick, 2022).

A trauma-aware approach to leadership would also consider interpersonal respect and perceived or real power differentials between leaders and those being led, as this can impact working relationships and emotional regulation. This is very important when working with people who already feel deprived of power or have reason to mistrust authority. Perceived or real power differentials can be defined by social constructs including culture, gender, sexual orientation and gender identities, age, skin colour, socioeconomic status, qualifications and degrees, and even the experience of trauma. These differentials can also occur due to physical characteristics such as height and social characteristics such as familiarity and interpersonal history. The greater the perception of power differential, the more likely this could impact interpersonal respect and emotions and therefore the functioning of colleagues. So, trauma-aware leadership would purposefully address perceived or real power differentials experienced by staff members, offer interactions and processes that help people feel safe and give them a voice that is respected and validated (Perry & Jackson, 2018).

It is also helpful for site leaders to develop their personal and professional capacities, and the capacities of other designated staff members, to work with the caregivers of trauma-impacted learners. These caregivers include biological parents or relatives, foster carers, and workers within child protection organisations or residential facilities. Sometimes interactions with these caregivers can be challenging, so developing the skills to interact in a trauma-aware manner can be important. Also, site leaders might consider embedding caregivers' support into their service delivery. For example, some schools or programs might engage professionals to deliver parenting support programs or provide support and resources (for example, food and uniforms) for students whose families are experiencing hardship.

Summary

The more education systems encompass trauma-aware education as an important aspect of service delivery, the more individual education sites and education site leaders, staff, and learners benefit. Through an informed, respected, and systemic approach to trauma-aware education, leaders will develop strong capacities to lead both the work and the people involved. Education systems and sites are complex and ever-changing institutions that present challenges to a comprehensive and sustained implementation of trauma-aware education. However, this should not stop us from forging forward to engage in vital conversations and activities that will progress trauma-aware education in all our education sites and systems.

Chapter 10

A final word from the author

As I finish writing this book, I am already aware of its inadequacies. Many other areas could be (and deserve to be) explored in a book such as this. Perhaps one day, I will be able to explore these areas. However, I am forever grateful to all the other researchers and authors who are already dedicating themselves to particular topics of vital importance that feed into the 'big picture' of 'complex childhood trauma' and 'trauma-aware education'. It is reassuring seeing how interest continues to grow regarding these topics and this body of critical work within research, education, and other areas in human services.

This book was developed over three (long) years and was primarily written on weekends and after-hours (the life of a busy academic)! At no time did I begrudge giving this time to this project, as in the forefront of my thinking were all the marvellous educators I have met or taught over the years who would love a comprehensive, easily accessible resource to which they could refer, to inform their thinking and their practice. I also reminded myself that this book might help other educators who have not yet had access to important information about their trauma-impacted learners, why they behave and sometimes suffer in the way they do, and what educators could potentially do in response.

I hope this book will serve several important (initial) purposes and prove helpful for educators, education sites, and education systems across Australia and beyond. From a proactive stance, I am truly hoping this text will prove helpful for universities and other higher education providers who are seeking to train up and qualify educators and other support personnel so that they are equipped even before they graduate to support our most vulnerable and victimised children and young people; those who have lived through complex childhood trauma. I hope the book will be helpful for educators leading schools and early childhood services so that they can better support the knowledge and skill development of their staff. I am hoping this text might prove useful to education system leaders who could perhaps benefit from a readily available text to explain and justify the importance of trauma-aware education. Overall, I am hoping the book will be helpful for anyone working with children, young people, and families living with the ongoing impacts of complex trauma.

So, I have provided some basic information in this book about important 'pieces of the trauma-aware education puzzle'. Each piece has a vital role in the success or otherwise of our attempts as educators to deliver education differently and more effectively for trauma-impacted learners. I have discussed the research and science that informs trauma-aware education. I have discussed considerations for the 'behaviour management' of learners in education sites and the importance of viewing behaviours through a 'neuroscience' rather than a 'behaviourist' lens. I have shared ways that educators can respond to support trauma-impacted learners to enhance their perceptions of safety, their capacities for relating and emotional regulation, and, therefore, their capacities to engage in learning. I have discussed the complex intersection between disability and trauma, an area very much deserving of more research and attention. I have examined trauma-aware education from an early childhood education perspective and explored the vitally important topic of educator wellbeing. The final chapter of this book looks into leadership in trauma-aware education and whole-site and systemic responses. Leadership is a vitally important 'piece of the puzzle,' Much of my current work focuses on growing the next generation of leaders in trauma-aware education.

Thank you to all the 'grown-ups' out there who go to work each day to support and educate trauma-impacted children and young people. Your job is not easy, and you are most likely feeling under-resourced and under-appreciated. I want to clearly express just how important you are, and how valued is the work that you do! The theory and the science are clear. It is through your generosity in allowing the nervous systems of trauma-impacted learners to engage with you and your nervous system that the magic happens! You are not only a source of education but a source of healing. You don't have to be a neuroscientist or mental health expert to achieve this. You just have to be a warm, relationally available, trauma-aware educator.

Thank you also to all the many hundreds (or maybe more) educators I have met over the years (and those I have not yet met), who have lived through complex childhood trauma themselves, and yet completed their studies to gain qualifications to educate and support young learners. This is a huge accomplishment, and you should always remember this. Thank you that you turn up to work each day, despite the challenges you face. Thank you that you don't give up on the trauma-impacted learners with whom you work, despite their behaviours and responses perhaps triggering unwanted emotions and memories for you. Thank you that you chose to 'give back'. You could have begrudged what you went through as a child, as you certainly did not deserve this, and it certainly should never have happened. However, you have worked through this and made the purposeful choice to become an educator and supporter of children and young people. Good on you! You are part of a group that continues to inspire my work, as you are the evidence that our young trauma-impacted learners in classrooms today can make it! They have a future waiting for them that could present some challenges but could also be ultimately rewarding and wonderful. They just need to connect with and be supported by terrific people like you!

Thank you to all the wonderful kids out there who have been impacted by complex trauma. You are so very deserving of all the efforts we can possibly bestow to help you access your education. The young learners I have worked with over the years have truly been my greatest teachers. They have been able to explain to me (whether through their behaviour or words) what they are experiencing coming to school, walking through the classroom door, engaging with adults and peers, and trying to engage with learning tasks. They have clearly explained the importance of educators helping them feel safe and helping them to connect to other people, and developing the capacities to trust and believe in them. Although they might not know or understand the term 'unconditional positive regard', this is exactly what they need. They have clearly explained how they are prone to hyperarousal or hypoarousal (for good reason) and how much they need help to practice emotional co-regulation and self-regulation in a safe, non-judgmental way. They have helped me to understand that we need to change thinking and practice to that which addresses their neurobiological concerns rather than thinking we have the power to change, address, modify, reinforce, or extinguish the behaviours that we don't find acceptable. I sincerely hope that all societies become so equipped and effective in child protection processes that the (far too high) numbers of trauma-impacted children and young people in our classrooms will diminish dramatically. However, we can't wait for this. We need to view the words and actions of our trauma-impacted learners through a trauma-aware lens and respond in a trauma-informed way. Every last one of them deserves this!

Finally, thank you to you, the reader. Thank you for your interest and thank you for the important work that you do. I am sincerely grateful for each one of you and am honoured that you have taken the time to read this book.

Dr Judith Howard

References

Chapter 1

Amin, R., Nadeem, E., Iqbal, K., Asadullah, M., & Hussain, B. (2020). Support for Students Exposed to Trauma (SSET) Program: An approach for building resilience and social support among flood-impacted children. *School Mental Health*, 12, 493–506. https://doi.org/10.1007/s12310-020-09373-y

Astitene, K., Aguenaou, H., Lahlour, L., & Barkat, A. (2020). Prevalence of post traumatic stress disorder among school-age adolescents. *International Neuropsychiatric Disease Journal*, 14(1), 40–49. https://doi.org/10.9734/INDJ/2020/v14i130121

Atkinson, J. (2013). *Trauma-informed services and trauma-specific care for Indigenous Australian children.* Canberra: Australian Institute of Health and Welfare.

Barr, D. A. (2018). When trauma hinders learning. *Phi Delta Kappa*, 99(6), 39–44.

Barrett, & Berger, E. (2021). Teachers' experiences and recommendations to support refugee students exposed to trauma. *Social Psychology of Education*, 24(5), 1259–1280. https://doi.org/10.1007/s11218-021-09657-4

Berger. E. (2019). Multi-tiered approaches to trauma-informed care in schools: A systematic review. *School Mental Health*, 11(4), 650–664. https://doi.org/10.1007/s12310-019-09326-0

Berger, E., Carroll, M., Maybery, D., & Harrison, D. (2018). Disaster impacts on students and staff from a specialist, trauma-informed Australian school. *Journal of Child & Adolescent Trauma*, 11(4), 521–530. https://doi.org/10.1007/s40653-018-0228-6

Berger, E., Jamshidi, N., Reupert, A., Jobson, L., & Miko, A. (2021). Review: The mental health implications for children and adolescents impacted by infectious outbreaks — a systematic review. *Child and Adolescent Mental Health, 26*(2), 157–166. https://doi.org/10.1111/camh.12453

Bellis, Hughes, K., Ford, K., Ramos Rodriguez, G., Sethi, D., & Passmore, J. (2019). Life course health consequences and associated annual costs of adverse childhood experiences across Europe and North America: a systematic review and meta-analysis. *The Lancet. Public Health, 4*(10), e517–e528. https://doi.org/10.1016/S2468-2667(19)30145-8

Biglan, A., Van Ryzin, M. J., & Hawkins, J. D. (2017). Evolving a More Nurturing Society to Prevent Adverse Childhood Experiences. Academic Pediatrics, 17(7), S150–S157. https://doi.org/10.1016/j.acap.2017.04.002

Bomber, L. M. (2009). Survival of the fittest! — Teenagers finding their way through the labyrinth of transitions in schools. In A. Perry. (Ed.), *Teenagers and attachment: Helping adolescents engage with life and learning* (pp. 31–62). Worth Publishing.

Boxall, H., Morgan, A. & Brown, R. (2020). *The prevalence of domestic violence among women during the COVID-19 pandemic.* Statistical Bulletin no. 28. Canberra: Australian Institute of Criminology. https://www.aic.gov.au/publications/sb/sb28

Caruana, C. (2010). Healing services for Indigenous people. *Family Relationships Quarterly no 17.* Retrieved from http://www.aifs.gov.au/afrc/pubs/newsletter/frq017/index.html

Chafouleas, S. M., Koriakin, T. A., Roundfield, K. D., & Overstreet, S. (2018). Addressing childhood trauma in school settings: A framework for evidence-based practice. *School Mental Health, 11*(1), 40–53. https://doi.org/10.1007/s12310-018-9256-5

Choi, K. J., & Kangas, M. (2020). Impact of maternal betrayal trauma on parent and child wellbeing: Attachment style and emotion regulation as moderators. *Psychological Trauma: Theory, Research, Practice, and Policy, 12*(2), 121–130. http://dx.doi.org/10.1037/tra0000492

Conti, G., Pizzo, E., Morris, S., & Melnychuk, M. (2021). The economic costs of child maltreatment in UK. *Health Economics, 30*(12), 3087–3105. https://doi.org/10.1002/hec.4409

Craig, S. (2017). *Trauma sensitive schooling for the adolescent years.* Teachers College Press.

Crouch, E., Radcliff, E., Merrell, M. A., Hung, P., & Bennett, K. J. (2021). Positive Childhood Experiences Promote School Success. Maternal and Child Health Journal, 25(10), 1646–1654. https://doi.org/10.1007/s10995-021-03206-3

Davidson, P., Saunders, P., Bradbury, B. and Wong, M., (2020). *Poverty in Australia 2020: Part 1, Overview*. ACOSS/UNSW Poverty and Inequality Partnership Report No. 3, Sydney: ACOSS

Desautels, L. L. (2020) *Connections over compliance: Rewiring our perceptions of discipline*. Wyatt-MacKenzie Publishing.

Dorado, Martinez, M., McArthur, L. E., & Leibovitz, T. (2016). Healthy Environments and Response to Trauma in Schools (HEARTS): A whole-school, multi-level, prevention and intervention program for creating trauma-informed, safe and supportive schools. *School Mental Health, 8*(1), 163–176. https://doi.org/10.1007/s12310-016-9177-0

Fang, X., Brown, D. S., Florence, C. S., & Mercy, J. A. (2011). The economic burden of child maltreatment in the United States and implications for prevention. *Child Abuse & Neglect, 36*(2), 156–165. https://doi.org/10.1016/j.chiabu.2011.10.006

Fang, X., Fry, D. A., Ji, K., Finkelhor, D., Chen, J., Lannen, P., & Dunne, M. P. (2015). The burden of child maltreatment in China: A systematic review. *Bulletin of the World Health Organization, 93*(3), 176–185C. https://doi.org/10.2471/BLT.14.140970

Fondren, K., Lawson, M., Speidel, R., McDonnell, C. G., & Valentino, K. (2020). Buffering the effects of childhood trauma within the school setting: A systematic review of trauma-informed and trauma-responsive interventions among trauma-affected youth. *Children and Youth Services Review, 109*, 104691–. https://doi.org/10.1016/j.childyouth.2019.104691

Hertel, R. & Johnson, M. M. (2013). How the traumatic experiences of students manifest in school settings. In E. Rossen & R. Hull. (Eds.), *Supporting and educating traumatised students: a guide for school-based professionals* (23 – 35). Oxford University Press.

Hughes, D. A., & Baylin, J. (2012). *Brain-based parenting: The neuroscience of caregiving for healthy attachment*. W. W. Norton & Company.

Jaffee, S. R., Ambler, A., Merrick, M., Goldman-Mellor, S., Odgers, C. L., Fisher, H. L., Danese, A., & Arseneault, L. (2018). Childhood maltreatment predicts poor economic and educational outcomes in the transition to adulthood. *American Journal of Public Health (1971), 108*(9), 1142–1147. https://doi.org/10.2105/AJPH.2018.304587

Jensen, F. E. & Nutt, H. E. (2015). *The teenage brain: A neuroscientist's survival guide to raising adolescents and young adults*. Harper Collins.

Kelly, K., Dudgeon, P., Gee, G., & Galaskin, B. (2009). *Living on the edge: Social and emotional wellbeing and risk and protective factors for seriouspsychological distress among Aboriginal and Torres Strait Islander people. Discussion paper 10.* Retrieved from http://www.Indigenouspsychology.com.au/publications

Kezelman, C., Hossack, N., Stavropoulos, P., Burley, P., (2015) *The Cost of Unresolved Childhood Trauma and Abuse in Adults in Australia*, Adults Surviving Child Abuse and Pegasus Economics, Sydney.

Kimble, M., Sripad, A., Fowler, R., Sobolewski, S., & Fleming, K. (2018). Negative world views after trauma: Neurophysiological evidence for negative expectancies. *Psychological Trauma: Theory, Research, Practice, and Policy, 10* (5), 576–584. https://doi.org/10.1037/tra0000324

Kirmayer, L. J., Gone, J. P., & Moses, J. (2014). Rethinking historical trauma. *Transcultural Psychiatry, 51*(3), 299–319. doi:10.1177/1363461514536358

Koea, J. B. (2008). Indigenous trauma: A New Zealand perspective. *International Journal of the Care of the Injured, 39*(5), 511–518.

Mathews, B., Pacella, R., Dunne, M., Scott, J., Finkelhor, D., Meinck, F., Higgins, D. J., Erskine, H., Thomas, H. J., Haslam, D., Tran, N., Le, H., Honey, N., Kellard, K., & Lawrence, D. (2021). The Australian Child Maltreatment Study (ACMS): protocol for a national survey of the prevalence of child abuse and neglect, associated mental disorders and physical health problems, and burden of disease. *BMJ Open, 11*(5), e047074–e047074. https://doi.org/10.1136/bmjopen-2020-047074

McCarthy, M.M., Taylor, P., Norman, R. E., Pezzullo, L., Tucci, J., & Goddard, C. (2016). The lifetime economic and social costs of child maltreatment in Australia. *Children and Youth Services Review, 71*, 217–226. https://doi.org/10.1016/j.childyouth.2016.11.014

Miller, J. & Berger, E. (2020). A review of school trauma-informed practice for Aboriginal and Torres Strait Islander children and youth. *The Educational and Developmental Psychologist, 37*(1), 39–46. https://doi.org/10.1017/edp.2020.2

Milroy, H. (2005). Preface. In S. R. Zubrick, S. R. Silburn, D. M. Lawrence, F. G. Mitrou, R. B. Dalby, E. M. Blair, J. Griffin, H. Milroy, J. A. De Maio, A. Cox, & L. J. (Eds.), *The Western Australian Aboriginal child health survey: The social and emotional wellbeing of Aboriginal children and young people*. Perth: Curtin University of Technology and Telethon Institute for Child Health Research.

Milroy. H. (2013). Beyond cultural security; towards sanctuary: Building an oasis in the desert for the health and wellbeing of our children. *Medical Journal of Australia, 199*(1), 14–. https://doi.org/10.5694/mja13.10796

Mo, S., Gai, R. T., Tachibana, Y., Bolt, T., Takahashi, Y., & Nakayama, T. (2020). The burden of disease and the cost of illness attributable to child maltreatment in Japan: long-term health consequences largely matter. *BMC Public Health, 20*(1), 1296–1296. https://doi.org/10.1186/s12889-020-09397-8

Moore, S. E., Scott, J. G., Ferrari, A. J., Mills, R., Dunne, M. P., Erskine, H. E., Devries, K. M., Degenhardt, L., Vos, T., Whiteford, H. A., McCarthy, M., & Norman, R. E. (2015). Burden attributable to child maltreatment in Australia. *Child Abuse & Neglect, 48*(Oct 2015), 208–220. https://doi.org/10.1016/j.chiabu.2015.05.006

Morgan, A., Pendergast, D., Brown, R., & Heck, D. (2015). Relational ways of being an educator: Trauma-informed practice supporting disenfranchised young people. *International Journal of Inclusive Education, 19*(10), 1037–1051.

National Scientific Council on the Developing Child (2010). *Early Experiences Can Alter Gene Expression and Affect Long-Term Development: Working Paper No. 10*. Retrieved from www.developingchild.harvard.edu.

National Scientific Council on the Developing Child (2004). *Young Children Develop in an Environment of Relationships: Working Paper No. 1*. Retrieved from www.developingchild.harvard.edu.

Newby, J. M., O'Moore, K., Tang, S., Christensen, H., & Faasse, K. (2020). Acute mental health responses during the COVID-19 pandemic in Australia. *PloS one, 15*(7), e0236562.

Nicolai, S., & Saus, M. (2013). Acknowledging the past while looking to the future: Conceptualising Indigenous child trauma. *Child Welfare, 92*(4), 55–74.

O'Donohue, Berger, E., McLean, L., & Carroll, M. (2021). Psychological outcomes for young adults after disastrous events: A mixed-methods scoping review. *Social Science & Medicine (1982), 276*, 113851–113851. https://doi.org/10.1016/j.socscimed.2021.113851

Office of the Advocate for Children and Young People (2020). *Children and young people's experience of disaster 2020*. https://f.hubspotusercontent20.net/hubfs/522228/docs/ ACYP-children-and-young-peoples-experience-of-disaster-2020_(160720).pdf

Siegel, D. (2014). *Brainstorm: The power and purpose of the teenage brain*. Scribe Publications.

Thompson, K. L., Hannan, S. M., & Miron, L. R. (2014). Fight, flight, and freeze: Threat sensitivity and emotion dysregulation in survivors of chronic childhood maltreatment. *Personality and Individual Differences, 69*, 28–32. https://doi.org/10.1016/j.paid. 2014.05.005

Teo, S., & Griffiths, G. (2020). Child protection in the time of COVID-19. *Journal of Paediatrics and Child Health, 56*(6), 838–840.

Thielen, ten Have, M., de Graaf, R., Cuijpers, P., Beekman, A., Evers, S., & Smit, F. (2016). Long-term economic consequences of child maltreatment: a population-based study. *European Child & Adolescent Psychiatry, 25*(12), 1297–1305. https://doi.org/10.1007/s00787-016-0850-5

Tran, T., Hammarberg, K., Kirkman, M., Nguyen, H., & Fisher, J. (2020). Alcohol use and mental health status during the first months of COVID-19 pandemic in Australia. *Journal of Affective Disorders, 277*, 810–813. https://doi.org/10.1016/j.jad.2020.09.012

Wada, I & & Igarashi, A. (2014) The social costs of child abuse in Japan. *Children and Youth Services Review, 46*, 72–77. doi:http://dx.doi.org/10.1016/j.childyouth.2014.08.002

White, R. D. (2015). Indigenous young people and hyperincarceration in Australia. *Youth Justice: An International Journal, 15*(3), 256–270. doi:10.117/14 732254145 62293

Yellow Horse Brave Heart, M., Chase, J., Elkins, J., & Altschul, D. (2011). Historical trauma among Indigenous people of the Americas: Concepts, research, and clinical considerations. *Journal of Psychoactive Drugs, 43*(4), 282–290. doi:10.1080/02791072.2011.628913

Zubrick, S., Silburn, S. R., Lawrence, D., Mitrou, F. G., Dalby, R. B., Blair, E. M., Griffin, J., Milroy, H., De Maio, J. A., & Cox, A. (2005). *The Western Australian Aboriginal Child Health Survey: Measuring the social and emotional wellbeing of Aboriginal children and the intergenerational effects of forced separation.* Curtin University of Technology & Telethon Institute for Child Health Research.

Chapter 2

Australian Institute of Health and Welfare. (2021). *Child Protection Australia 2019–20*. Child welfare series no. 74. Cat. no. CWS 78. Canberra: AIHW

Australian Institute of Health and Welfare. (2020). *Young people under youth justice supervision and in child protection 2018–19*. Data linkage series no. 26. Cat. no. CSI 28. Canberra: AIHW

Barrett, N. & Berger, E. (2021). Teachers' experiences and recommendations to support refugee students exposed to trauma. *Social Psychology of Education, 24*(5), 1259–1280. https://doi.org/10.1007/s11218-021-09657-4

Beebe, B. & Lachmann, F. M. (2015). The expanding world of Edward Tronick. *Psychoanalytic Inquiry, 35*(4), 328–336. https://doi.org/10.1080/07351690.2015.1022476

Berger. E. (2019). Multi-tiered Approaches to Trauma-Informed Care in Schools: A Systematic Review. *School Mental Health, 11*(4), 650–664. https://doi.org/10.1007/s12310-019-09326-0

Bowlby, J. (1951). *Maternal care and mental health*. World Health Organization Monograph (Serial No. 2).

Bowlby, J. (1958). The nature of the child's tie to his mother. *International Journal of Psychoanalysis, 39*(5), 350–373.

Bowlby, J. (1988). *A secure base: Parent-child attachment and healthy human development*. Basic Books.

Bowlby J., & Ainsworth, M. D. S. (1951). *Maternal care and mental health*. World Health Organization.

Bretherton, I. (1992). The origins of attachment theory: John Bowlby and Mary Ainsworth. *Developmental Psychology, 28*, 759–775.

Cashmore. J. (2011). The link between child maltreatment and adolescent offending: Systems neglect of adolescents. *Family Matters, 89*, 31–41.

Chafouleas, S. M., Koriakin, T. A., Roundfield, K. D., & Overstreet, S. (2018). Addressing childhood trauma in school settings: A framework for evidence-based practice. *School Mental Health, 11*(1), 40–53. https://doi.org/10.1007/s12310-018-9256-5

Cooper, G., Hoffman, K., & Powell, B. (2017). Circle of Security in child care: Putting attachment theory into practice in preschool classrooms, *ZERO TO THREE, 37* (3), 27–34.

Currie, J. M. & Tekin, E. (2012). Understanding the cycle: Childhood maltreatment and future crime. *The Journal of Human Resources, 47*(2), 509–549. https://doi.org/10.3368/jhr.47.2.509

Cyr, C., Euser, E. M., Bakermans-Kranenburg, M. J., & van IJzendoorn, M. H. (2010). Attachment security and disorganisation in maltreating and high-risk families. *Development and Psychopathology, 22*, 87–108. doi:10.1017/s0954579409990289

Dunedin Multidisciplinary Health and Development Research Unit. (n.d.). *The Dunedin Study.* https://dunedinstudy.otago.ac.nz/

Fondren, K., Lawson, M., Speidel, R., McDonnell, C. G., & Valentino, K. (2020). Buffering the effects of childhood trauma within the school setting: A systematic review of trauma-informed and trauma-responsive interventions among trauma-affected youth. *Children and Youth Services Review, 109*, 104691–. https://doi.org/10.1016/j.childyouth.2019.104691

Fong. K. (2019). Neighborhood inequality in the prevalence of reported and substantiated child maltreatment. *Child Abuse & Neglect, 90*, 13–21. https://doi.org/10.1016/j.chiabu.2019.01.014

Forsman, H. & Jackisch, J. (2021). Cumulative childhood adversity and long-term educational outcomes in individuals with out-of-home care experience: Do multiples matter for a population defined by adversity? *The British Journal of Social Work.* https://doi.org/10.1093/bjsw/bcab194

Gehred, M. Z., Knodt, A. R., Ambler, A., Bourassa, K. J., Danese, A., Elliott, M. L., Hogan, S., Ireland, D., Poulton, R., Ramrakha, S., Reuben, A., Sison, M. L., Moffitt, T. E., Hariri, A. R., & Caspi, A. (2021). Long-term neural embedding of childhood adversity in a population-representative birth cohort followed for 5 decades. *Biological Psychiatry (1969), 90*(3), 182–193. https://doi.org/10.1016/j.biopsych.2021.02.971

Gindis, B. (2019). *Child development mediated by Trauma: The dark side of international adoption.* Routledge.

Granqvist, P., Sroufe, L. A., Dozier, M., Hesse, E., Steele, M., van Ijzendoorn, M., Solomon, J., Schuengel, C., Fearon, P., Bakermans-Kranenburg, M., Steele, H., Cassidy, J., Carlson, E., Madigan, S., Jacobvitz, D., Foster, S., Behrens, K., Rifkin-Graboi, A., Gribneau, N., ... Duschinsky, R. (2017). Disorganised attachment in infancy: a review of the phenomenon and its implications for *clinicians and policymakers.* Attachment & Human Development, 19(6), 534–558. https://doi.org/10.1080/14616734.2017.1354040

Gray, S. (2015). Widening the Circle of Security: A quasi-experimental evaluation of attachment-based professional development for family child care providers. *Infant Mental Health Journal, 36*(3), 308–319.2

Harlow, H. F. (1958). The nature of love. *American Psychologist, 13*(12), 673–85. https://doi.org/10.1037/h0047884

Harlow, H. F., Harlow, M. K., Dodsworth, R. O., & Arling, G. L. (1966). Maternal behavior of rhesus monkeys deprived of mothering and peer associations in infancy. *Proceedings of the American Philosophical Society, 110*(1), 58–66. http://www.jstor.org/stable/986002

Hughes, K., Bellis, M. A., Hardcastle, K. A., Sethi, D., Butchart, A., Mikton, C., Jones, L., & Dunne, M. P. (2017). The effect of multiple adverse childhood experiences on health: a systematic review and meta-analysis. *The Lancet. Public Health, 2*(8), e356–e366. https://doi.org/10.1016/S2468-2667(17)30118-4

Hunt, T. K. A., Slack, K. S., & Berger, L. M. (2017). Adverse childhood experiences and behavioral problems in middle childhood. *Child Abuse & Neglect, 67*, 391–402. https://doi.org/10.1016/j.chiabu.2016.11.005

Jimenez, M., Wade, R., Lin, Y., Morrow, L., & Reichman, N. (2016). Adverse experiences in early childhood and kindergarten outcomes. *Pediatrics, 137*(2). https://doi.org/10.1542/peds.2015-1839

Kim, H., Wildeman, C., Jonson-Reid, M., & Drake, B. (2017). Lifetime prevalence of investigating child maltreatment among US children. *American Journal of Public Health (1971), 107*(2), 274–280. https://doi.org/10.2105/AJPH.2016.303545

Kim, M., Woodhouse, S. S., & Dai, C. (2018). Learning to provide children with a secure base and a safe haven: The Circle of Security-Parenting (COS-P) group intervention. *Journal of Clinical Psychology, 74*(8), 1319–1332. https://doi.org/10.1002/jclp.22643

Main., M. (2000). The organised categories of infant, child, and adult attachment: Flexible vs. inflexible attention under attachment-related stress. *Journal of the American Psychoanalytic Association, 48*(4), 1055–1096. https://doi.org/10.1177/00030651000480041801

Main, M. & Hesse, E. (1990). Parents' unresolved traumatic experiences are related to infant disorganised attachment status. In Greenberg, M. T., Cicchetti, D., & Cummings, E. M. (Eds.), *Attachment in the preschool years* (pp. 161–181). University of Chicago Press.

Main M., Kaplan N., & Cassidy J. (1985). Security in infancy, childhood, and adulthood: A move to the level of representation. *Monographs of the Society for Research in Child Development, 50*, 66–104. doi:10.2307/3333827

Main, M. & Solomon, J. (1986). Discovery of a new, insecure-disorganised/disoriented attachment pattern. In Yogman, M., & Brazelton, T. B. (Eds.), *Affective development in infancy* (pp. 95–124). Ablex.

Main, M., & Solomon, J. (1990). Procedures for identifying infants as disorganised/disoriented during the Ainsworth Strange Situation. In Greenberg, M.

T., Cicchetti, D., & Cummings, E. M. (Eds.), *Attachment in the preschool years* (pp. 121–160). University of Chicago Press.

Malvaso, C. G., Delfabbro, P. H., & Day, A. (2017). Child maltreatment and criminal convictions in youth: The role of gender, ethnicity and placement experiences in an Australian population. *Children and Youth Services Review, 73*, 57–65. https://doi.org/10.1016/j.childyouth.2016.12.001

Mathews, B., Pacella, R., Dunne, M., Scott, J., Finkelhor, D., Meinck, F., Higgins, D. J., Erskine, H., Thomas, H. J., Haslam, D., Tran, N., Le, H., Honey, N., Kellard, K., & Lawrence, D. (2021). The Australian Child Maltreatment Study (ACMS): Protocol for a national survey of the prevalence of child abuse and neglect, associated mental disorders and physical health problems, and burden of disease. *BMJ Open, 11*(5), e047074–e047074. https://doi.org/10.1136/bmjopen-2020-047074

Maxwell, A., Reay, R. E., Huber, A., Hawkins, E., Woolnough, E., & McMahon, C. (2021). Parent and practitioner perspectives on Circle of Security Parenting (COS-P): A qualitative study. *Infant Mental Health Journal, 42*(3), 452–468. https://doi.org/10.1002/imhj.21916

Maynard, B. R., Farina, A., Dell, N. A., & Kelly, M. S. (2019). Effects of trauma-informed approaches in schools: A systematic review. *Campbell Systematic Review, 15*(1-2). https://doi.org/10.1002/cl2.1018

Metzler, M., Merrick, M. T., Klevens, J., Ports, K. A., & Ford, D. C. (2017). Adverse childhood experiences and life opportunities: Shifting the narrative. *Children and youth services review, 72*, 141–149. https://doi.org/10.1016/j.childyouth.2016.10.021

Miller, L. (2005). *The handbook of international adoption medicine: A guide for physicians, parents, and providers*. Oxford University Press.

Morgan, A., Pendergast, D., Brown, R., & Heck, D. (2015). Relational ways of being an educator: Trauma-informed practice supporting disenfranchised young people. *International Journal of Inclusive Education, 19*(10), 1037–1051.

Powell, B., Cooper, G., Hoffman, K., & Marvin, B. (2014). *The Circle of Security Intervention: enhancing attachment in early parent-child relationships*. Guilford Press.

Roseby, S. & Gascoigne, M. (2021). A systematic review on the impact of trauma-informed education programs on academic and academic-related functioning for students who have experienced childhood adversity. *Traumatology, 27*(2), 149–167. https://doi.org/10.1037/trm0000276

Sempowicz, T. (2017). *Examining the primary school experiences of intercountry adoptees: perspectives of adoptive parents and children.* Queensland University of Technology.

Sempowicz, T., Howard, J., Tambyah, M., & Carrington, S. (2018). Identifying Obstacles and Opportunities for Inclusion in the School Curriculum for Children Adopted from Overseas: Developmental and Social Constructionist Perspectives. *International Journal of Inclusive Education, 22*(6), 606–621. https://doi.org/10.1080/13603116.2017.1390004

Solomon, J., & George, C. (2011). Disorganisation of maternal caregiving across two generations. In Solomon, J., & George, C. (Eds.), *Disorganised attachment & caregiving* (pp. 25–51). Guilford Press.

Stratford, B., Cook, E., Hanneke, R., Katz, E., Seok, D., Steed, H., Fulks, E., Lessans, A., & Temkin, D. (2020). A scoping review of school-based efforts to support students who have experienced trauma. *School Mental Health, 12*(3), 442–477. https://doi.org/10.1007/s12310-020-09368-9

Tronick, E., Als, H., Adamson, L., Wise, S., & Brazelton, T. B. (1978). The infant's response to entrapment between contradictory messages in face-to-face interaction. *Pediatrics, 62*(3), 403–403. https://doi.org/10.1542/peds.62.3.403

Zakszeski, B. N., Ventresco, N. E., & Jaffe, A. R. (2017). Promoting resilience through trauma-focused practices: A critical review of school-based implementation. *School Mental Health, 9,* 310–321. https://doi.org/10.1007/s12310-017-9228-1

Chapter 3

Anderson, C., Polcari, A., & Teicher, M. (2012). Childhood maltreatment is associated with altered large-scale cortical network structural connectivity. *Biological Psychiatry, 71*(8), 197S–197S.

Anderson, S.A.S., Hawes, D. J., & Snow, P. C. (2016). Language impairments among youth offenders: A systematic review. *Children and Youth Services Review, 65*, 195–203. https://doi.org/10.1016/j.childyouth.2016.04.004

Ansell, E., Rando, K., Tuit, K., Guarnaccia, J., & Sinha, R. (2012). Cumulative adversity and smaller gray matter volume in medial prefrontal, anterior cingulate, and insula regions. *Biological Psychiatry, 72*(1), 57–64.

Arden, J. B. (2019). *Mind-Brain-Gene: Toward psychotherapy integration*. WW Norton and Co.

Atkinson, J. (2002). *Trauma trails, recreating song lines: The transgenerational effects of trauma in Indigenous Australia*: Spinifex Press.

Barlow, M.R., Pezdek, K. & Blandon-Gitlin, K. (2017). Trauma and Memory. In Gold, S.N. (ed.) *APA Handbook of Trauma Psychology: Foundations in Knowledge*. American Psychological Association, pp.307–331.

Beaney. J. (2021). *Autism through a sensory lens: Sensory assessment and strategies (2nd ed.)*. Routledge.

Blanche. E. (2022). *An evidence-based guide to combining interventions with sensory integration in pediatric practice*. Routledge.

Brewin, C.R. (2005). Encoding and retrieval of traumatic memories. In J. Vasterling & C. Brewin, (eds). *Neuropsychology of PTSD: Biological, cognitive and clinical perspectives*. Guilford Press, pp.131–152.

Cabrera, C., Torres, H., & Harcourt, S. (2020). The neurological and neuropsychological effects of child maltreatment. *Aggression and Violent Behavior, 54*, 101408–. https://doi.org/10.1016/j.avb.2020.101408

Cary, N. (2012). *The epigenetics revolution: How modern biology is rewriting our understanding of genetics, disease, and inheritance*. Columbia University Press.

Cashmore. J. (2011). The link between child maltreatment and adolescent offending: Systems neglect of adolescents. *Family Matters, 89*, 31–41.

Center on the Developing Child at Harvard University (2011). *Building the Brain's "Air Traffic Control" System: How Early Experiences Shape the Development of Executive Function: Working Paper No. 11*. Retrieved from www.devhcdc.wpengine.com.

Center on the Developing Child at Harvard University (2014). *A Decade of Science Informing Policy: The Story of the National Scientific Council on the Developing Child.* http://www.developingchild.net.

Champagne, T. (2011). Attachment, trauma, and occupational therapy practice. OT Practice, 16(5), 1–8.

Choi, J., Jeong, B., Polcari, A.M., Rohan, M.L. & Teicher M.H. (2012). Reduced fractional anisotropy in the visual limbic pathway of young adults witnessing domestic violence in childhood. *Neuroimage, 59*(2), 1071–1079.

Cohen, N.J. (2001). *Language impairment and psychopathology in infants, children and adolescents.* Thousand Oaks, CA: Sage.

Cohen, N. J., Barwick, M. A., Horodezky, N. B., Vallance, D. D., & Im, N. (1998). Language, achievement, and cognitive processing in psychiatrically disturbed children with previously identified and unsuspected language impairments. *Journal of Child Psychology and Psychiatry, 39*(6), 865–877. https://doi.org/10.1111/1469-7610.00387

Corrigan, F.M., Fisher, J.J., Nutt, D.J. (2010). Autonomic dysregulation and the Window of Tolerance model of the effects of complex emotional trauma. *Journal of Psychopharmacology, 25* (1) 17–25

Cozolino, L. (2002). *The neuroscience of psychotherapy: Building and rebuilding the human brain.* Norton.

Cozolino, L. (2013). *The social neuroscience of education: Optimizing attachment and learning in the classroom.* W.W. Norton and Co.

Cozolino, L. (2014). *The neuroscience of human relationships: Attachment and the developing social brain (2nd edn).* W.W. Norton and Company.

Demers, L., Mckenzie, K., Hunt, R., Cicchetti, D., Cowell, R., Rogosch, F., Toth, S., & Thomas, K. (2018). Separable effects of childhood maltreatment and adult adaptive functioning on amygdala connectivity during emotion processing. *Biological Psychiatry. Cognitive Neuroscience and Neuroimaging, 3*(2), 116–124.

Dods, J. (2013). Enhancing understanding of the nature of supportive school-based relationships for youth who have experienced trauma. *Canadian Journal of Education, 36*(1), 71–95.

Engel-Yeger, B., Palgy-Levin, D. & Lev-Wiesel, R. (2013), The sensory profile of people with posttraumatic stress symptoms, *Occupational Therapy in Mental Health, 29*(3), 266–278.

Felitti, V. J., Anda, R. F., Nordenberg, D., Williamson, D. F., Spitz, A. M., Edwards, V., & Marks, J. S. (1998). Relationship of childhood abuse and household dysfunction to many of the leading causes of death in adults: The

Adverse Childhood Experiences (ACE) Study. *American Journal of Preventive Medicine, 14*(4), 245–258.

Forneris, C. A., Gartlehner, G., Brownley, K. A., Gaynes, B. N., Sonis, J., Coker-Schwimmer, E., et al. (2013). Interventions to prevent post-traumatic stress disorder: A systematic review. *American Journal of Preventive Medicine, 44* (6), 635–650.

Forsman, H. & Jackisch, J. (2021). Cumulative childhood adversity and long-term educational outcomes in individuals with out-of-home care experience: Do multiples matter for a population defined by adversity? *The British Journal of Social Work.* https://doi.org/10.1093/bjsw/bcab194

Fraser, K., MacKenzie, D., & Versnel, J. (2017). Complex Trauma in Children and Youth: A Scoping Review of Sensory-Based Interventions. *Occupational Therapy in Mental Health, 33*(3), 199–216. https://doi.org/10.1080/0164212X.2016.1265475

Freyd, J. & Birrell, P. (2013). *Blind to betrayal: How we fool ourselves we're not being fooled.* Wiley & Sons.

Gehred, M. Z., Knodt, A. R., Ambler, A., Bourassa, K. J., Danese, A., Elliott, M. L., Hogan, S., Ireland, D., Poulton, R., Ramrakha, S., Reuben, A., Sison, M. L., Moffitt, T. E., Hariri, A. R., & Caspi, A. (2021). Long-term neural embedding of childhood adversity in a population-representative birth cohort followed for 5 decades. *Biological Psychiatry (1969), 90*(3), 182–193. https://doi.org/10.1016/j.biopsych.2021.02.971

Glackin, E. B., Hatch, V., Drury, S.S. & Gray S.A.O. (2020). Linking pre-schoolers' parasympathetic activity to maternal early adversity and child behavior: An intergenerational perspective. *Dev Psychobiol. 2020;00:1–12.* https://doi.org/10.1002/dev.22012

Glod, C., Teicher, M., Hartman, C., Harakal, T., & Mcgreenery, C. (1997). Enduring effects of early abuse on locomotor activity, sleep, and circadian rhythms. *Annals of the New York Academy of Sciences,* 821, 465–467.

Goodman-Delahunty, J., Nolan, M.A., & Van Gijn-Grosvenor. (2017). *Empirical Guidance on the Effects of Child Sexual Abuse on Memory and Complainants' Evidence (Report for the Royal Commission into Institutional Responses to Child Sexual Abuse).* Commonwealth of Australia.

Haase, L., Thom, N. J., Shukla, A., Davenport, P. W., Simmons, A. N., Stanley, E. A., Paulus, M. P., & Johnson, D. C. (2015). Mindfulness-based training attenuates insula response to an aversive interoceptive challenge. *Social Cognitive and Affective Neuroscience, 11*(1), 182–190. https://doi.org/10.1093/scan/nsu042

Hall, A., Perez, A., West, X., Brown, M., Kim, E., Salih, Z., & Aronoff, S. (2021). The association of adverse childhood experiences and resilience with health outcomes in adolescents: An observational study. *Global Pediatric Health, 8,* https://doi.org/10.1177/2333794X20982433

Harms. (2015). *Understanding trauma and resilience.* Palgrave.

Herringa, R., & Teicher, M. (2018). Neurobiological mechanisms of resilience and vulnerability to childhood adversity. *Journal of the American Academy of Child & Adolescent Psychiatry, 57*(10), S305–S305.

Ho, S. S., MacDonald, A., & Swain, J. E. (2014). Associative and sensorimotor learning for parenting involves mirror neurons under the influence of oxytocin. *Behavioral and Brain Sciences, 37*(2), 203–204.

Howell, E. (2005). *The Dissociative Mind.* Routledge.

Hudson, L., Beilke, S., & Many, M. (2016). "If you're brave enough to live it, the least I can do is listen": Overcoming the consequences of complex trauma. *ZERO TO THREE, 36(5), 4–11.* Retrieved from http://search.proquest.com/docview/1969007950/

Hunt, T. K. A., Slack, K. S., & Berger, L. M. (2017). Adverse childhood experiences and behavioral problems in middle childhood. *Child Abuse & Neglect, 67,* 391-402. https://doi.org/10.1016/j.chiabu.2016.11.005

Hurren, E., Stewart, A., & Dennison, S. (2017). Transitions and turning points revisited: A replication to explore child maltreatment and youth offending links within and across Australian cohorts. *Child Abuse & Neglect, 65,* 24–36.

Iacoviello, B. M., & Charney, D. S. (2014). Psychosocial facets of resilience: Implications for preventing posttrauma psychopathology, treating trauma survivors, and enhancing community resilience. *European Journal of Psychotraumatology ,* 5 , 23970, doi: http://dx.doi.org/10.3402/ejpt.v5.23970

Ismail, F. Y., Fatemi, A., & Johnston, M. V. (2016). Cerebral plasticity: Windows of opportunity in the developing brain. *European Journal of Paediatric Neurology, 21*(1), 23–48. https://doi.org/10.1016/j.ejpn.2016.07.007

Jedd, K., Hunt, R., Cicchetti, D., Hunt, E., Cowell, R., Rogosch, F., Toth, S., & Thomas, K. (2015). Long-term consequences of childhood maltreatment: Altered amygdala functional connectivity. *Development and Psychopathology, 27*(4 Pt 2), 1577–1589.

Jimenez, M., Wade, R., Lin, Y., Morrow, L., & Reichman, N. (2016). Adverse experiences in early childhood and kindergarten outcomes. *Pediatrics, 137*(2). https://doi.org/10.1542/peds.2015-1839

Johnson, S., Riley, A., Granger, D., & Riis, J. (2013). The science of early life toxic stress for pediatric practice and advocacy. *Pediatrics, 131*(2).

Kaiser, R., Clegg, R., Goer, F., Pechtel, P., Beltzer, M., Vitaliano, G., Olson, D., Teicher, M., & Pizzagalli, D. (2018). Childhood stress, grown-up brain networks: Corticolimbic correlates of threat-related early life stress and adult stress response. *Psychological Medicine, 48*(7), 1157–1166.

Karr-Morse, R. & Wiley, M. S. (2012). *Scared sick: The role of childhood trauma in adult disease.* Basic Books.

Koomar, J. A. (2009). Trauma- and attachment-informed sensory integration assessment and intervention. *Sensory Integration Special Interest Section Quarterly, 32*(4), 1-4.

Kraaijenvanger, E., Pollok, T., Monninger, M., Kaiser, A., Brandeis, D., Banaschewski, T., & Holz, N. (2020). Impact of early life adversities on human brain functioning: A coordinate-based meta-analysis. *Neuroscience and Biobehavioral Reviews, 113*, 62–76.

Lanius, U., Paulsen, S., & Corrigan, F. (2014). *Neurobiology and treatment of traumatic dissociation: Toward an embodied self.* Springer Publishing Company.

Levine, P. (1997) *Waking the Tiger: Healing Trauma.* North Atlantic Books.

Levine P. A. (2015). *Trauma and memory: Brain and body in a search for the living past.* North Atlantic Books.

Luthar, S. S., Cicchetti, D., & Becker, B. (2000). The construct of reslilience: A critical evaluation and guidelines for future work. *Child Development, 71* (3), 543–562.

Lyons-Ruth, K., Pechtel, P., Yoon, S.A., Anderson, C. M. & Teicher, M. H. (2016). Disorganized attachment in infancy predicts greater amygdala volume in adulthood. *Behavioural Brain Research, 308* (July), 83–-93.

Malvaso, C. G., Delfabbro, P. H., & Day, A. (2017). The child protection and juvenile justice nexus in Australia: a longitudinal examination of the relationship between maltreatment and offending. *Child Abuse & Neglect, 64,* 32–46.

Malvaso, C. G., Delfabbro, P. H., Day, A., & Nobles, G. (2018). The maltreatment-violence link: exploring the role of maltreatment experiences and other individual and social risk factors among young people who offend. *Journal of Criminal Justice, 55,* 35–45.

Marusak, H. A., Etkin, A. & Thomason, M. E. (2015). Disrupted insula-based neural circuit organization and conflict interference in trauma-exposed youth. *NeuroImage Clinical, 8*(C), 516–525.

Masten, A. (2001). *Ordinary magic: Resilience processes in development.* The American Psychologist, 56(3), 227–238. https://doi.org/10.1037/0003-066X.56.3.227

Masten. (2014). *Ordinary magic: Resilience in development.* The Guilford Press.

May-Benson, T. & Teasdale, A. (2019). Validation of a Sensory-Based Trauma-Informed Intervention Program Using Qualitative Video Analysis. *The American Journal of Occupational Therapy, 73*(4_Supplement_1), 7311520393–7311520393p1. https://doi.org/10.5014/ajot.2019.73S1-PO2034

McDonnell, C., & Valentino, K. (2016). Intergenerational effects of childhood trauma: Evaluating pathways among maternal ACEs, perinatal depressive symptoms, and infant outcomes. *Child Maltreatment, 21(4), 317–326.* https://doi.org/10.1177/1077559516659556_

Mcgowan, P. (2012). Epigenetic clues to the biological embedding of early life adversity. *Biological Psychiatry, 72*(1), 4–5.

McGreevy, S. & Boland, P. (2020). Sensory-based interventions with adult and adolescent trauma survivors. *The Irish Journal of Occupational Therapy, 48*(1), 31–54. https://doi.org/10.1108/IJOT-10-2019-0014

Metzler, M., Merrick, M. T., Klevens, J., Ports, K. A., & Ford, D. C. (2017). Adverse childhood experiences and life opportunities: Shifting the narrative. *Children and Youth Services Review, 72,* 141–149. https://doi.org/10.1016/j.childyouth.2016.10.021

Mitchell, J., Tucci, J. & Tronick, E. (2019). *The Handbook of Therapeutic Care for Children: Evidence-Informed Approaches to Working with Traumatized Children and Adolescents in Foster, Kinship and Adoptive Care.* Jessica Kingsley Publishers.

Music, G. (2017). *Nurturing Natures: Attachment and children's emotional, sociocultural and brain development (2nd edn.).* Routledge.

Nash, W. P., & Watson, P. J. (2012). Review of VA/DOD clinical practice guideline on management of acute stress and interventions to prevent posttraumatic stress disorder. *Journal of Rehabilitation Research and Development, 49* (5), 637.

National Scientific Council on the Developing Child (2015). *Supportive Relationships and Active Skill-Building Strengthen the Foundations of Resilience: Working Paper No. 13.* Retrieved from www.developingchild.harvard.edu.

Ogden, P., & Fisher, J. (2015). *Sensorimotor psychotherapy: Interventions for trauma and attachment* (Norton series on interpersonal neurobiology). W.W. Norton & Company.

Ogden, P., Minton, K., & Pain, C (2006). *Trauma and the body: a sensorimotor approach to psychotherapy.* W.W. Norton & Co.

Ogden, P., Pain, C., & Fisher, J. (2006). A sensorimotor approach to the treatment of trauma and dissociation. *The Psychiatric Clinics of North America, 29*, 263–279. doi:10.1016/j.psc.2005.10.012

Ohashi, K., Anderson, C., Polcari, A., Khan, A., & Teicher, M. (2014). Psychopathology and impaired brain network architecture: The importance of childhood maltreatment. *Biological Psychiatry, 75*(9).

Ohashi, K., Anderson, C., Polcari, A., Rohan, M., & Teicher, M. (2012). Developmental sensitive periods for the association between childhood maltreatment and fiber tract integrity. *Biological Psychiatry, 71*(8).

Ohashi, K., Anderson, C., & Teicher, M. (2015). Specific vulnerability of amygdala - prefrontal cortex resting state functional connectivity to peer victimization. *Biological Psychiatry, 77*(9), 344S–345S.

Pechtel, P., Teicher, M., Anderson, C., & Lyons-Ruth, K. (2013). Sensitive periods of amygdala development: The role of adversity in preadolescence. *Biological Psychiatry, 73*(9), 83S–83S.

Perry, B., Griffin, G., Davis, G., Perry, J., & Perry, R. (2018). The impact of neglect, trauma, and maltreatment on neurodevelopment: Implications for juvenile justice practice, programs, and policy. In *The Wiley Blackwell Handbook of Forensic Neuroscience* (Vols. 2-2, pp. 813–835). Wiley Blackwell.

Pineda, J. (2009). *Mirror Neuron Systems: The Role of Mirroring Processes in Social Cognition.* Humana Press.

Porges, S. W. (2011). *The Polyvagal Theory: Neurophysiological foundations of emotions, attachment, communication, and self-regulation.* WW Norton & Co.

Porges, S. W. (2017). *The pocket guide to the Polyvagal Theory: The transformative power of feeling safe.* W.W. Norton & Co.

Praszkier, R. (2016). Empathy, mirror neurons and sync. *Mind & Society, 15*(1), 1–25.

Radley, B., Davis, T. A., Wingo, A. P., Mercer, K. B., & Ressler, K. J. (2013). Family environment and adult resilience: Contributions of positive caregiving and the oxytocin receptor gene. *European Journal of Psychotraumatology , 4* , 21659, doi: http://dx.doi.org/10.3402/ejpt.v4i0.21659

Rodger, S., Ashburner, J. & Hinder, E. (2012). Sensory interventions for children: Where does our profession stand?". *Australian Occupational Therapy Journal, 59*(5), 337–338.

Rothschild, B. (2000) *The Body Remembers: The Psychophysiology of Trauma and Trauma Treatment.* Norton.

Russo, S. J., Murrough, J. W., Han, M.-H., Charney, D. S., & Nestler, E. J. (2012). Neurobiology of resilience. *Nature Neuroscience, 15*(11), 1475–1484. https://doi.org/10.1038/nn.3234

Rydberg, J.A. (2017) Research and Clinical Issues in Trauma and Dissociation. *European Journal of Trauma and Dissociation*,1 (2), 89-99.

Schalinskia, I., Teicher, M.H., Rockstroham B. (2019). Early neglect is a key determinant of adult hair cortisol concentration and is associated with increased vulnerability to trauma in a transdiagnostic sample. *Psychoneuroendocrinology, 108* (October), 35–42.

Schore, A. N. (2003). *Affect dysregulation and disorders of the self:* Norton.

Schore, A. N. (2012). *The Science of the Art of Psychotherapy.* W.W. Norton & Co.

Schore, A. N. (2019). *Right Brain Psychotherapy.* W.W. Norton & Co.

Schore, A. N. (2020). *Reader's Guide to Affect Regulation and Neurobiology.* W.W. Norton & Co.

Sege, R., & Harper Browne, C. (2017). Responding to ACEs With HOPE: Health Outcomes from Positive Experiences. *Academic Pediatrics, 17*(7), S79–S85. https://doi.org/10.1016/j.acap.2017.03.007

Shonkoff, J., & Phillips, D. (2000). *From neurons to neighborhoods: The science of early child development.* National Academy Press.

Siegel, D. J. (2009). *Mindsight.* Random House.

Siegel, D. J. (2012). *The developing mind: How relationships and the brain interact to shape who we are* (2nd ed.). Guilford Press.

Siegel, D. J. (2012). *Pocket guide to interpersonal neurobiology.* Norton.

Silberg, J. (2013). *The child survivor: Healing developmental trauma and dissociation.* Routledge.

Snedden, D. (2012), Trauma-informed practice: An emerging role of occupational therapy. *Occupational Therapy Now, 14*(6), 26–28.

Snow, P. C. (2009). Child maltreatment, mental health and oral language competence: Inviting speech language pathology to the prevention table. *International Journal of Speech Language Pathology 11*(12): 95–103.

Snow, P. & Powell, M. (2012). Youth (in)justice: Oral language competence in early life and risk for engagement in antisocial behaviour in adolescence. *Trends and Issues in Crime and Criminal Justice, 435,* 1–6. https://doi.org/10.3316/agispt.20122719

Snow., P. C. (2019). Speech-language pathology and the youth offender: Epidemiological overview and roadmap for future speech-language pathology research and scope of practice. *Language, Speech & Hearing Services in Schools, 50*(2), 324–339. https://doi.org/10.1044/2018_LSHSS-CCJS-18-0027

Snyder, C. R., & Heinze, L. S. (2005). Forgiveness as a mediator of the relationship between PTSD and hostility in survivors of childhood abuse. *Cognition & Emotion, 19* (3), 413–431.

Stavropoulos, P.A. & Kezelman, C. A. (2018). *The truth of memory and the memory of truth: Different types of memory and the significance for trauma.* Blue Knot Foundation. https://www.blueknot.org.au/resources/publications/trauma-and-memory

Steele, W. & Kuban, C. (2013). *Working with grieving and traumatized children and adolescents discovering what matters most through evidence-based, sensory interventions.* Wiley.

Tedeschi, R. G., Calhoun, L. G., Shakespeare-Finch, J., & Taku, K. (2018). *Posttraumatic growth: theory, research, and applications.* Routledge.

Teicher, M. H. (2002). Scars that won't heal: The neurobiology of child abuse. *Scientific American, 286*(3), 68–75.

Teicher, M. (2012). Childhood maltreatment is associated with gray matter volume alterations in hippocampal dentate gyrus, CA3 and subiculum. *Biological Psychiatry, 71*(8), 112S–112S.

Teicher, M. (2015). Gender-specific influence of type and timing of childhood maltreatment on caudate, putamen and nucleus accumbens volume. *Biological Psychiatry, 77*(9), 42S–42S.

Teicher, M. (2018). A structural network model that accurately predicts susceptibility versus resilience to psychopathology in individuals with maltreatment. *Journal of the American Academy of Child & Adolescent Psychiatry, 57*(10), S306–S306.

Teicher. M. (2019). Neurobiological consequences of childhood maltreatment: Importance of sensitive periods and network architecture. *Journal of the American Academy of Child and Adolescent Psychiatry, 58*(10), S145–S145.

Teicher, Samson, J. A., Polcari, A., & McGreenery, C. E. (2006). Sticks, stones, and hurtful words: Relative effects of various forms of childhood maltreatment. *The American Journal of Psychiatry, 163*(6), 993–1000. https://doi.org/10.1176/appi.ajp.163.6.993

Teicher, M., Anderson, C., Ohashi, K., Khan, A., Mcgreenery, C., Bolger, E., Rohan, M., & Vitaliano, G. (2018). Differential effects of childhood neglect and abuse during sensitive exposure periods on male and female hippocampus. *NeuroImage, 169*, 443–452. https://doi.org/10.1016/j.neuroimage.2017.12.055

Teicher, M. H., Ito, Y., Glod, C.A., Andersen, S. L., Dumont, N. & Ackerman, E. (1997), Preliminary evidence for abnormal cortical development in physically and sexually abused children using EEG Coherence and MRI. *The Psychobiology of Posttraumatic Stress Disorder, 821* (1), 160–175.

Teicher, M., Parigger, A., & Schmahl, C. (2015). The "Maltreatment and Abuse Chronology of Exposure" (MACE) scale for the retrospective assessment of abuse and neglect during development. *PLoS ONE, 10*(2).

Teicher M. H. & Vitaliano, G.D. (2011). Witnessing violence toward siblings: An understudied but potent form of early adversity. *PLoS ONE, 6*(12).

Tomoda, A., Navalta, C.P., Polcari, A., Sadato, N., and Teicher, M.H. (2009) Childhood sexual abuse is associated with reduced gray matter volume in visual cortex of young women. *Biol Psychiatry 66*, 642–648

Tomoda, A., Polcari, A., Anderson, C.M. & Teicher, M.H. (2012). Reduced visual cortex gray matter volume and thickness in young adults who witnessed domestic violence during childhood. *PloS One, 7*(12).

Tomoda, A., Sheu, Y-S., Rabi, K., Suzuki, H., Navalta, C.P., Polcari, A. & Teicher, M.H. (2011). Exposure to caregiver verbal abuse is associated with increased gray matter volume in superior temporal gyrus. *Neuroimage, 54*(1), 260–8.

Tomoda, A., Suzuki, H., Rabi, K., Sheu, Y-S., Polcari, A., and Teicher, M.H. (2009) Reduced prefrontal cortical gray matter volume in young adults exposed to harsh corporal punishment. *Neuroimage 47*(2), 66–71.

Tottenham, N., Hare, T., Quinn, B., Mccarry, T., Nurse, M., Gilhooly, T., Millner, A., Galvan, A., Davidson, M., Eigsti, I., Thomas, K., Freed, P., Booma, E., Gunnar, M., Altemus, M., Aronson, J., & Casey, B. (2010). Prolonged institutional rearing is associated with atypically large amygdala volume and difficulties in emotion regulation. *Developmental Science, 13*(1), 46–61.

Uher, R., Caspi, A., Houts, R., Sugden, K., Williams, B., Poulton, R., & Moffitt, T. (2011). Serotonin transporter gene moderates childhood maltreatment's effects on persistent but not single-episode depression: Replications and implications for resolving inconsistent results. *Journal of Affective Disorders, 135*(1-3), 56–65. https://doi.org/10.1016/j.jad.2011.03.010

van der Hart, O., Nijenhuis, E., & Steele, K. (2006) *The haunted self: Structural dissociation and the treatment of chronic traumatization.* Norton.

van der Kolk, B.A. (2015) *The body keeps the score: Brain, mind and body in the healing of trauma.* Viking.

Warner, E., Koomar, J., Lary, B. & Cook, A. (2013). Can the body change the score? Application of sensory modulation principles in the treatment of traumatized adolescents in residential settings. *Journal of Family Violence. 28*(7), 729-738. doi: 10.1007/s10896-013-9535-8

Warner, E., Spinazzola, J., Westcott, A., Gunn, C. & Hodgdon, H. (2014). The body can change the score: Empirical support for somatic regulation in the treatment of traumatized adolescents. *Journal of Child and Adolescent Trauma, 7*(4), 237–246.

Weiland, S. (ed.). (2015). *Dissociation in traumatized children and adolescents: Theory and clinical interventions* (2nd edn.). Routledge.

Willis, J., (2009). *How your child learns best: Brain-friendly strategies you can use to ignite your child's learning and increase school success.* Sourcebooks, Inc.

Wilmot. K. (2020). Wired differently: A teacher's guide to understanding sensory-processing challenges. Gryphone House.

Wolan, T., Delaney, M. A., & Weller, A. (2015). Group work with children who have experienced trauma using a sensorimotor framework. *Children Australia, 40,* 205–208. doi:10.1017/cha.2015.16

Xavier, G., Spindola, L., Ota, V., Carvalho, C., Maurya, P., Tempaku, P., Moretti, P., Mazotti, D., Sato, J., Brietzke, E., Miguel, E., Grassi-Oliveira, R., Mari, J., Bressan, R., Gadelha, A., Pan, P., & Belangero, S. (2018). Effect of male-specific childhood trauma on telomere length. *Journal of Psychiatric Research, 107,* 104–109. https://doi.org/10.1016/j.jpsychires.2018.10.012

Yehuda, R., & Lehrner, A. (2018). Intergenerational transmission of trauma effects: Putative role of epigenetic mechanisms. *World Psychiatry, 17*(3), 243–257. https://doi.org/10.1002/wps.20568

Ziegler, D. (2011). *Traumatic experience and the brain: A handbook for understanding and treating those traumatized as children.* Acacia Publishing.

Zhai, Z.W., Yip, S. W., Lacadie, C. M., Sinha, R., Mayes, L. C., & Potenza, M. N. (2019). Childhood trauma moderates inhibitory control and anterior cingulate cortex activation during stress. NeuroImage (Orlando, Fla.), 185, 111–118. https://doi.org/10.1016/j.neuroimage.2018.10.049

Chapter 4

Berger. E. (2019). Multi-tiered approaches to Trauma-Informed Care in schools: A systematic review. *School Mental Health, 11*(4), 650–664. https://doi.org/10.1007/s12310-019-09326-0

Berger, E. & Martin, K. (2021). Embedding trauma-informed practice within the education sector. *Journal of Community & Applied Social Psychology, 31*(2), 223–227. https://doi.org/10.1002/casp.2494

Bomber, L. M. (2009). Survival of the fittest! — Teenagers finding their way through the labyrinth of transitions in schools. In A. Perry. (Ed.), *Teenagers and attachment: Helping adolescents engage with life and learning* (pp. 31-62). Worth Publishing.

Chafouleas, S. M., Koriakin, T. A., Roundfield, K. D., & Overstreet, S. (2018). Addressing childhood trauma in school settings: A framework for evidence-based practice. *School Mental Health, 11*(1), 40–53. https://doi.org/10.1007/s12310-018-9256-5

Doll. B. (2019). Addressing student internalising behavior through multi-tiered systems of support. *School Mental Health, 11*(2), 290–293. https://doi.org/10.1007/s12310-019-09315-3

Glasberg, B. A. & LaRue, R. H. (2015). *Functional Behavior Assessment for people with autism: Making sense of seemingly senseless behavior (Second edition.)*. Woodbine House.

Hadaway, S. M. & Brue, A. W. (2016). *Practitioner's guide to Functional Behavioral Assessment: Process, purpose, planning, and prevention*. Springer.

Jones, A. M., West, K. B., & Suveg, C. (2017). Anxiety in the school setting: A framework for evidence-based practice. *School Mental Health, 11*(1), 4–14. https://doi.org/10.1007/s12310-017-9235-2

Kearney, C. A. (2016). *Managing school absenteeism at multiple tiers: An evidence-based and practical guide for professionals*. Oxford University Press.

Matson, J. L. (2021). *Functional Assessment for challenging behaviors and mental health disorders (2nd ed.)*. Springer.

Miltenberger. R. G. (2016). *Behavior modification: Principles and procedures (6th ed.)*. Cengage Learning.

National Association of School Psychologists. (2016). *Ensuring high quality, comprehensive, and integrated specialised instructional support services* [Position Statement]. Bethesda, MD: Author.

Nickerson, A. B. (2019). Preventing and intervening with bullying in schools: A framework for evidence-based practice. *School Mental Health 11*, 15–28 (2019). https://doi.org/10.1007/s12310-017-9221-8

Nohelty K., Burns C. & Dixon D. (2021). A brief history of Functional Analysis: An update. In Matson J.L. (eds.) *Functional Assessment for challenging behaviors and mental health disorders. Autism and Child Psychopathology Series.* Springer. https://doi.org/10.1007/978-3-030-66270-7_2

Preston, A. I., Wood, C. L., & Stecker, P. M. (2016). Response to Intervention: Where it came from and where it's going. *Preventing School Failure, 60*(3), 173–182. https://doi.org/10.1080/1045988X.2015.1065399

Ratner, H., George, E., & Iveson, C. (2012). *Solution Focused Brief Therapy: 100 key points and techniques.* Routledge.

Rawson. S. (2020). *Applying trauma-sensitive practices in school counselling: Interventions for achieving change.* Routledge.

Singer, J.B., Erbacher, T.A. & Rosen, P. (2019) School-based suicide prevention: A framework for evidence-based practice. *School Mental Health 11*, 54–71. https://doi.org/10.1007/s12310-018-9245-8

Sugai, G. & Horner, R. R. (2006). A promising approach for expanding and sustaining School-Wide Positive Behavior Support. *School Psychology Review, 35*(2), 245–259. https://doi.org/10.1080/02796015.2006.12087989

Sugai, G. Horner, R. H., Dunlap, G., Hieneman, M., Lewis, T. J., Nelson, C. M., Scott, T., Liaupsin, C., Sailor, W., Turnbull, A. P., Turnbull, H. R., Wickham, D., Wilcox, B., & Ruef, M. (2000). Applying Positive Behavior Support and Functional Behavioral Assessment in schools. *Journal of Positive Behavior Interventions, 2*(3), 131–143. https://doi.org/10.1177/109830070000200302

Thomeer, M. L., McDonald, C. A., Rodgers, J. D., & Lopata, C. (2017). High-Functioning Autism Spectrum Disorder: A Framework for Evidence-Based Practice. *School Mental Health, 11*(1), 29–39. https://doi.org/10.1007/s12310-017-9236-1

Walker. (2018). *Learning Theory and Behaviour Modification.* Routledge.

Chapter 5

Bannink, F. (2015). *Solution-focused questions for help with trauma.* W.W. Norton and Co.

Berg, I. K. & Steiner, T. (2003). *Children's solution work.* Norton.

Brelsford, V. L., Meints, K., Gee, N. R., & Pfeffer, K. (2017). Animal-Assisted Interventions in the Classroom-A Systematic Review. *International Journal of Environmental Research and Public Health, 14*(7), 669–. https://doi.org/10.3390/ijerph14070669

Broderick, P. C. (2019). Mindfulness in the secondary classroom: *A guide for teaching adolescents.* W. W. Norton and Co.

Cozolino, L. (2013) T*he Social neuroscience of education: Optimising attachment and learning in the classroom.* W.W. Norton and Co.

Dimolareva, M., & Dunn, T. J. (2020). Animal-Assisted Interventions for School-Aged Children with Autism Spectrum Disorder: A Meta-Analysis. *Journal of Autism and Developmental Disorders, 51*(7), 2436–2449. https://doi.org/10.1007/s10803-020-04715-w

Dravsnik, J., Signal, T., & Canoy, D. (2018). Canine co-therapy: The potential of dogs to improve the acceptability of trauma-focused therapies for children. *Australian Journal of Psychology, 70*(3), 208–216. https://doi.org/10.1111/ajpy.12199

Farb, N., Segal, Z., Mayberg, H., Bean, J., McKeon, D., Fatima, Z., & Anderson, A. (2007). Attending to the present: Mindfulness meditation reveals distinct neural modes of self-reference. *Social Cognitive and Affective Neuroscience, 2*(4), 313–322. https://doi.org/10.1093/scan/nsm030

Gee, N. R., Rodriguez, K. E., Fine, A. H., & Trammell, J. P. (2021). Dogs Supporting Human Health and wellbeing: A Biopsychosocial Approach. *Frontiers in Veterinary Science, 8*, 630465–630465. https://doi.org/10.3389/fvets.2021.630465

Hawkins, R. D., Robinson, C., & Brodie, Z. P. (2022). Child-dog attachment, emotion regulation and psychopathology: The mediating role of positive and negative behaviours. *Behavioral Sciences, 12*(4), 109–. https://doi.org/10.3390/bs12040109

Hediger, K., Wagner, J., Künzi, P., Haefeli, A., Theis, F., Grob, C., Pauli, E., & Gerger, H. (2021). Effectiveness of animal-assisted interventions for children and adults with post-traumatic stress disorder symptoms: A systematic review and meta-analysis. *European Journal of*

Psychotraumatology, 12(1), 1879713–1879713. https://doi.org/10.1080/20008198.2021.1879713

Hoagwood, K. E., Acri, M., Morrissey, M., & Peth-Pierce, R. (2017). Animal-assisted therapies for youth with or at risk for mental health problems: A systematic review. *Applied Developmental Science, 21*(1), 1–13. https://doi.org/10.1080/10888691.2015.1134267

Jenkins, & Tedeschi, P. (Eds) (2019). *Transforming Trauma Resilience and Healing Through Our Connections with Animals.* Purdue University Press.

Jennings, P. A. (2015). *Mindfulness for teachers: Simple skills for peace and productivity in the classroom.* W. W. Norton and Co.

Joss, D., Khan, A., Lazar, S. W., & Teicher, M. H. (2019). Effects of a mindfulness-based intervention on self-compassion and psychological health among young adults with a history of childhood maltreatment. *Frontiers in Psychology, 10*, 2373–2373. https://doi.org/10.3389/fpsyg.2019.02373

Joss, D., Khan, A., Lazar, S. W., & Teicher, M. H. (2021). A pilot study on amygdala volumetric changes among young adults with childhood maltreatment histories after a mindfulness intervention. *Behavioural Brain Research, 399*, 113023–113023. https://doi.org/10.1016/j.bbr.2020.113023

Joss, D., Lazar, S. W., & Teicher, M. H. (2020). Effects of a mindfulness based behavioral intervention for young adults with childhood maltreatment history on hippocampal morphometry: A pilot MRI study with voxel-based morphometry. Psychiatry Research. *Neuroimaging, 301*, 111087–111087. https://doi.org/10.1016/j.pscychresns.2020.111087

Joss, D., & Teicher, M. H. (2021). Clinical effects of mindfulness-based interventions for adults with a history of childhood maltreatment: A scoping review. *Current Treatment Options in Psychiatry, 8*(2), 31–46. https://doi.org/10.1007/s40501-021-00240-4

Karl, S., Boch, M., Zamansky, A., van der Linden, D., Wagner, I. C., Voelter, C. J., Lamm, C., & Huber, L. (2020). Exploring the dog-human relationship by combining fMRI, eye-tracking and behavioural measures. *Scientific Reports, 10*(1), 22273–22273. https://doi.org/10.1038/s41598-020-79247-5

Kivlen, C. A., Quevillon, A., & Pasquarelli, D. (2022). Should Dogs Have a Seat in the Classroom? The Effects of Canine Assisted Education on College Student Mental Health. *The Open Journal of Occupational Therapy, 10*(1), COV11–14. https://doi.org/10.15453/2168-6408.1816

Kral, T.R.A., Schuyler, B. S., Mumford, J. A., Rosenkranz, M. A., Lutz, A., & Davidson, R. J. (2018). Impact of short- and long-term mindfulness meditation training on amygdala reactivity to emotional stimuli. *NeuroImage, 181,* 301–313. https://doi.org/10.1016/j.neuroimage.2018.07.013

Kropp, J. J. & Shupp, M. M. (2017). Review of the Research: Are Therapy Dogs in Classrooms Beneficial? *Forum on Public Policy, 2017*(2).

Milner, J. & Bateman, J. (2011). *Working with children and teenagers using solution focused approaches: Enabling children to overcome challenges and achieve their potential.* Jessica Kingsley Publishers.

Mims, D. & Waddell, R. (2016). Animal Assisted Therapy and Trauma Survivors. *Journal of Evidence-Informed Social Work, 13*(5), 452–457. https://doi.org/10.1080/23761407.2016.1166841

Muela, A., Balluerka, N., Amiano, N., Caldentey, M. A., & Aliri, J. (2017). Animal-assisted psychotherapy for young people with behavioural problems in residential care. *Clinical Psychology and Psychotherapy, 24*(6), O1485–O1494. https://doi.org/10.1002/cpp.2112

Murakami, H., Nakao, T., Matsunaga, M., Kasuya, Y., Shinoda, J., Yamada, J., & Ohira, H. (2012). The structure of mindful brain. *PloS One, 7*(9), e46377–e46377.

Rush, K. S., Golden, M. E., Mortenson, B. P., Albohn, D., & Horger, M. (2017). The effects of a mindfulness and biofeedback program on the on-and off-task behaviors of students with emotional behavioral disorders. *Contemporary School Psychology, 21*(4), 347–357. https://doi.org/10.1007/s40688-017-0140-3

Seigel, D. J. (2007). *The mindful brain: Reflection and attunement in the cultivation of wellbeing.* W. W. Norton and Co.

Sempowicz, T., Howard, J., Tambyah, M., & Carrington, S. (2018). Identifying obstacles and opportunities for inclusion in the school curriculum for children adopted from overseas: developmental and social constructionist perspectives. *International Journal of Inclusive Education, 22*(6), 606–621. https://doi.org/10.1080/13603116.2017.1390004

Signal, T., Taylor, N., Prentice, K., McDade, M., & Burke, K. J. (2017). Going to the dogs: A quasi-experimental assessment of animal assisted therapy for children who have experienced abuse. *Applied Developmental Science, 21*(2), 81–93. https://doi.org/10.1080/10888691.2016.1165098

Thompkins, A., Lazarowski, L., Ramaiahgari, B., Gotoor, S. S. R., Waggoner, P., Denney, T. S., Deshpande, G., & Katz, J. S. (2021). Dog–human social relationship: representation of human face familiarity and emotions in the dog brain. *Animal Cognition, 24*(2), 251–266. https://doi.org/10.1007/s10071-021-01475-7

Vibe, M., Bjørndal, A., Fattah, S., Dyrdal, G., Halland, E., & Tanner-Smith, E. (2017). Mindfulness-based stress reduction (MBSR) for improving health, quality of life and social functioning in adults: A systematic review and meta-analysis. *Campbell Systematic Reviews, 13*(1), 1–264. https://doi.org/10.4073/csr.2017.11

Villafaina-Dominguez, B., Collado-Mateo, D., Merellano-Navarro, E., & Villafaina, S. (2020). Effects of Dog-Based Animal-Assisted Interventions in Prison Population: A Systematic Review. *Animals (Basel), 10*(11), 2129–. https://doi.org/10.3390/ani10112129

Weishaar. (1992). *Aaron T. Beck.* Sage Publications.

Wills. F. (2021). *Beck's Cognitive Therapy: Distinctive features (2nd edn.).* Routledge. https://doi.org/10.4324/9781003055792

Willis, J., (2006). *Research based strategies to ignite student learning: Insights from a neurologist and classroom teacher.* ASCD.

Willis, J., (2007). *Brain-friendly strategies for the inclusion classroom.* ASCD.

Willis, J., (2009). *How your child learns best: Brain-friendly strategies you can use to ignite your child's learning and increase school success.* Sourcebooks, Inc.

Yeigh, T. (2020). *Managing with mindfulness: Connecting with students in the 21st century.* Cambridge University Press.

Chapter 6

Administration on Children, Youth and Families (2013). *Child maltreatment 2012.* Retrieved from http://www.acf.hhs.gov/programs/cb/resource/child-maltreatment-2012

Afifi., T.O. (2018). Continuing conversations: Debates about adverse childhood experiences (ACEs) screening. *Child Abuse & Neglect, 85,* 172–173. https://doi.org/10.1016/j.chiabu.2018.06.012

Alisic, E., Zalta, A. K., Van Wesel, F., Larsen, S. E., Hafstad, G. S., Hassanpour, K., & Smid, G. E. (2014). Rates of post-traumatic stress disorder in trauma-exposed children and adolescents: Metaanalysis. *British Journal of Psychiatry, 204,* 335–340.

American Psychiatric Association. (2013). *Diagnostic and statistical manual of mental disorders* (5th ed.). Author.

American Psychological Association. (2016). *Resolution on the maltreatment of children with disabilities.* http://www.apa.org/about/policy/maltreatment-children.aspx. https://www.cdc.gov/ncbddd/developmentaldisabilities/facts.html

Baidawi, S. & Piquero, A. R. (2020). Neurodisability among children at the nexus of the child welfare and youth justice system. *Journal of Youth and Adolescence, 50*(4), 803–819. https://doi.org/10.1007/s10964-020-01234-w

Baweja, S. Santiago, C. D., Vona, P., Pears, G., Langley, A., & Kataoka, S. (2016). Improving implementation of a school-based program for traumatized students: Identifying factors that promote teacher support and collaboration. *School Mental Health, 8,* 120–131.

Benson, P. R., & Karlof, K. L. (2009). Anger, stress proliferation, and depressed mood among caregivers of children with ASD: A longitudinal replication. *Journal of Autism and Developmental Disorders, 39,* 350–362.

Berger, E., D'Souza, L., & Miko, A. (2021). School-based interventions for childhood trauma and autism spectrum disorder: a narrative review. *The Educational and Developmental Psychologist, 38*(2), 186–193. https://doi.org/10.1080/20590776.2021.1986355

Blake, J. J., Kim, E. S., Lund, E. M., Zhou, Q., Kwok, O., & Benz, M. R. (2014). Predictors of bully victimization in students with disabilities: A longitudinal examination using a national data set. *Journal of Disability Policy Studies, 26*(4), 199-208. doi: 10.1177/1044207314539012

Blodgett, C. (2012). *Adopting ACEs screening and assessment in child serving systems.* Working Paper. WSU Area Health Education Center.

Bruhn, A. L., Woods-Groves, S., & Huddle, S. (2014). A preliminary investigation of emotional and behavioral screening practices in K-12 schools. *Education and Treatment of Children, 37*, 12 611–634.

Centre of Research Excellence in Disability and Health. (2021). *Nature and extent of violence, abuse, neglect and exploitation against people with disability in Australia.* Author.

Chafouleas, S. M., Kilgus, S. P., & Wallach, N. (2010). Ethical dilemmas in school-based behavioral screening. *Assessment for Effective Intervention, 35*, 245–252.

Crandall, Magnusson, B. M., Hanson, C. L., & Leavitt, B. (2021). The effects of adverse and advantageous childhood experiences on adult health in a low-income sample. *Acta Psychologica, 220*, 103430–103430. https://doi.org/10.1016/j.actpsy.2021.103430

D'Andrea, W., Ford, J., Stobach, B., Spinazolla, J., & van der Kolk, B. A. (2012). Understanding interpersonal trauma in children: Why we need a developmentally appropriate trauma diagnosis. *American Journal of Orthopsychiatry, 82*, 187–200.

Dion, J., Paquette, G., Tremblay, K. N., Collin-Vézina, D., & Chabot, M. (2018). Child maltreatment among children with intellectual disability in the Canadian incidence study. *American Journal on Intellectual and Developmental Disabilities, 123*(2), 176–188. https://doi.org/10.1352/1944-7558-123.2.176

Disability Discrimination Act 1992 (Australia).

Dodds, R. L. (2020). An exploratory review of the associations between adverse experiences and autism. *Journal of Aggression, Maltreatment & Trauma*, 1–20. https://doi.org/ 10.1080/10926771.2020.1783736

Dube. S. R. (2018). Continuing conversations about adverse childhood experiences (ACEs) screening: A public health perspective. *Child Abuse & Neglect, 85*, 180–184. https://doi.org/10.1016/j.chiabu.2018.03.007

Dubowitz, H., Roesch, S., Arria, A. M., Metzger, R., Thompson, R., Kotch, J. B., & Lewis, T. (2019). Timing and chronicity of child neglect and substance use in early adulthood. *Child Abuse & Neglect, 94*, 104027–104027. https://doi.org/10.1016/j.chiabu.2019.104027

Earl, R. K., Peterson, J., Wallace, A. S., Fox, E., Ma, R., Pepper, M., & Haidar, G. (2017). *Trauma and autism disorder: A reference guide.* Bernier Lab, Centre for Human Development and Disability, University of Washington. https://tfcbt.org/wpcontent/uploads/2019/05/Bernier-Lab-UW-Trauma-andASD-Reference-Guide-2017.pdf

Eklund K. & Dowdy, E. (2014). Screening for behavioral and emotional risk versus traditional school identification methods. *School Mental Health, 6,* 40–49.

Eklund, K. & Rossen, E. (2016). Guidance for trauma screening in schools: *A product of the defending childhood state policy initiative.* The National Center for Mental Health and Juvenile Justice.

Eklund, K. R., Rossen, E., Koriakin, T., Chafouleas, S. M., & Resnick, C. (2018). A systematic review of trauma screening measures for children and adolescents. *School Psychology Quarterly, 33*(1), 30–43. https://doi.org/10.1037/spq0000244

Felitti, V. J., Anda, R. F., Nordenberg, D., Williamson, D. F., Spitz, A. M., Edwards, V., Koss, M. P., & Marks, J. S. (1998). Relationship of Childhood Abuse and Household Dysfunction to Many of the Leading Causes of Death in Adults: The Adverse Childhood Experiences (ACE) Study. *American Journal of Preventive Medicine, 14*(4), 245–258. https://doi.org/10.1016/S0749-3797(98)00017-8

Ford, J. D., Spinazzola, J., Kolk, B., & Chan, G. (2022). Toward an empirically based Developmental Trauma Disorder diagnosis and semi-structured interview for children: The DTD field trial replication. *Acta Psychiatrica Scandinavica, 145*(6), 628–639. https://doi.org/10.1111/acps.13424

Ford, K., Hughes, K., Hardcastle, K., Di Lemma, L. C., Davies, A. R., Edwards, S., & Bellis, M. A. (2019). The evidence base for routine enquiry into adverse childhood experiences: A scoping review. *Child Abuse & Neglect, 91,* 131–146. https://doi.org/10.1016/j.chiabu.2019.03.007

Forness, S. R., Freeman, S. F., N. Paparella, T., Kauffman, J. M., & Walker, H. M. (2012). Special education implications of point and cumulative prevalence for children with emotional or behavioral disorders. *Journal of Emotional and Behavioral Disorders, 20,* 4–18.

Frederick, Devaney, J., & Alisic, E. (2019). Homicides and maltreatment-related deaths of disabled children: A systematic review. *Child Abuse Review, 28*(5), 321–338. https://doi.org/10.1002/car.2574

Glover, T. A., & Albers, C. A. (2007). Considerations for evaluating universal assessments. *Journal of School Psychology, 45,* 117–135. doi: 10.1016/j.jsp.2006.05.005

Goldson. E. (2001). Maltreatment among children with disabilities. *Infants and Young Children, 13*(4), 44–54. https://doi.org/10.1097/00001163-200113040-00010

Gonzalez, A., Monzon, N., Solis, D., Jaycox, L., & Langley, A. K., (2016). Trauma exposure in elementary school children: Description of screening procedures, level of exposure, and stress symptoms. *School Mental Health, 8*, 77–88.

Hartley, M. T., Bauman, S., Nixon, C. L., & Davis, S. (2015). Comparative study of bullying victimization among students in general and special education. *Exceptional Children, 81*, 176–193.

Hibbard, R. A. & Desch, L. W. (2007). Maltreatment of children with disabilities. *Pediatrics, 119*(5), 1018–1025. https://doi.org/10.1542/peds.2007-0565

Heinonen, A., & Ellonen, N. (2013). Are children with disabilities and long-term illnesses at increased risk of disciplinary violence? *Journal of Scandinavian Studies in Criminology and Crime Prevention, 14*, 172–187.

Heller, T., & Ganguly, R. (2002). *Grandcaregivers raising grandchildren with developmental disabilities*. Washington, DC: Administration on Aging.

Helton, J. J. & Cross, T. P. (2011). The relationship of child functioning to parental physical assault: Linear and curvilinear models. *Child Maltreatment, 16*, 126–136.

Hershkowitz, I., Lamb, M. E., & Horowitz, D. (2007). Victimization of children with disabilities. *American Journal of Orthopsychiatry, 77*(4), 629–635. https://doi.org/10.1037/0002-9432.77.4.629.

Holden, G. W., Gower, T. & Chmielewski, M. (2020). Methodological considerations in ACEs research. In Asmundson, G. J. G. & Afifi, T. O. (Eds.), *Adverse Childhood Experiences: Using evidence to advance research, practice, policy, and prevention* (pp. 161–182). Academic Press.

Hoover, D. W. (2015). The effects of psychological trauma on children with autism spectrum disorders: A research review. *Journal of Autism and Developmental Disorders, 2*(3), 287–299. https://doi.org/10.1007/s40489-015-0052-y

Hughes, N. (2015). Understanding the influence of neurodevelopmental disorders on offending: Utilizing developmental psychopathology in biosocial criminology. Criminal Justice Studies, 28(1), 39-60. https://doi.org/10.1080/1478601X.2014.1000004

Hughes, N., & O'Byrne, K. P. (2016). Disabled inside: Neurodevelopmental impairments among young people in custody. *Prison Service Journal, 226*, 14–21.

Hughes, N., Williams, H., Chitsabesan, P., Davies, R., & Mounce, L. (2012). *Nobody made the connection: The prevalence of neurodisability in young people who offend*. London: Office of the Children's Commissioner.

Hurren, E., Stewart, A., & Dennison, S. (2017). Transitions and turning points revisited: A replication to explore child maltreatment and youth offending links within and across Australian cohorts. *Child Abuse & Neglect, 65,* 24–36.

Jackson, A. L., Waters, S., & Abell, T. (2015). *Taking Time — A Literature Review: Background for a trauma-informed framework for supporting people with intellectual disability.* Melbourne, Australia: Berry Street.

Jaudes, P. K., & Mackey-Bilaver, L. (2008). Do chronic conditions increase young children's risk of being maltreated? *Child Abuse & Neglect, 32,* 671–681.

Jones, C., Stalker, K., Franklin, A., Fry, D., Cameron, A., & Taylor, J. (2017). Enablers of help-seeking for deaf and disabled children following abuse and barriers to protection: A qualitative study. *Child & Family Social Work, 22*(2), 762–771. https://doi.org/10.1111/cfs.12293

Jones, L., Bellis, M. A., Wood, S., Hughes, K., McCoy, E., & Eckley, L., et al. (2012). Prevalence and risk of violence against children with disabilities: A systematic review and meta-analysis of observational studies. *Lancet, 380,* 899–907.

Karni-Visel, Y., Hershkowitz, I., Hershkowitz, F., Flaisher, M., & Schertz, M. (2020). Increased risk for child maltreatment in those with developmental disability: A primary health care perspective from Israel. *Research in Developmental Disabilities, 106,* 103763–103763. https://doi.org/10.1016/j.ridd.2020.103763

Keesler. J. M. (2014). A call for the integration of trauma-informed care among intellectual and developmental disability organizations. *Journal of Policy and Practice in Intellectual Disabilities, 11*(1), 34–42. https://doi.org/10.1111/jppi.12071

Kendall-Tackett, K., Lyon, T., Taliaferro, G., & Little, L. (2005). Why child maltreatment researchers should include children's disability status in their maltreatment studies. *Child Abuse & Neglect, 29,* 147–151.

Kerns, C. M., Newschaffer, C. J., & Berkowitz, S. J. (2015). Traumatic childhood events and autism spectrum disorder. *Journal of Autism and Developmental Disorders, 45*(11), 3475–3486. https://doi.org/10.1007/s10803-015-2392-y

Leeb, R. T., Bitsko, R. H., Merrick, M. T., & Armour, B. S. (2012). Does childhood disability increase risk for child abuse and neglect? *Journal of Mental Health Research in Intellectual Disabilities, 5,* 4–31.

Lightfoot, E. B., & LaLiberte, T. L. (2006). Approaches to child protection case management for cases involving people with disabilities. *Child Abuse & Neglect, 30,* 381–391.

Lightfoot, E., Hill, K., & LaLiberte, T. (2011). Prevalence of children with disabilities in the child welfare system and out of home placement: An examination of administrative records. *Children and Youth Services Review, 33*(11), 2069–2075.

Maclean, M. J., Sims, S., Bower, C., Leonard, H., Stanley, F. J., & O'Donnell, M. (2017). Maltreatment risk among children with disabilities. *Pediatrics (Evanston), 139*(4).

Manders, J. E., & Stoneman, Z. (2009). Children with disabilities in the child protective services system: An analogue study of investigation and case management. *Child Abuse & Neglect, 33*, 229–237.

McCallion, P., & Janicki, M. (2000). *Grandcaregivers as caregivers of children with disabilities: Facing the challenges.* Taylor & Francis.

McDonnell, C. G., Boan, A. D., Bradley, C. C., Seay, K. D., Charles, J. M., & Carpenter, L. A. (2019). Child maltreatment in autism spectrum disorder and intellectual disability: Results from a population-based sample. *Journal of Child Psychology and Psychiatry, 60*(5), 576–584. https://doi.org/10.1111/jcpp.12993

McLennan, J. D., McTavish, J. R. & Harriet L. MacMillan, H. L. (2020) Routine screening of ACEs: Should we or shouldn't we?. In Asmundson, G. J. G., & Afifi, T. O. (Ed.), *Adverse childhood experiences: Using evidence to advance research, practice, policy, and prevention* (pp. 145–159). Academic Press

McNally, P., Taggart, L., & Shevlin, M. (2021). Trauma experiences of people with an intellectual disability and their implications: A scoping review. *Journal of Applied Research in Intellectual Disabilities, 34*(4), 927–949. https://doi.org/10.1111/jar.12872

Mersky, J. P., Berger, L. M., Reynolds, A. J., & Gromoske, A. N. (2009). Risk factors for child and adolescent maltreatment. *Child Maltreatment, 14*, 73–88.

Murphy, N. (2011). Maltreatment of children with disabilities: The breaking point. *Journal of Child Neurology, 26*, 1054-1056.

National Child Traumatic Stress Network. https://www.nctsn.org/

National Child Traumatic Stress Network. (n.d.). *Standardized measures to assess complex trauma.* Retrieved from http://www.nctsnet.org/trauma-types/complex-trauma/standardizedmeasures-assess-complex-trauma

Neece, C. L. Shulamite, A. G., & Baker, B. L. (2012). Caregiving stress and child behavior problems: A transactional relationship across time. *American Journal on Intellectual and Developmental Disabilities, 117*, 48–68.

Nelson, C. A., Bhutta, Z. A., Burke Harris, N., Danese, A., & Samara, M. (2020). Adversity in childhood is linked to mental and physical health throughout life. *BMJ, 371*, m3048–m3048. https://doi.org/10.1136/bmj.m3048

Oh, D. L., Jerman, P., Silvério Marques, S., Koita, K., Purewal Boparai, S. K., Burke Harris, N., & Bucci, M. (2018). Systematic review of pediatric health outcomes associated with childhood adversity. *BMC Pediatrics, 18*(1), 83–19. https://doi.org/10.1186/s12887-018-1037-7

O'Leary, C., Leonard, H., Bourke, J., D'antoine, H., Bartu, A., & Bower, C. (2013). Intellectual disability: Population-based estimates of the proportion attributable to maternal alcohol use disorder during pregnancy. *Developmental Medicine and Child Neurology, 55*(3), 271–277.

Raja, Rabinowitz, E. P., & Gray, M. J. (2021). Universal screening and trauma informed care: Current concerns and future directions. Families Systems & Health, 39(3), 526–534. https://doi.org/10.1037/fsh0000585

Resch, J. A., Elliott, T. R., & Benz, M. R. (2012). Depression among caregivers of children with disabilities. *Families, Systems, & Health, 30*, 291–301.

Robinson, S. (2012). *Enabling and protecting: Proactive approaches to addressing the abuse and neglect of children and young people with a disability*. Children with Disability Australia.

Rose, C. A., Monda-Amaya, L. E., & Espelage, D. L. (2011). Bullying perpetration and victimization in special education: A review of the literature. *Remedial and Special Education, 32*, 114–130.

Rossen, E., & Cowan, K. C. (2013). The role of schools in supporting traumatized students. Principal's Research Review, 8(6), 1–7.

Schmid, M., Petermann, F., & Fegert, J.M. (2013). Developmental trauma disorder: Pros and cons of including formal criteria in the psychiatric diagnostic systems. *BMC Psychiatry, 13*, 3–3.

Seppälä, P., Vornanen, R., & Toikko, T. (2021). Multimorbidity and polyvictimization in children — An analysis on the association of children's disabilities and long-term illnesses with mental violence and physical violence. *Child Abuse & Neglect, 122*, 105350–105350. https://doi.org/10.1016/j.chiabu.2021.105350

Shannon, P., & Tappan, C. (2011). A qualitative analysis of child protective service practice with children with developmental disabilities. *Children and Youth Services Review, 33*, 1469–1475.

Shemesh, E., Newcorn, J. H., Rockmore, L., Shneider, B. L., Emre, S., Gelb, B. D., & Yehuda, R. (2005). Comparison of caregiver and child reports of emotional trauma symptoms in pediatric outpatient settings. *Pediatrics, 115*, e582–e589. doi:10.1542/peds.2004-2201

Spencer, N., Devereux, E. Wallace, A., Sundrum, R., Shenoy, M., Bacchus, C., & Logan, S. (2005). Disabling conditions and registration for child abuse and neglect: A population-based study. *Pediatrics, 116*, 609–613.

Stalker, K., & McArthur, K. (2012). Child abuse, child protection and disabled children: A review of recent research. *Child Abuse Review, 21*, 24–40.

Stover, C. S., Hahn, H., Im, J. J. Y., & Berkowitz, S. (2010). Agreement of caregiver and child reports of trauma exposure and symptoms in the early aftermath of a traumatic event. *Psychological Trauma: Theory, Research, Practice, and Policy, 2*, 159–168. doi:10.1037/a0019156

Sullivan, P. M., & Knutson, J. F. (2000). Maltreatment and disabilities: A population-based epidemiological study. *Child Abuse & Neglect, 24*(10), 1257–1273. https://doi.org/10.1016/S0145-2134(00)00190-3

Taylor, J. L., & Gotham, K. O. (2016). Cumulative life events, traumatic experiences, and psychiatric symptomatology in transition-aged youth with autism spectrum disorder. *Journal of Neurodevelopmental Disorders, 8*(1), 28–38. https://doi.org/10.1186/s11689-016-9160-y

Trauma and Intellectual/Developmental Disability Collaborative Group. (2020). *The impact of trauma on youth with intellectual and developmental disabilities: A fact sheet for providers.* National Center for Child Traumatic Stress.

Turner, H. A., Finkelhor, D., Mitchell, K. J., Jones, L. M., & Henly, M. (2020). Strengthening the predictive power of screening for adverse childhood experiences (ACEs) in younger and older children. *Child Abuse & Neglect, 107*, 104522–. https://doi.org/10.1016/j.chiabu.2020.104522

Turner, H. A., Vanderminden, J., Finkelhor, D., Hamby, S., & Shattuck, A. (2011). Disability and victimization in a national sample of children and youth. *Child Maltreatment, 16*, 275–286.

U.S. Department of Health and Human Services, Children's Bureau Child Welfare Information Gateway. (2012). *The risk and prevention of maltreatment of children with disabilities.* Retrieved from https://www.childwelfare.gov/pubs/prevenres/focus

van den Heuvel, L. L. & Seedat, S. (2013). Screening and diagnostic considerations in childhood post-traumatic stress disorder. *Neuropsychiatry, 3*(5), 497–511. https://doi.org/10.2217/npy.13.61

van der Kolk, B.A. Pynoos, R.S. Cicchetti, D. Cloitre, M. D'Andrea, W. Ford, J.D. & Teicher, M. (2009). Proposal to include a developmental trauma disorder diagnosis for children and adolescents in DSM-V: Official submission from the national child traumatic stress network developmental trauma disorder taskforce to the American Psychiatric Association. available at: www. cathymalchiodi.com/dtd_nctsn.p (accessed 20 April 2019).

Victorian Ombudsman. (2010). *Own motion investigation into child protection — out of home care*. http://www.forgottenaustralians.com/pdf/Own_motion.pdf

Westcott, H. L., & Jones, D. P. H. (1999). Annotation: The abuse of disabled children. *Journal of Child Psychology and Psychiatry, 40*, 497–506.

Woodbridge, M. W., Sumi, W. C., Thornton, S. P., Fabrikant, N., Rouspil, K. M., Langley, A. K., & Kataoka, S. H. (2015). Screening for trauma in early adolescence: Findings from a diverse school district. *School Mental Health, 8*(1), 89–105. https://doi.org/10.1007/s12310-015-9169-5

Ziviani, J., Darlington, Y., Feeney, R., Meredith, P., & Head, B. (2013). Children with disabilities in out of-home care: Perspectives on organizational collaborations. *Children and Youth Services Review, 35*, 797–805.

Chapter 7

Arden, J. B. (2019). *Mind-Brain-Gene: Toward psychotherapy integration.* WW Norton and Co.

Asmussen, K., McBride, T., & Waddell, S. (2019). The potential of early intervention for preventing and reducing ACE-related trauma. *Social Policy and Society: Journal of the Social Policy Association, 18*(3), 425–434. https://doi.org/10.1017/S1474746419000071

Australian Institute of Health and Welfare (2021). *Child protection Australia 2019-20.* Child welfare series no. 74. Cat. no. CWS 78. Canberra: AIHW

Bartlett, J. D. & Smith, S. (2019). The role of early care and education in addressing early childhood trauma. *American Journal of Community Psychology, 64*(3–4), 359–372. https://doi.org/10.1002/ajcp.12380

Brandt, K., Perry, B. D., Seligman, S., Tronick, E., & Brazelton, T. B. (2014). *Infant and early childhood mental health: Core concepts and clinical practice.* American Psychiatric Publishing.

Chu, A. T. & Lieberman, A. F. (2010). Clinical implications of traumatic stress from birth to age five. *Annual Review of Clinical Psychology, 6*(1), 469–494. https://doi.org/10.1146/annurev.clinpsy.121208.131204

Cozolino, L. (2013) *The social neuroscience of education: Optimizing attachment and learning in the classroom.* W.W. Norton and Co.

Davidson, B. C., Davis, E., Cadenas, H., Barnett, M., Sanchez, B. E. L., Gonzalez, J. C., & Jent, J. (2021). Universal teacher-child interaction training in early special education: A pilot cluster-randomized control trial. *Behavior Therapy, 52*(2), 379–393. https://doi.org/10.1016/j.beth.2020.04.014

De Bellis, M. D. & Zisk, A. (2014). The biological effects of childhood trauma. *Child and Adolescent Psychiatric Clinics of North America, 23*(2), 185–222. https://doi.org/10.1016/j.chc.2014.01.002

Dolby, R. (2017). *The circle of security: Roadmap to building supportive relationships.* Early Childhood Australia Inc.

Forsman, H. & Jackisch, J. (2021). Cumulative childhood adversity and long-term educational outcomes in individuals with out-of-home care experience: Do multiples matter for a population defined by adversity? *The British Journal of Social Work.* https://doi.org/10.1093/bjsw/bcab194

Gil, E. & Terr, L. C. (2010). *Working with children to heal interpersonal trauma: The power of play.* Guilford Press.

Harvard Centre on the Developing Child. *5 Steps for brain-building: Serve and Return.* https://developingchild.harvard.edu/resources/how-to-5-steps-for-brain-building-serve-and-return/

Howard, J. (2020). *Trauma-aware early childhood education and care.* Early Childhood Australia.

Hughes, D. A., & Baylin, J. (2012). *Brain-based parenting: The neuroscience of caregiving for healthy attachment.* W. W. Norton & Company.

Jimenez, M., Wade, R., Lin, Y., Morrow, L., & Reichman, N. (2016). Adverse experiences in early childhood and kindergarten outcomes. *Pediatrics, 137*(2). https://doi.org/10.1542/peds.2015-1839

Kanine, R. M., Jackson, Y., Huffhines, L., Barnett, A., & Stone, K. J. (2018). A pilot study of universal teacher–child interaction training at a therapeutic preschool for young, maltreated children. *Topics in Early Childhood Special Education, 38*(3), 146–161. https://doi.org/10.1177/0271121418790012

Loomis. A. M. (2018). The role of preschool as a point of intervention and prevention for trauma-exposed children: Recommendations for practice, policy, and research. *Topics in Early Childhood Special Education, 38*(3), 134–145. https://doi.org/10.1177/0271121418789254

Loomis, A. M. & Felt, F. (2020). Knowledge, skills, and self-reflection: Linking trauma training content to trauma-informed attitudes and stress in preschool teachers and staff. *School Mental Health, 13*(1), 101–113. https://doi.org/10.1007/s12310-020-09394-7

National Scientific Council on the Developing Child. (2004). *Young children develop in an environment of relationships.* Working Paper No. 1. Retrieved from http://www.developingchild.net.

Neitzel. J. (2020). Addressing Trauma in Early Childhood Classrooms: Strategies and Practices for Success. *Young Exceptional Children, 23*(3), 157–168. https://doi.org/10.1177/1096250619850137

Porges, S. W., & Furman, S. A. (2011). The early development of the autonomic nervous system provides a neural platform for social behaviour: A polyvagal perspective. *Infant and Child Development, 20*(1), 106–118.

Powell, B., Cooper, G., Hoffman, K., & Marvin, B. (2014). *The Circle of Security intervention: Enhancing attachment in early parent-child relationships.* Guilford Press.

Praszkier, R. (2016). Empathy, mirror neurons and SYNC. *Mind & Society, 15*, 1–25.

Ryan, K., Lane, S. J., & Powers, D. (2017). A multidisciplinary model for treating complex trauma in early childhood. *International Journal of Play Therapy, 26*(2), 111–123. https://doi.org/10.1037/pla0000044

Statman-Weil., K. (2015). Creating trauma-sensitive classrooms. *Young Children, 70*(2), 72–79.

Twardosz, S., & Lutzker, J. R. (2010). Child maltreatment and the developing brain: A review of neuroscience perspectives. *Aggression and Violent Behavior, 15*(1), 59–68.

Whitters, H. G. (2020). *Adverse childhood experiences, attachment, and the early years learning environment: Research and inclusive practice*. Routledge.

Yogman, M., Garner, A., Hutchinson, J., Hirsh-Pasek, K., Golinkoff, R. M., Baum, R., Gambon, T., Lavin, A., Mattson, G., & Wissow, L. (2018). The power of play: A pediatric role in enhancing development in young children. *Pediatrics, 142*(3), 1–. https://doi.org/10.1542/peds.2018-2058

Chapter 8

Abraham-Cook. S. (2012). *The prevalence and correlates of compassion fatigue, compassion satisfaction, and burnout among teachers working in high-poverty urban public schools*. ProQuest Dissertations Publishing.

Borntrager, C., Caringi, J. C., van den Pol, R., Crosby, L., O'Connell, K., Trautman, A., et al. (2012). Secondary traumatic stress in school personnel. *Advances in School Mental Health Promotion, 5*(1), 38–50.

Bowlby, J. (1988). *A secure base: Parent-child attachment and healthy human development*. Basic Books.

Brunsting, N., Sreckovic, M. A., & Lane, K. L. (2014). Special Education Teacher Burnout: A Synthesis of Research from 1979 to 2013. *Education & Treatment of Children, 37*(4), 681–711. https://doi.org/10.1353/etc.2014.0032

Caringi, J., Stanick, C., Trautman, A., Crosby, L., Devlin, M., & Adams, S. (2015). Secondary traumatic stress in public school teachers: Contributing and mitigating factors. *Advances in School Mental Health Promotion, 8*(4), 244–256.

Castro Schepers, O. & Young, K. S. (2022). Mitigating secondary traumatic stress in preservice educators: A pilot study on the role of trauma-informed practice seminars. *Psychology in the Schools, 59*(2), 316–333. https://doi.org/10.1002/pits.22610

Christian-Brandt, A., Santacrose, D., & Barnett, M. (2020). In the trauma-informed care trenches: Teacher compassion satisfaction, secondary traumatic stress, burnout, and intent to leave education within underserved elementary schools. *Child Abuse & Neglect, 110*(Pt 3), 104437–104437. https://doi.org/10.1016/j.chiabu.2020.104437

Craig, S. (2015). *Trauma-sensitive schools: Learning communities transforming children's lives K-5*. Teachers College Press.

Craig, S. (2017). *Trauma sensitive schooling for the adolescent years: Promoting resiliency and healing, Grades 6-12*. Teachers College Press.

DuBois, A., & Mistretta, M. (2020). *Overcoming burnout and compassion fatigue in schools: A guide for counselors, administrators, and educators*. Routledge.

Essary, J. N., Barza, L., & Thurston, R. J. (2020). *Secondary traumatic stress among educators*. Kappa Delta Pi Record, 56(3), 116–121. https://doi.org/10.1080/00228958.2020.1770004

Figley, C. R. (2013). *Compassion fatigue: Coping with secondary traumatic stress disorder in those who treat the traumatized*. Routledge.

Fisher, M. (2011). Factors influencing stress, burnout, and retention of secondary teachers. *Current Issues in Education, 14*(1), 1–37.

Gultom, S. Endriani, D., & Harahap, A. S. (2022). Less emotion but more fatigue: Social-Emotional Learning (SEL) competencies, and compassion fatigue among educators during the COVID-19 pandemic. *Kinestetik (Online), 6*(1), 146–158. https://doi.org/10.33369/jk.v6i1.21034

Holland. M.L. (2022). *Burnout and trauma related employment stress: Acceptance and commitment strategies in the helping professions.* Springer.

Hydon, S. P. (2016). *Exploring the prevalence and mitigating variables of secondary traumatic stress in K-12 educators.* ProQuest Dissertations Publishing.

Hupe, T. M. & Stevenson, M. C. (2019). Teachers' intentions to report suspected child abuse: The influence of compassion fatigue. *Journal of Child Custody, 16*(4), 364–386. https://doi.org/10.1080/15379418.2019.1663334

L'Estrange, L. & Howard, J. (2022) Trauma-informed initial teacher education training: A necessary step in a system-wide response to addressing childhood trauma. *Frontiers in Education, 7,* Article number: 929582. https://doi.org/10.3389/feduc.2022.929582

Powell, B., Cooper, G., Hoffman, K., & Marvin, B. (2014). *The Circle of Security intervention: Enhancing attachment in early parent-child relationships.* Guilford Press.

Robert-Bitar. N. (2020). *Compassion fatigue and compassion satisfaction in high poverty schools.* ProQuest Dissertations Publishing.

Rothschild, B. & Rand, M. L. (2006). *Help for the helper: The psychophysiology of compassion fatigue and vicarious trauma (1st ed.).* Norton.

Shaw. S. (2022). *Secondary traumatic stress in rural public school teachers: A qualitative phenomenological study.* ProQuest Dissertations Publishing.

Siegel, D. J. (2012). *The developing mind: How relationships and the brain interact to shape who we are (2nd ed.).* Guilford Press.

Skaalvik, E. M., & Skaalvik, S. (2011). Teacher job satisfaction and motivation to leave the teaching profession: Relations with school context, feeling of belonging, and emotional exhaustion. *Teaching and Teacher Education, 27*(6), 1029–1038.

Skaalvik, E. M., & Skaalvik, S. (2015). Job satisfaction, stress and coping strategies in the teaching profession — What do teachers say? *International Education Studies, 8*(3), 181–192.

Skovholt, T.M. & Trotter-Mathison, M. (2016). *The resilient practitioner: Burnout and compassion fatigue prevention and self-care strategies for the helping professions (3rd ed.).* Routledge.

Sprang, G. & Garcia, A. (2022). An Investigation of secondary traumatic stress and trauma-informed care utilization in school personnel. *Journal of Child & Adolescent Trauma.* https://doi.org/10.1007/s40653-022-00465-2

You, S., & Conley, S. (2015). Workplace predictors of secondary school teachers' intention to leave: An exploration of career stages. *Educational Management Administration & Leadership, 43*(4), 561–581. https://doi.org/10.1177/1741143214535741

Chapter 9

Allison, A. C., & Ferreira, R. J. (2017). Implementing cognitive behavioral intervention for trauma in schools (CBITS) with Latino youth. *Child and Adolescent Social Work Journal*, 34(2), 181–189.

Atkinson, J. (2013). *Trauma-informed services and trauma-specific care for Indigenous Australian children.* Canberra: Closing the Gap Clearinghouse.

Balch, T., & Balch, B. (2019). *Building great school counselor-administrator teams: A systematic approach to supporting students, staff, and the community.* Solution Tree Press.

Berger, E. (2019). Multi-tiered approaches to trauma-informed care in schools: A systematic review. *School Mental Health* 11, 650–664.

Berger, E., Martin, K., & Phal, A. (2020). Dealing with student trauma: Exploring school leadership experiences and impact. *Leadership and Policy in Schools*, 1–11.

Berger, E., & Samuel, S. (2020). A qualitative analysis of the experiences, training, and support needs of school mental health workers regarding student trauma. *Australian Psychologist*, 55(5), 498–507.

Chafouleas, S. M., Johnson, A. H., Overstreet, S., & Santos, N. M. (2016). Toward a blueprint for trauma-informed service delivery in schools. *School Mental Health*, 8(1), 144–162.

Chafouleas, S. M., Koriakin, T. A., Roundfield, K. D., & Overstreet, S. (2019). Addressing childhood trauma in school settings: A framework for evidence-based practice. *School Mental Health*, 11(1), 40–53. https://doi.org/10.1007/s12310-018-9256-5

Costa, D. A. (2017). Transforming traumatised children within NSW Department of Education schools: One school counsellor's model of practice — REWIRE. *Children Australia*, 42(2), 113–126.

Cozolino, L. (2014). *The neuroscience of human relationships: Attachment and the developing social brain (2nd edn).* W.W. Norton and Company.

DuBois, A., & Mistretta, M. (2020). *Overcoming burnout and compassion fatigue in schools: A guide for counselors, administrators, and educators.* Routledge.

Emerick. (2022). *Become a trauma informed leader.* linkedin.com.

Glasser. W. (1992). *The quality school: Managing students without coercion (2nd, expanded ed.).* Harper Perennial.

Greig, J., Bailey, B., Abbott, L., & Brunzell, T. (2021). Trauma-informed integral leadership: Leading school communities with a systems-aware approach. *International Journal of Whole Schooling, 17*(1), 62–97.

Howard, J. A. (2019) A Systemic Framework for Trauma-Informed Schooling: Complex but Necessary!, *Journal of Aggression, Maltreatment & Trauma, 28*:5, 545–565, https://doi.org/10.1080/10926771.2018.1479323

Howard, J., L'Estrange, L., & Brown, M. (2021). The School Counsellor's Role in Trauma-Aware Education. *Journal of Psychologists and Counsellors in Schools*, 1–11. https://doi.org/10.1017/jgc.2021.32

Howard, J., L'Estrange, L., & Brown, M. (2022). National Guidelines for Trauma-Aware Education in Australia. *Frontiers in Education. 7*. 1–11.

Howell, P. B., Thomas, S., Sweeney, D., & Vanderhaar, J. (2019). Moving beyond schedules, testing and other duties as deemed necessary by the principal: The school counselor's role in trauma informed practices. *Middle School Journal, 50*(4), 26-34.

Kezelman, C. & Stavropoulos, P. (2016). Dealing with trauma: acknowledgement of trauma and implementation of trauma-informed practice within legal practice and systems is long overdue. Doing so will enhance both individual and community wellbeing. *Law Institute Journal, 90*(10), 36–.

Martinez Jr, R. R., Williams, R. G., & Green, J. (2020). The role of school counselors delivering a trauma-informed care approach to supporting youth --10.

O'Gorman, S. (2018). The case for integrating trauma informed family therapy clinical practice within the school context. *British Journal of Guidance & Counselling, 46*(5), 557–565.

Ormiston, H. E., Nygaard, M. A., & Heck, O. C. (2020). The role of school psychologists in the implementation of trauma-informed multi-tiered systems of support in schools. *Journal of Applied School Psychology*, 1–33.

Parker, M., & Henfield, M. S. (2012). Exploring school counselors' perceptions of vicarious trauma: A qualitative study. *Professional Counselor, 2*(2), 134–142.

Perry, B. D & Jackson, A.L. (2018). Trauma Informed Leadership. In Federico, M., Long, M. & Cameron, N. Eds.). *Leadership in child and family practice* (pp. 146–162). Routledge.

References Chapter 9

Powell. A. M. (2021). *Best Practices for Trauma-Informed School Counseling.* IGI Global.

Quadara, A. & Hunter, C. (2016). Principles of Trauma-Informed Approaches to Child Sexual Abuse: *A Discussion Paper. Sydney: Royal Commission into Institutional Responses to Child Sexual Abuse.*

Queensland University of Technology & Australian Childhood Foundation (2021). *National Guidelines for Trauma-Aware Education.* https://eprints.qut.edu.au/207800/

Rawson, S. (2020). *Applying Trauma-Sensitive Practices in School Counseling.* Routledge.

Reinbergs, E. J., & Fefer, S. A. (2018). Addressing trauma in schools: Multitiered service delivery options for practitioners. *Psychology in the Schools, 55*(3), 250–263.

Rumsey, A. D., & Milsom, A. (2019). Supporting school engagement and high school completion through trauma-informed school counseling. *Professional School Counseling, 22*(1), 1-10.

Stokes, H. & Brunzell, T. (2020). Leading trauma-informed practice in schools. *Leading & Managing, 26*(1), 70–77. https://doi.org/10.3316/informit.437893476165410

Substance Abuse and Mental Health Services Administration (SAMHSA). (2014). SAMHSA's concept of Trauma and Guidance for a Trauma-Informed Approach. *HHS Publication No. (SMA) 14-4884.* Retrieved from https://store.samhsa.gov/sites/default/files/d7/priv/sma14-4884.pdf.

Tang, A. (2020). The impact of school counseling supervision on practicing school counselors' self-efficacy in building a comprehensive school counseling program. *Professional School Counseling, 23*(1), 1–11.

Wubbolding. R.E. (2007). Glasser Quality School. *Group Dynamics, 11*(4), 253–261. https://doi.org/10.1037/1089-2699.11.4.253

www.ingramcontent.com/pod-product-compliance
Lightning Source LLC
Chambersburg PA
CBHW051633230426
43669CB00013B/2280